Turf Culture

Turf Culture

A Complete Manual for the Groundsman

Frank Hope

N.D.H., N.D.Arbor., Cert.Ed.B'ham.

BLANDFORD PRESS

POOLE   DORSET

First published 1978

Copyright © 1978 Blandford Press Ltd.

Link House, West Street
Poole, Dorset BH15 1LL

ISBN 0 7137 0873 5

Printed in Great Britain by
Unwin Brothers Limited, Old Woking, Surrey
Colour plates printed by Tindal Press Ltd., Chelmsford, Essex

Contents

Foreword

There are relatively few books about the work of the groundsman and even fewer which have been written to assist him in his studies for various horticultural and groundsmens examinations. However, here is such a book and one which can also be used by the enthusiastic amateur gardener.

It has been planned with a view to bringing the art of groundsmanship to the inexperienced but also to bring new ideas and technology to the practicing groundsman and keen gardener.

This book is also different in that for the first time a section has been allocated to the managerial aspects relating to the organisation of the industry; this section will be of particular interest to candidates attempting the various specialist examinations in groundsmanship.

I believe that this book will not only find its place with experienced groundsmen but also with students and will come to be regarded as a text book as well as a standard work of reference.

P. M. Phillips, NDH

TO MY PARENTS

Preface

Turf culture and management represents a growing industry in more ways than one. It must provide and maintain facilities for a wide range of sports and ornamental situations. The recent increase in leisure time has meant that such facilities are in an ever increasing demand, resulting in over use and a reduction in the time allowed for the normal maintenance operations. This book shows how modern ideas and practices can help to overcome some of these difficulties.

It must be remembered that one is dealing with living materials and therefore the chapters relating to botany and plant nutrition are every bit as important as those on weed control and pest and disease prevention. When the grass has grown, the cultural operations become of vital importance; the range of available machinery for these operations is far more extensive than ever before and the groundsman's expertise in handling and maintaining these implements must therefore be of the highest order.

A great deal of recent legislation has necessitated a rationalisation of practices to minimise accidents and possible prosecutions. The safe use of chemicals is therefore a topic of vital importance to the operator and supervisor. The expanding range of suitable chemicals makes it necessary for the groundsman to be up to date and aware of the precautions which must be taken in their use.

The managerial aspects of the industry are introduced and these will be of interest to both supervisors and students. Further reading is recommended for management practices and other topics which have been mentioned to show their application to the practical situation.

Since groundsmanship encompasses a wide range of horticultural practices, some guides are included in the Appendices to stimulate interest and arouse curiosity.

It is hoped that this book will prove that the technical knowledge and practical competence which is required of the groundsman will make him a craftsman equal to any other, no matter what the industry.

Acknowledgements

I would like to thank the following people and organisations for all the kind assistance and suggestions which they have given during the compilation of this book: Mr. P. Drury and the Nottinghamshire County Council for the donation of their article on Management in the Sportsground Industry; Mr. D. G. Gooding and Syn-Chemicals for their notes on the Safe Use of Chemicals and help with transparencies of turf diseases; Mr P. Gillard, N.D.T. for his notes on pests; Mr. T. V. Davies for supplying many of the line drawings; Mr. T. Deans for his help in compiling the chapter on levelling; Mr. D. Hargreaves for his line drawings and the checking of the final manuscript.

I would also like to thank Mr. P. M. Phillips, formerly the Head Groundsman of Rolls-Royce Motors Ltd. for all the kind assistance and notes which he has so unselfishly donated.

Finally, I am grateful to Mrs. J. Thomas for her assistance in typing the manuscript and I wish to thank Margaret for all her patience during the preparation and writing of this book.

Illustrations

Most of the illustrations in the book were supplied by the author. Other sources, which are gratefully acknowledged, were Shell Chemicals (U.K.) Ltd (Plates 19 and 21), The Natural History Photographic Agency/G. E. Hyde (Plates 20 and 24), The Glasshouse Crops Research Institute (Plate 22) and The Royal Horticultural Society, Wisley (Plate 18).

1   Soils

The inorganic fraction of the soil has been produced by the break-down of igneous, sedimentary and metamorphic rocks. Even though these rocks are formed in different ways, they can be seen to be broken down (to a greater or lesser degree) by the actions of chemical, physical and biological processes—collectively termed 'weathering agents.'

Weathering Agents

As rain falls, it dissolves oxygen and carbon dioxide from the atmosphere; this absorption makes the rain water slightly acid, so that it acts as a solvent, causing the gradual disintegration of the rocks by chemical reaction. Frost and ice are both powerful weathering agents; water expands when it is frozen, producing a terrific force capable of cracking large boulders.

Rock is made up from a number of minerals that expand and contract at varying rates. When exposed to extreme variations in temperature, an uneven expansion and contraction takes place to produce a crumbling effect.

Other types of weathering, such as abrasion from dust-laden winds, or the activity of colonising plants, produce a continual disintegration of the parent rock. It is this never-ending breakdown that produces a distinct layer of light coloured material; the subsoil, on top of the weathered rock.

Above the subsoil, a dark coloured mass is formed which is quite different in appearance from the lower layers. This is the soil proper. If a close look is taken, it will be seen that the roots of plants are almost entirely confined to this layer and that the dark colour is due to the presence of decaying vegetable matter and humus. It is here that earthworms can be found continually aerating the soil by the

1

excavation of their burrows and the lifting up of freshly divided earth. Plant roots can aid aeration in two ways. Firstly, to obtain their moisture and mineral salts they make their way between the soil particles; secondly, when they die their remains are broken down to produce humus, which helps to bind the soil particles together.

Soils produced *in situ* from the parent rock in the manner described above are called 'sedentary'—as opposed to 'transported' soils that have been carried to their final positions by the actions of wind and water.

The characteristics of each individual soil depend to a large extent upon its chemical and physical composition.

Soils are a mixture of mineral particles of all sizes. Where one size is more abundant than the others, e.g. clay, the soil is referred to as that type of soil—clay soil.

The mineral particles are divided up according to their size:

Sand 2–0·2 mm diameter
Fine sand 0·2–0·02 mm diameter
Silt 0·02–0·002 mm
Clay 0·002 and below

The major types of soil are described below.

Clay Soils

Clay soils have tiny air spaces between the particles which are capable of retaining a high proportion of moisture. The minute particles have colloidal properties enabling them to hold on to large quantities of nutrients. They are commonly referred to as 'cold soils' because the water which lies in the spaces between the soil particles warms up slowly in spring. As they absorb water they have the tendency to become very sticky and unworkable, whilst when dry they shrink, becoming hard and cracked.

Soils containing a high percentage of clay and which have a poor crumb structure are difficult to cultivate. To improve the workability of this type of soil, the groundsman can incorporate lime. Adding lime to a soil causes the clay particles to join together to form *floccules*. Application of sandy top dressings will also improve surface drainage. The benefit of these treatments is that the soil becomes better drained and aerated and easier to work than a poorly structured clay. However, to sustain this improvement, large amounts of bulky manure must be incorporated.

Sandy Soils

Sandy soils are formed from quartz or silica grains which are resistant to weathering. All but the finest sands contain large air spaces and have a poor water-holding capacity, which makes them rather sterile. However, because of the lack of excess soil moisture, sandy soils tend to warm up quickly in spring, and so they are referred to as warm or early soils. They are rarely sticky, are easy to cultivate and are valuable additives for poorly drained clays.

In general, soils which contain a high percentage of sand particles will be well drained and aerated. However, their water-holding capacity will be poor and during periods of drought grass swards may suffer from lack of moisture. Well-drained, sandy soils produce ideal conditions for the breakdown of organic matter by bacteria. This is why they are sometimes called 'hungry soils'. To improve the water-holding capacity and to maintain high fertility, hungry soils require feeding with large amounts of organic matter such as peat, garden compost or farmyard manure.

Silty Soils

Silts are similar to sand, but they are often stone-free and very deep. They are composed of the same materials as sands and have the same nutrient-holding capacity. However, unlike sands they have small pore spaces and this enables them to retain large quantities of water. They can be difficult to cultivate and have a tendency to cause blocking of drains. To improve their workability, the groundsman must incorporate bulky organic materials such as garden compost, peat and farmyard manure.

Chalky Soils

Chalky soils are characterised by the presence of large quantities of calcium in either amorphous or crystalline forms. Lime, which is composed basically of calcium carbonate, is a very variable factor in soil as it is both a plant nutrient and soil conditioner. In pure water,

3

calcium carbonate is insoluble, but when mixed with weak acids it dissolves as calcium bicarbonate and so is easily leached from the soil.

Chalks are alkaline and have a naturally high pH, low nutrient holding capacity and the tendency to become sticky when wet. Many plants such as the Greater Celandine (*Chelidonium majus*), Wayfaring Tree (*Viburnum lanata*) and the Common Beech (*Fagus sylvatica*) are able to thrive in chalky soils whereas other plants such as Rhododendrons and most of the Heathers are incapable of extracting the correct amounts of nutrients.

Lime, as mentioned above, is continually being leached from the soil and the more that is lost the more acid the conditions become. The reduction of the calcium content of a soil can produce the following effects:

1 Certain plant nutrients, may be unavailable to the plants;
2 Increased activity of some soil borne fungi;
3 Reduction of bacterial activity;
4 Reduction in the rate of breakdown of organic matter;
5 Increase in the number of acid loving plants.

The calcium content of a soil can be maintained by incorporating a variety of materials, the commonest of which are as follows:

Ground limestone (calcium carbonate)

This is the cheapest form of lime available. It is slow acting, pleasant to handle and easy to store. Applications are usually made during the winter months to allow the material to be washed in before the spring.

Hydrated lime (calcium hydroxide)

Hydrated lime is produced by burning chalk in kilns and then slaking it by spraying with water. It is comparatively expensive to buy but is readily available to plants.

Gypsum (calcium sulphate)

This material is frequently used to reduce the salinity of soils which have been flooded by salt water. It provides calcium but has very little effect on the pH of the soil.

Fertilisers containing calcium

Chemicals such as Nitro-chalk, and bonemeal contain some calcium. These materials should be used where the soil is already known to be acid.

Soil pH

The pH scale is a method used to indicate the *acidity* or *alkalinity* of a soil. The scale ranges from 0 to 14. A soil which is neutral will have a reading of pH 7·0. Readings below 7·0 indicate acidity, whereas readings above 7·0 indicate alkalinity.

The pH of a soil can be rapidly determined by means of liquids (indicators) which change colour in accordance with the degree of acidity or alkalinity. However, more accurate results can be obtained by electrical methods which depend on the fact that if two electrodes of appropriate type are immersed in a suspension of soil in water, a difference in electrical potential exists between them. This difference can be measured and used to calculate the pH of the soil suspension.

Soil pH can be altered by applying lime. When lime is added it raises the pH value, that is it makes the soil more alkaline. It is important to maintain the correct pH (approx. 5·5–6·5) as the indiscriminate use of lime can discourage fine-leaved grasses and in certain circumstances can encourage the establishment of broad-leaved species.

Organic Soils

Organic soils can be formed from either peaty bogland or mosslands. They consist of partially decomposed organic matter capable of retaining large quantities of soil moisture. As these soils originate from bogs or mossland they have the tendency to be badly drained, flat and very acid. However, once drained they produce high quality soils that are rich in nutrients and easy to work.

Organic Matter

Organic matter has two contrasting effects upon the soil. One effect is the release of nutrients when the matter has broken down; the other is the improvement in the structure which is due to the formation of humus. Humus is colloidal; in the soil it coats all the particles and helps stick them together, forming a sound structure. This is very important with sand and silt soils, because with insufficient clay or humus colloidal particles, a stable structure will not be produced. Similarly, when humus is present in clay soils, it coats the soil particles which inhibits deflocculation—thus producing a more stable structure.

Nitrification

Nitrogen in its natural state is a gas making up approximately 79% by volume of the atmosphere. Unfortunately, in this form, it is unavailable to plants. Plants obtain the majority of their nitrogen from the soil as nitrates and use the nitrogen in the production of proteins, e.g. chorophyll, which aid the formation of healthy, green growth.

The nitrogen in plant and animal residues is present in complex forms which are insoluble in water and cannot be directly used by plants. Before the residues become available for growth, they must be converted to nitrates. This conversion is brought about by bacteria.

The main controlling factor in bacterial activity and consequently availability of nitrogen is temperature. The conversion of organic nitrogen to available inorganic forms will only take place when soil temperature is adequate. This is usually from early spring to late autumn. The conversion of organic nitrogen to available nitrates takes place in three distinct stages. These are described below.

Ammonification

When plants and animals decay they decompose and are broken down to produce ammonia gas. This is brought about by the action of ammonifying bacteria and some fungi that are active in well-drained and aerated soils. Once produced, nitrogen is converted to ammonium compounds in the soil.

Production of nitrites

The ammonium material is oxidised to nitrites by bacteria called *Nitrosomonas*. Nitrites are toxic to plant growth, but fortunately the action of the next bacteria in the cycle quickly converts the toxic nitrites to available nitrates.

Production of nitrates

The formation of nitrates from nitrites is brought about by bacteria known as *Nitrobacter*. All plant growth relies on this conversion as nitrates are the main form of nitrogen for plant growth (see Fig. 1.1).

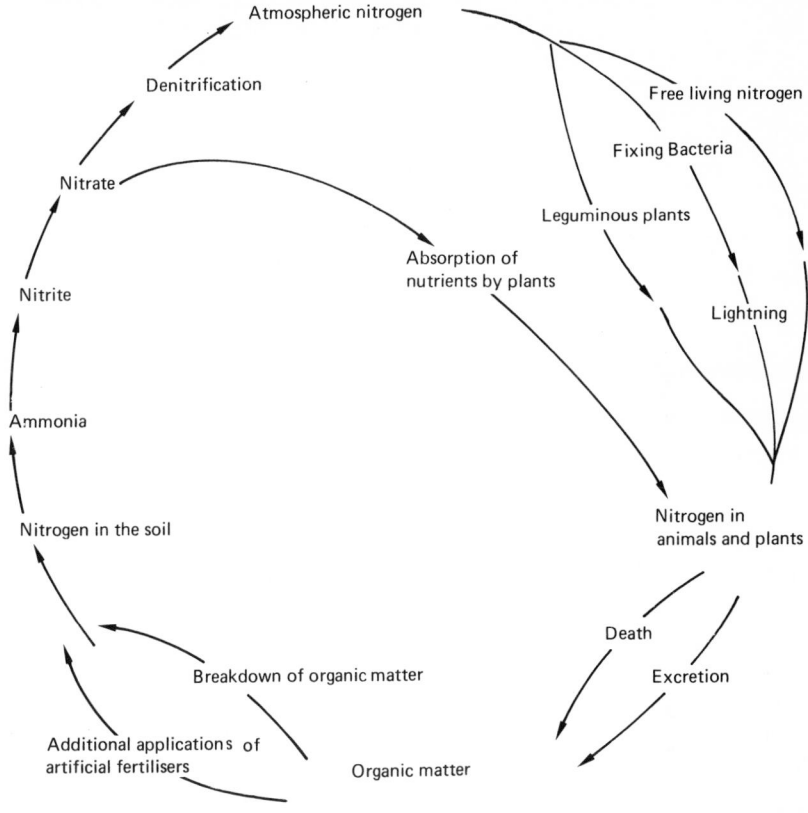

Fig. 1.1   The nitrogen cycle.

Nitrogen fixation

As well as the nitrogenous compounds produced by nitrification, additional nitrogen is produced by the activity of certain groups of bacteria. The three main types capable of fixing nitrogen are *Rhizobium* bacteria, found in the root nodules of leguminous plants, and *Azobacter* and *Clostridia*, both of which live freely in the soil and can fix atmospheric nitrogen.

7

De-nitrification

It must be remembered that, in certain circumstances, de-nitrification can take place whereby the soil nitrates are converted first to nitrites and then to nitrogen gas, which is then released to the atmosphere.

Soil Micro-Organisms

Fertile soils contain a large number of organisms consisting of both plants (flora) and animals (fauna). All play an important part in the breakdown of organic matter, with the subsequent release of nutrients and improved soil structure. Micro-organisms found in the soil include the bacteria, fungi, actinomycetes, algae and protozoa, the majority living saprophytically, although a number can be parasitic. Of the above, the most important groups are the bacteria and fungi.

Bacteria

These are present in the soil in large numbers and are commonly put into two main groups namely, *autotrophic* and *heterotrophic* bacteria. Autotrophic types obtain their carbon from the carbon dioxide in the soil and their energy from simple substances, such as ammonium compounds, which do not contain carbon. They are fairly simple kinds of organisms but some are extremely useful as they can fix atmospheric nitrogen. Examples of these are the *Azobacter*, which are active in aerobic soils, and the *Clostridia* that are active in anaerobic conditions. These bacteria take in atmospheric nitrogen to make up protein and release it to the soil after their death. Heterotrophic bacteria are a little more sophisticated than autotrophic types and unlike the latter they have to obtain both their carbon and energy by breaking down complicated compounds. If the soil conditions are ideal for bacterial growth (e.g. plenty of food, water and correct temperature), a build up of this type of bacteria will take place and cause the rapid decomposition of organic matter.

Fungi

Fungi are simple plants that are devoid of chlorophyll. Because of this they must obtain their food either as saprophytes feeding on dead matter, or as parasites growing on living tissues. In general, their role is most important in acid soils and under conditions where a large quantity of organic matter is present. However, they can also be active in neutral to alkaline soils. Some fungi have the ability of living in association with higher plants, the plants supplying the fungi with food, whilst the fungi increase the water and nutrient uptake of the plants. This type of relationship is called a *mycorrhizal association*.

Soil Moisture

Water is one of the most important constituents of any soil. It is essential for plant growth and is used in many processes including nutrient uptake, maintenance of turgidity, cooling the plant and photosynthesis. A lack of moisture is not only detrimental to plant growth, it also affects the activity of soil organisms, thus reducing the breakdown of organic matter and so preventing nutrients from becoming available to the plants. Excess moisture, on the other hand, reduces the amount of air in a soil and produces anaerobic conditions unsuitable for the growth of plants. Soil standing in water will tend to lose its structure, thus making any drainage problem much worse.

In free-draining soil, the moisture is held in a film around the soil particles. When water is applied, some of the spaces between the particles become filled and a corresponding amount of air is driven out of the soil. If water is continued to be applied, all the spaces between the particles are filled and all the air is expelled from the soil. When this occurs, puddles form on the surface and the soil is said to be *saturated*. The formation of puddles, however, can also indicate that the water is being applied at too fast a rate for the soil to accept it. Thus, care should always be taken to ensure that the amount of water applied is equal to the infiltration rate of the soil, otherwise a false indication of the moisture status will be given.

When the application of water to a saturated soil ceases, the excess moisture will drain away and a point will be reached where the soil is holding the maximum amount of water against the force of gravity. The soil is then said to be at *field capacity*. This is the ideal state for plant growth, as the soil will be holding the correct amounts of moisture and air.

As further water is removed from the soil, a point will be reached where the plants can no longer extract water and so they wilt. Plants in such conditions may recover overnight or, when placed in a humid atmosphere, but if they do not the soil is said to be at *permanent*

9

wilting point, i.e. no more water is available to the plants. At permanent wilting point the plants will not recover unless water is applied to the soil. The soil is not completely dry at permanent wilting point, it just means that the moisture is held so tightly around the soil particles that the plants cannot remove enough to maintain healthy growth.

Water is occasionally prevented from percolating through the soil by the occurrence of some form of impervious stratum, such as rock or clay. When this happens, the water collects and produces a saturated layer beneath the soil surface. The level at which the water stands is termed the *water table*. It is of the utmost importance to plants since moisture is able to rise from the water table to moisten the soil above.

To summarize, water should be applied at such a rate as will allow it to be absorbed without the formation of puddles; the ideal condition for growth is when the soil moisture status is between field capacity and wilting point, remembering that serious damage or death can occur if this latter stage is reached.

Soil Nutrients

The nutrients essential for plant growth have two main functions:

1   As a part of plant structure;
2   In the control of plant metabolism.

The elements required and their functions are as follows.

Major nutrients

Nitrogen   used mainly for structural purposes, e.g. the production of proteins such as protoplasm and chlorophyll.

Phosphorus   used in the formation of nucleo-proteins and energy transfer during cell division.

Potassium   used to regulate osmotic potential and transport nutrients around the plant.

Calcium   utilised in both metabolism and structure, i.e. cell walls.

Magnesium   a constituent of chlorophyll and affects the movement of Phosphorus in plants.

Sulphur   production of amino-acids and oils in plants.

Minor nutrients

Iron used as a catalyst in the production of chlorophyll.
Manganese activates enzymes and protein synthesis.
Copper activator of enzymes.
Zinc activator of enzymes.
Boron used by the plant to move sugars.
Molybdenum essential for nitrate producing enzymes.

A brief description of the uses and functions of substances in plants is given in Table 1, which follows on pages 12–15.

Table 1.1 Plant Substances

Substance	Method of Entry and Movement	Main Functions	Notes
Major Elements			
Nitrogen	Enters plants in the form of nitrates or ammonium ions. Moved as amino-acids and other organic N compounds.	Constituent of protein, Nucleic acids, pigments and auxins.	Found in all parts of the plant especially in meristematic tissues. Deficiency can lead to chlorosis and poor spindly growth.
Phosphorus	Enters plants in the form of phosphates. Moved in the plant as complex phosphates, or as simple inorganic phosphate.	Used in energy transfer, nucleic acids and proteins.	Found in active tissues, encouraging the healthy production of young roots. Can be inhibited by applications of nitrogen. Becomes unavailable if the pH is high or low.
Potassium	Enters the plant and is moved around as potassium ions.	Affects enzyme activity and osmotic pressure.	Required mainly in meristematic tissue. More available in the lighter soils.
Calcium	Enters the plant as calcium from plant residues and various forms of inorganic calcium. Translocated as calcium ions—only in xylem immobile in phloem.	Forms calcium pectate in the middle lamella of the cell wall. Facilitates meristem functioning and works in relationship with boron.	Found in meristematic tissues and is relatively high in leaf tissues.
Sulphur	Enters the plants as sulphates and is moved about in the same form, or as amino-acids.	Found in proteins and amino-acids. Functions in enzymes and is a constituent of vitamins.	Found in young growing points, can be used as flowers of sulphur to lower the pH of a soil.

Magnesium	Enters the plant and is moved around in the form of magnesium ions.	A constituent element of chlorophyll and is used by the plant to transport phosphorus. Important in the functions of enzymes and is fairly mobile within a plant.	Found in plant leaves, but can be moved to areas of high need. A deficiency leads to chlorosis of leaves and poor growth with brilliant colour tints.

Minor elements

Iron	Enters the plant in the ferrous form and is translocated as complex iron compounds. Ferric form not taken in.	Mainly metabolic, acting as a catalyst for the production of chlorophyll and respiration processes.	Found everywhere in the plant. Its availability is dependent upon pH with deficiencies occurring in alkaline soils. Deficiency can give severe chlorosis of leaves.
Boron	Enters the plant as borate ions and is translocated as boron.	Concerned with sugar movement within the plant.	Found everywhere in the plant. Deficiency causes the death of the apical meristems. Can be corrected by applications of borax.
Copper	Enters the plant and is translocated as copper ions.	Constituent of enzymes especially for respiration and oxidation.	Found everywhere in the plant. Deficiencies can lead to a type of chlorosis and die-back of shoots.
Zinc	Enters the plant and is translocated as zinc ions.	Used in enzyme systems.	Found everywhere in the plant. Deficiencies lead to malformation of leaves. Can be unavailable under conditions of high pH.
Manganese	Taken into the plant and is translocated in the form of manganese ions.	Found mainly in enzyme systems in leaves and seeds.	Deficiency usually leads to chlorisis in the older leaves. Availability is dependent upon pH. Shortages can be alleviated by sprays of manganese sulphate.

13

Table 1.1—*continued*

Substance	Method of Entry and Movement	Main Functions	Notes
Molybdenum	Taken into the plant and is translocated in the form of molybdenum ions.	Found mainly in enzyme systems especially in nitrate assimilation and nitrogen fixation.	Deficiency symptoms show up as reduced leaf size. Sometimes found lacking in acid soils
Elements that are not essential for growth			
Silicon	Taken into the plant via its roots and is translocated in the form of silicon salts.	Has no specific function in the plant—accumulated by grasses.	Can be absorbed by grasses.
Sodium	Taken into the plant and translocated in the form of sodium ions.	Serves the same function as potassium in halophytes (salt-loving plants).	
Water	Taken into the plant by the process of osmosis and is translocated as water through the xylem and phloem.	Main functions include turgidity, cooling, solvent action, structural and metabolism—carbohydrates.	Found everywhere in the plant, a deficiency leading to wilting and death.
Carbon	Enters the plant in the form of carbon dioxide gas and is translocated in the form of complex sugars.	Essential part of sugar, protein, fats, pigments and auxins.	Found everywhere in the plant.

Oxygen	Enters the plant in the form of water and is translocated in the form of water and sugars.	As for carbon.	Found everywhere in the plant.
Hydrogen	Enters the plant via its roots in the form of water and is translocated as water or sugars.	As for carbon.	Found everywhere in the plant.
Sugars	Manufactured by the leaves and translocated as sucrose in the phloem.	Source of energy.	Found everywhere in the plant, especially in storage organs.
Proteins	Manufactured in living cells and translocated in the phloem in the form of amino-acids.	Mainly structural and enzymes, e.g. chlorophyll.	Found everywhere in the plant.
Chlorophyll	Manufactured in the leaves and is not translocated around the plant.	Photosynthesis.	Used to absorb sunlight which is used as an energy source for sugar synthesis.
Vitamins	Manufactured in mature leaves and translocated in the phloem.	Used in enzyme systems.	Found everywhere in the plant.

15

2 Levelling

During the construction of a lawn, a number of operations may need to be carried out before the final preparation of the seedbed can be completed. If the site is uneven, it may be necessary to carry out some form of levelling. Sports, such as bowls require a very even playing surface, whereas amenity lawns may be quite acceptable with gentle undulations. One must remember, however, that undulations if too large may cause damage to mowers and cause 'scalping' of high points on the lawn.

There are a number of ways in which soil can be levelled. Some of these are suitable for small sites whilst others are only suitable for large areas. The method chosen will depend to a large extent on the size of the site and on the degree of accuracy required. The methods of levelling which are commonly used are described below.

Grading

This simply consists of levelling the topsoil with spades or tractor-mounted equipment. It is frequently used for land which contains only minor undulations, or which has already been levelled by some other means. On small sites, grading is carried out by hand-operated equipment, the final levels being set by visual judgement. On larger sites, such as motorway embankments, major grading is carried out by using specialised earth-moving machines, the final levels being set with sophisticated equipment.

Simple Levelling

On small areas of land, simple forms of levelling are required which can be carried out by one or two persons. There are two methods which are suitable for use on this type of site, both of which can, if necessary, be adapted for larger areas. The first technique consists of levelling the site by using pegs, spirit levels and straight edges whilst the second consists of using pegs and boning rods.

Method of simple levelling

The operations are as follows:

1 Remove the topsoil and store it for re-distribution (if necessary).
2 Select a point on the site which is to be the final level (called the *datum point*);
   Knock a peg into the soil at the datum point leaving the top 150 mm above ground level (Fig. 2.1);
3 Knock a series of pegs into the ground at intervals of approximately 3 m (9ft.).
4 Place a straight edge and spirit level on the datum peg and on one of the other pegs;
   Knock the second peg into the soil until it is level with the datum peg (first peg);
5 Level each peg on the site in the same way.

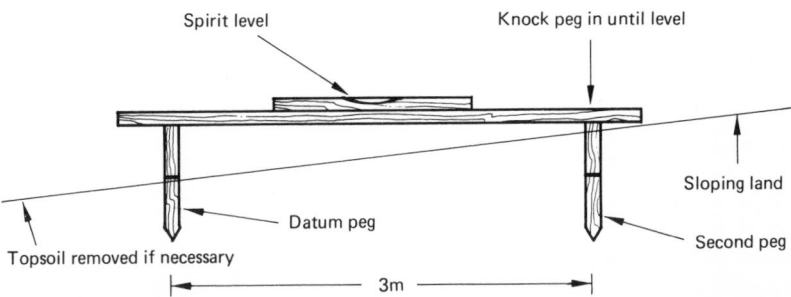

Fig. 2.1 Simple levelling using pegs and spirit levels.

When each of the pegs on the site has been levelled the subsoil can be moved until it is at the same height as the mark on the datum peg. Once the subsoil is level (see Cut-and-Fill method on p. 19) the topsoil can be redistributed evenly over the site and the pegs removed.

Use of boning rods for levelling

Boning rods are pieces of equipment which can be used for

17

simple levelling, or when putting in levels for drains. They are made in sets of three, each rod being identical. They are usually made of wood with dimensions of approximately 1 m (3 ft) long with a cross piece of 0·6 m (2 ft) (see Fig. 2.2).

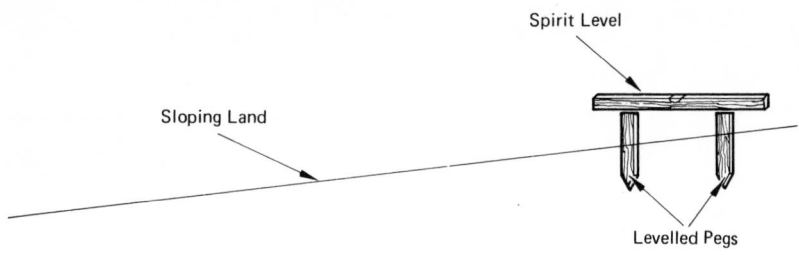

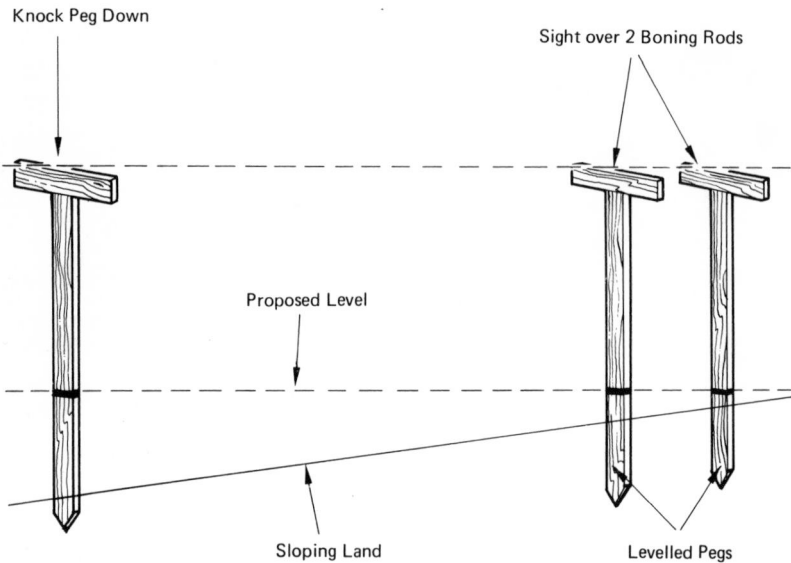

Fig. 2.2   Levelling with boning rods.

This system is faster and more suited to the larger site than the spirit level technique, but unfortunately it is not as accurate. When used for levelling the method adopted is as follows:

18

1   Knock two pegs into the ground at the highest point of the level required;
2   By means of a spirit level and straight edge adjust the two pegs until their tops are level (Fig. 2.2);
3   Place a boning rod on each of the two pegs;
4   Place the third rod on one of the remaining pegs on the site;
5   Sight over the first two pegs to see if the third peg is level;
6   If not, knock in the peg until it is;
7   Continue with the rest of the pegs on the site.

Cut-and-fill Technique of Soil Movement

On sites which require the movement of large amounts of soil, a system called the cut-and-fill technique is used. It consists of moving soil on the site from high places to low places. The system is used to minimise the movement of soil, its major utilization being on large, sloping sites.

Cut-and-fill is carried out during the process of levelling. For areas which have large gradients, it is recommended that the topsoil should be firstly removed, the subsoil levelled, and the topsoil re-distributed over the site. (See Fig. 2.3). If the sub-soil were not levelled the sward growth would be very uneven and at certain times of the year could be unsuitable for use.

Levelling of Large Areas—Terms and Equipment

It is quite possible that the preceding methods of levelling may be totally inadequate for large sites or, areas where major earth moving is necessary. When this is the case, specialised levelling techniques with sophisticated equipment should be carried out, however, this type of work should only be done by fully trained personnel.

Levelling terms

Levelling   This is the term given to the determination of relative heights or points on the earth's surface. A level surface in this context being one which is at all times normal (90°) to the direction of gravity.

Datum line   Two basic types exist.

   (a) *Ordnance datum*   Mean sea level. In the U.K. this is an official

datum above which all levels shown on ordnance survey maps are calculated. From this datum, a series of Ordnance Survey benchmarks (O.S.B.M.) are situated all over the U.K., the commonest ones being found on walls, fences and buildings indicated by ⋀.
(b) *Local datum*   A local datum is chosen by the surveyor purely for convenience and may be any arbitrary plane, i.e. a step, post, wall, etc. and given an assumed value.

Reduced level   A reduced level of a particular point is its height above or below the adopted datum line. Reduced levels can be repre-

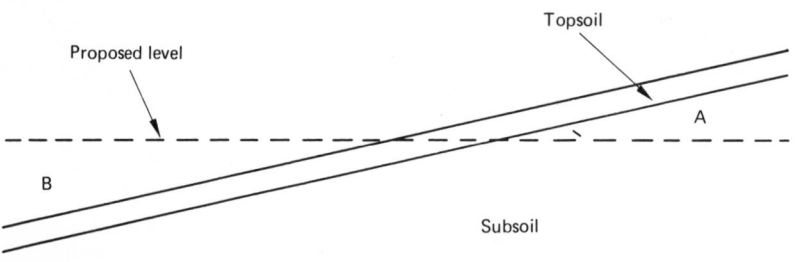

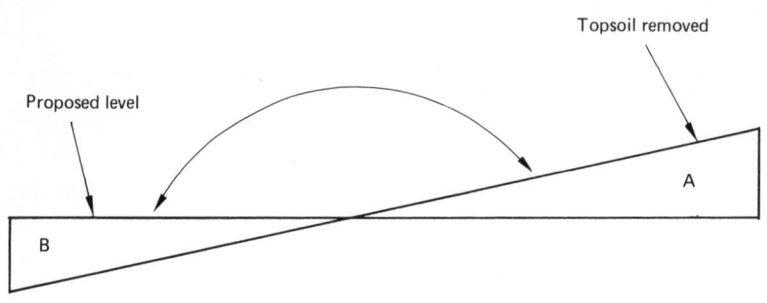

Fig. 2.3   The cut-and-fill technique of soil movement.

sented on a drawing in 3 ways, namely spot levels, sections and contours.

Height of instrument This can be described as the height of the line of collimation above the chosen datum (see Fig. 2.4).

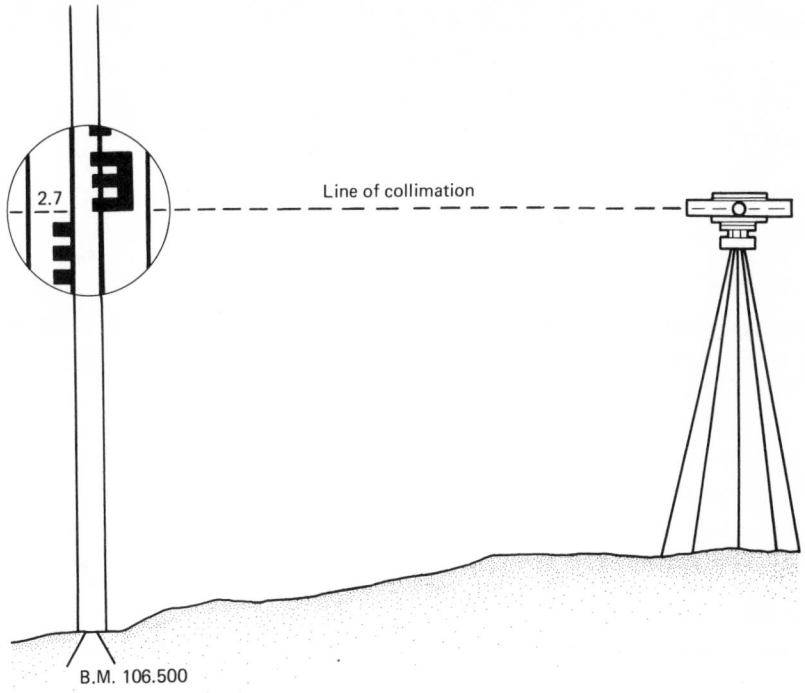

Fig. 2.4   Height of instrument = BM + staff reading
$$= 106 \cdot 500 + 2 \cdot 700$$
$$= 109 \cdot 200.$$

Backsight A backsight is the first reading taken after the level has been set up. It consists of taking a sight on to a point whose height is known or can be calculated, e.g. O.S.B.M.

Foresight A foresight is the last sight taken before the instrument is moved. It consists of taking a sight on to a point whose height is needed to carry on the line of levels.

Intermediate sight An intermediate sight is any reading other than

21

a backsight or foresight, taken when the instrument is in the same position.

Change Point   A change point occurs when the instrument is moved, the staff remains in the same position. The reading taken before moving the instrument is a foresight, and when the instrument is set up in the new position the first reading is a backsight, i.e. back to the position where the staff has been situated during the operation. Since these two readings are taken on to the same position, they are usually entered on the same line in the level book.

Levels

A level is a piece of equipment which is basically a telescope mounted on a tripod and which can be made to rotate in any direction in a horizontal or level plane.

The Dumpy level (see Fig. 2.5)

This piece of equipment has been used for a number of years and is an improvement on the old 'Y' type level. The telescope is fitted firmly to the base plate and the instrument is adjusted in a horizontal plane by 3 or 4 levelling screws. In theory, once the instrument is levelled no further adjustment is required. However, in practice, it is found that the settings do not remain correct for very long. This necessitates regular corrections of the levelling screws to re-centralise the bubble in the spirit level.

SETTING-UP A DUMPY LEVEL

1   Open up the tripod and firm the points into the soil ensuring that the legs are at an angle of approximately 60%;
2   Re-adjust the legs until the lower parallel plate is roughly horizontal;
3   Remove the instrument from the case, taking note of its position in the box (This will aid safe replacement after use);
4   Screw the level on the tripod ensuring that the threads do not get crossed;
5   (i) On three screw levels, turn the telescope in line with two of the adjusting screws;
    (ii) Grip the two screws with forefingers and thumbs and turn them in opposite directions until the bubble is centralised;

(iii) Next, turn the telescope at right angles to its original position, i.e. over the third screw and adjust the screw until the bubble is centralised once more;

(iv) Return the telescope to its original position to check that the bubble is still correct, if not, repeat the operation.

Fig. 2.5   The Dumpy level.

6 (i) On four screw levels, the telescope should be levelled over each pair of the screw threads in turn;
(ii) Repeat the operation until the telescope can be rotated in any direction with the bubble still centralised.

Fig. 2.6   The Quickset level.

The Quickset level (Fig. 2.6)

Because of the problems of maintaining the adjustment of the Dumpy level, the quickset level was developed. This differs from the Dumpy in that the telescope is not rigidly fixed to the base plate, but is hinged

Fig. 2.7   The Cowley level.

centrally instead, an elevating screw being used for the final adjustment of the spirit level before a reading is taken.

The Cowley level (Fig. 2.7)

Cowley levels differ from other instruments in that neither lenses nor bubble tubes are used in their construction. They are easy to use, requiring very little in the way of instructional training and are especially suited to the smaller site. The body of the instrument consists of two solidly constructed aluminium die castings, inside which is a unique system of mirrors, one of which is delicately but robustly pivoted on a pendulum. All the working parts are fully enclosed and there are no knobs, screws or controls whatsoever.

Diaphragms

A diaphragm is fitted to all levels next to the eyepiece and this can be focussed to the user's requirements. Many different types can be used, ranging from a number of strands of hair, to etched glass or, even metal pointers. A fairly typical example (Fig. 2.8) would consist of

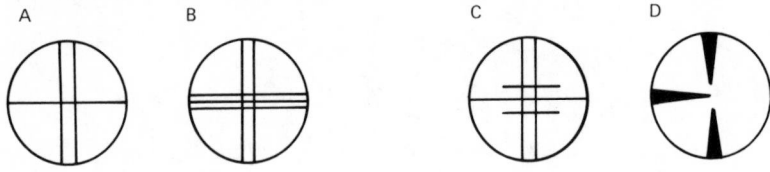

Fig. 2.8   Types of diaphram.

2 parallel, vertical lines and 1 or even 3 horizontals. The verticals are used as a guide to check that the staff is held correctly, whilst the central horizontal line is the one used to take the readings.

Levelling Staff

Levelling staffs (Fig. 2.9) are usually produced in mahogany or aluminium and are constructed in 3 telescoping sections, usually giving a total length of between 4·25–5 m (14–16½ ft). The graduations on the staff are marked off in metres, decimetres and centimetres, whilst millimetres are obtained by estimation. With most types of level, the staff will appear inverted in the telescope, this means that

26

great care must always be shown when taking readings, otherwise
errors can occur.

Reading the staff
To read the staff, the telescope is directed towards the staff and the

Fig. 2.9   The levelling staff

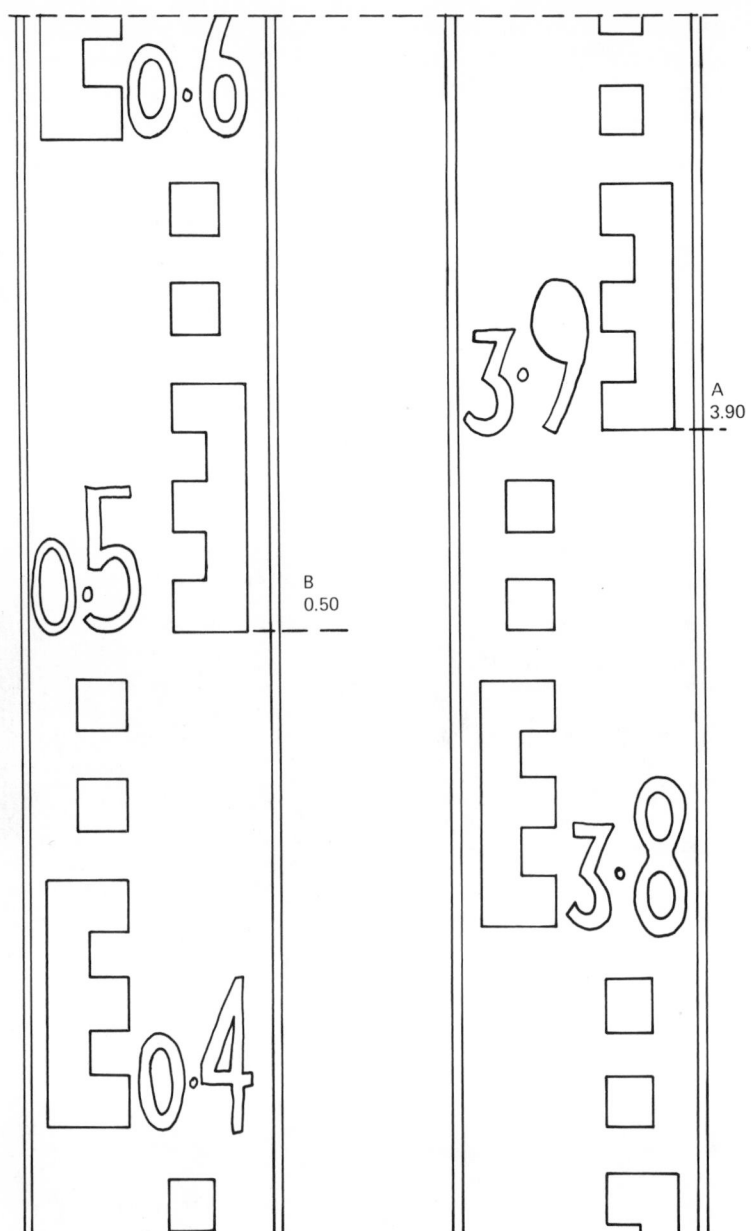

Fig. 2.10   Readings on a levelling staff.

focussing screw is used to bring the staff into clear focus. If the quickset level is being used, the main spirit level is accurately centred using the elevating screw. With the diaphragm in sharp focus, the axial line will be clearly seen against the staff, the reading is then noted (Fig. 2.10).

Levelling Procedure

Finding the difference in level between two points

1   Set up the instrument, preferably between the two points (see Fig. 2.11)
2   Adjust it until the telescope is horizontal
3   Read the staff held at each point in succession
4   By simple subtraction the difference in level can be found, i.e. Difference between points A and B = $3 \cdot 90 - 0 \cdot 50 = 3 \cdot 40$.

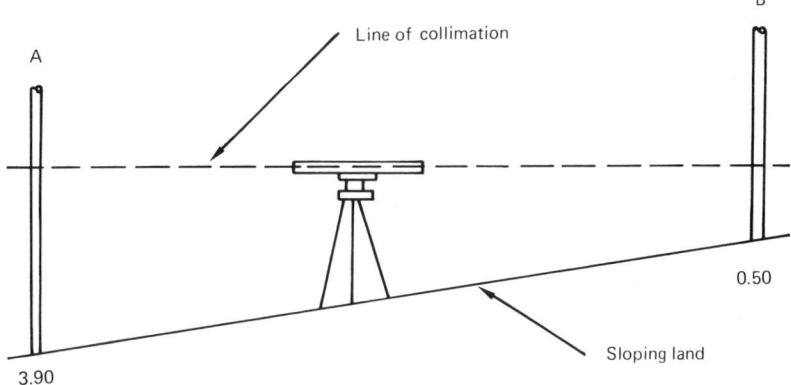

Fig. 2.11   Finding the difference in level between two points.
Difference between points A and B = $3 \cdot 90 - 0 \cdot 50$
$= 3 \cdot 40$.

It is essential that this simple example is understood otherwise more complicated calculations will not be followed.

When levelling, it is commonly necessary to obtain a series of heights over a sloping site. Where this is required the following method can be followed. Before describing the system however, it will be beneficial to recap on a number of terms:

Backsight   The first reading taken after setting up the level.

Foresight   The last reading taken before the instrument is moved.

Intermediate sight   Any reading other than a backsight or foresight taken when the instrument is in the same position.

Levelling a sloping site

1   Place the level at station 1 (see Fig. 2.12).
2   Put the staff at point A and take a backsight reading.
3   Move the staff to point B and take a foresight reading.
4   Place the level at station 2 and take another backsight reading on to point B.

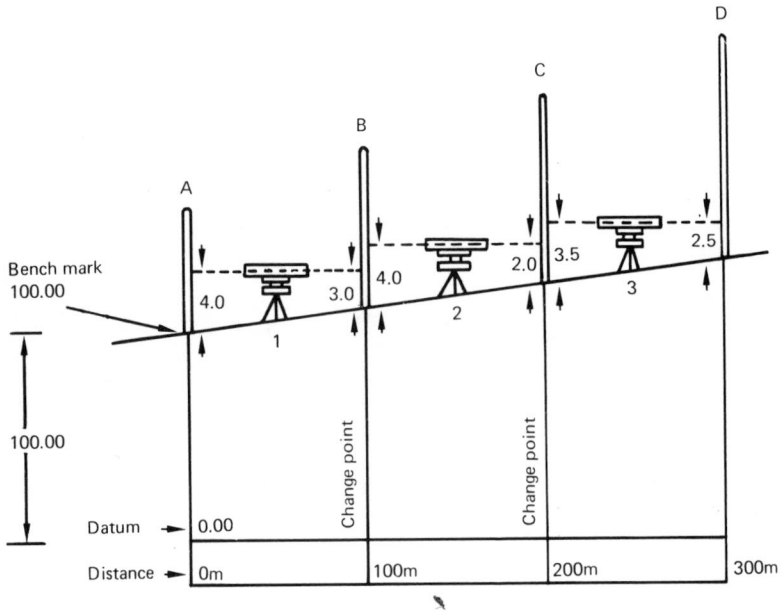

Fig. 2.12   Taking a series of levels up an incline.

5   Place the staff at point C and take a foresight reading.
6   Move the level to station 3 and take a backsight onto point C.
7   Transfer the staff to point D and take another reading.
8   This process can be continued until all the site is levelled.

In practice, a small error in reading is often unavoidable. However, it should never be allowed to exceed 0·01 per change point. In order to check whether the levels are correct, the difference between the

30

sums of the backsights and foresights should equal the difference between the first and last reduced levels (see below).

Booking the readings

There are two main systems of reducing levels, the height of collimation method and the rise and fall method.

COLLIMATION METHOD

So that further work can be carried out away from the site, it is necessary to book the various readings taken during the levelling process. Whatever system of logging is used, it is advantageous to use a field or level book. The collimation method of booking figures is as follows:

a) Point A is taken from a bench mark of a reduced level of 100·000. This should be placed in the Reduced Level column.

b) The first reading, a backsight of 4·000 was taken on to point A. This is placed in the Backsight column. The distance from 0·00 should be placed in the Distance column and the height of the instrument should be calculated by adding together the reduced level and the backsight, i.e. 100·000 + 4·000 = 104·000.

c) The second reading, a foresight of 3·000, should be entered in the Foresight column. The reading was taken onto point B 100 m away from point A. This distance should be placed in the Distance column.

The reduced level can be calculated by subtracting the foresight reading from the height of the instrument, i.e.

$$104\cdot000 - 3\cdot000 = 101\cdot000$$

d) The third reading taken from point B is a backsight of 4·000. This should be placed in the Backsight column and the height of instrument calculated by adding the backsight to the reduced level, i.e.

$$101\cdot000 + 4\cdot000 = 105\cdot000$$

e) The fourth reading, a foresight of 2·000 taken on to point C

31

should be placed in the Foresight column and the reduced level calculated as above, i.e.

$$105 \cdot 000 - 2 \cdot 000 = 103 \cdot 000$$

This figure should be placed in the Reduced Level column and the distance between C and A should be placed in the Distance column.

f) The fifth reading, a backsight of $3 \cdot 500$ should be entered in the Backsight column and the height of instrument calculated, i.e.

$$103 \cdot 000 + 3 \cdot 500 = 106 \cdot 500$$

g) The next reading, a foresight of $2 \cdot 500$ is booked in the Foresight column and the reduced level is calculated, i.e.

$$106 \cdot 500 - 2 \cdot 500 = 104 \cdot 000$$

The check to see if the figures are accurate is as follows:

$$\frac{\text{Difference between sums of backsight and foresight}}{} = \frac{\text{Difference between the first and last reduced levels.}}{}$$

Back-site	Intermediate sight	Fore-sight	Height of Instrument	Reduced Level	Dis-tance	Remarks
4·000			104·000	100·000	0·00	Taken off a bench mark
		3·000		101·000	100·000	
4·000			105·000			
		2·000		103·000	200·00	On to Point C
3·500			106·500			
		2·500		104·000	300·00	Bench Mark
11·500		7·500		100·000		
7·500						
4·000				4·000		

The rise-and-fall method of reducing readings is basically the same as the collimation method, the only difference between the two being that the former book has rise and fall columns whilst the latter has a height of instrument column. The rise and fall method can be described as calculating the difference in height of a station relative to the preceding station. The method can be booked as set out below.

Back-site	Intermediate sight	Fore-sight	Rise	Fall	Reduced Level	Dis-tance	Remarks
4·000					100·000	0·00	Bench Mark
4·000		3·000	1·000		101·000	100	
3·500		2·000	2·000		103·000	200	
		2·500	1·000		104·000	300	Bench Mark
11·500		7·500	4·000	0·000	104·000		
7·500					100·000		
4·000			4·000		4·000		

Notice that the rise column figures occur when the staff reading is less than the reading on the preceding station. Notice also that this example contains no fall figures. This is because the readings are taken up a steady incline. To check the accuracy of the bookings the following system can be followed. A further explanation of rise and fall can be seen in Fig. 2.13.

The difference in the sum = The difference between the sums of the
of the backsight   rise and falls or the difference between
                           the first and last reduced level.

It must be stated that the preceding chapter is only intended as a very brief introduction to the specialised operations of levelling. It is meant to give an insight into the equipment and calculations necessary for accurate levelling to take place. Where a serious study of the work is to be done, the author recommends that the reader should obtain a book on surveying and levelling.

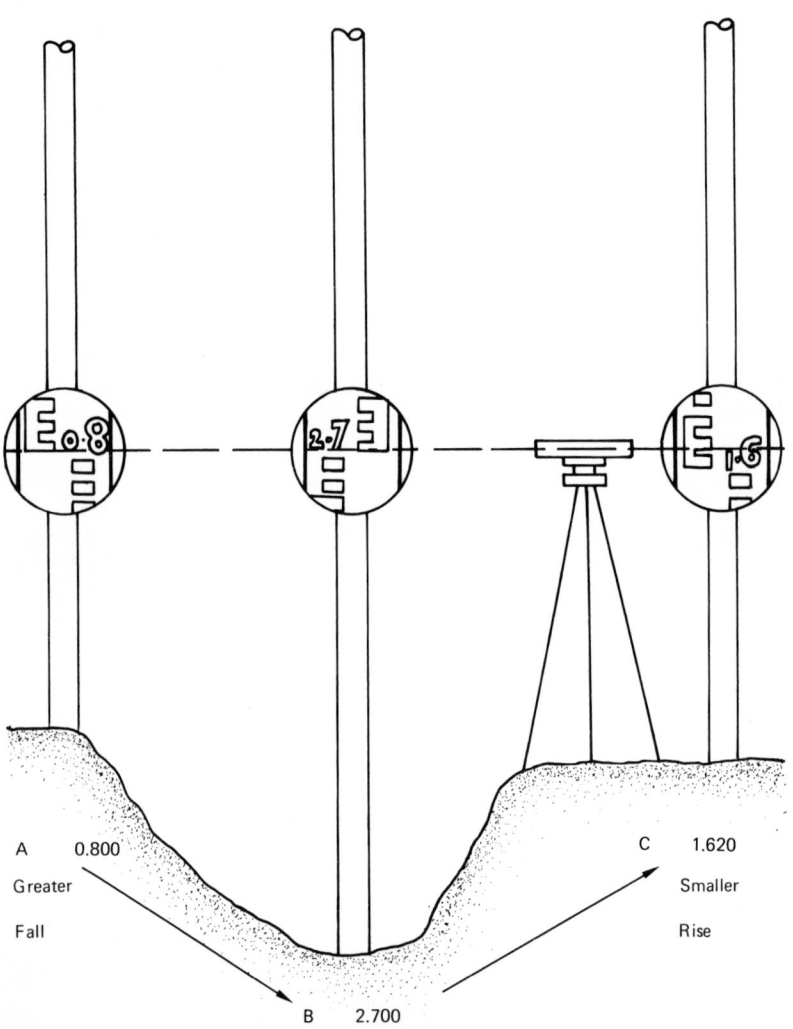

A   0.800
Greater
Fall

B   2.700

C   1.620
Smaller
Rise

Fig. 2.13   The rise-and-fall method of levelling.

3   Drainage

Signs of Poor Drainage

Poorly drained soils can often be seen to exhibit their own weed flora. If one looks around damp bogland, or even round the edges of ponds and lakes, plants which are flourishing are those which have adapted their growth habit to moist conditions. Rushes, mosses, buttercups, and sedges are all plants which grow in damp places. When these are seen growing on a site, it is a good indication that the soil will require some form of drainage.

On large sites it is possible to check if drainage problems exist by opening up a number of inspection pits and looking at the soil profiles. A soil profile can be considered as a cross-section through the soil layers. If the soil is a uniform brown colour throughout the depth of the profile, this will indicate that no drainage problem exists. On the other hand, if the soil is a dark greyish or bluish black colour then some form of impeded drainage is probably present.

Other signs of poor drainage which can be obtained from the inspection of soil profiles are the formation of impervious layers (commonly known as soil 'pans'), poor root growth, poor soil structure, and the production of rust coloured mottling which suggests that the soil is waterlogged at certain times of the year.

There are a number of different types of drainage problem and each type will have a different remedy. In heavy soils the problem is often one of surface water (due to a low infiltration rate), whereas on light soils it is more likely to be caused by a high water table (due to insufficient underdrains or poor outlets). If, for any reason, one cannot decide whether a site requires draining, advice should be sought from a qualified drainage contractor, the Ministry of Agriculture regional officers, or appropriate local authority.

35

Advantages of Good Drainage

There are many advantages obtained from drainage, many of which are common to all soils whilst others are only applicable to special sites. Some of the more important advantages are:

a) The removal of excess soil moisture;
b) Improvement of soil aeration;
c) Better distribution of plant foods;
d) Greater depth of soil available for root production;
e) Deeper rooting enables plants to obtain more moisture in summer;
f) Use of sports grounds can be extended;
g) Soil tends to warm up faster in the Spring.

Types of Drain

Drainage can be conveniently divided into two types; surface layer drainage and sub-surface drainage, or underdrainage as it is sometimes called. The main difference between the two is that sub-surface drainage is designed to remove excess water over a considerable depth of the soil, whereas surface layer drainage is more concerned with the rapid removal of water from the area close to the grass roots.

Surface layer drainage

Surface layer drainage mainly consists of ensuring that the soil is well structured. By this we mean that the sand, silt and clay particles are joined together in the best possible manner. This is most important as a weak structure can inhibit the movement of water, reduce aeration, and prevent healthy root growth. Some of the ways of preventing poor surface drainage in both bare soil and established turf are as follows:

a) Never carry out work on the site when the soil is wet;
b) Do not allow heavy equipment onto the site during construction unless some form of sub-soiling is to be carried out before sowing;
c) Do not 'over use' rotary cultivators as these can quickly ruin the soil structure;
d) Prevent soil 'capping' from occurring;

36

e) Improve the soil structure by incorporating bulky organic materials such as well rotted compost or farmyard manure;

f) On established turf, relieve soil compaction by using aeration and scarification equipment;

g) Incorporate bulky inorganic materials, e.g. sand;

h) Improve any existing sub-surface drainage.

SAND SLITTING

Areas such as football pitches, which are subjected to prolonged heavy wear, can become unusable because of excess surface moisture. This moisture collects because the structure is ruined by over compaction, or because the soil contains a high percentage of clay. To encourage healthy growth this excess moisture must be removed as quickly as possible.

A specialised form of surface drainage called sand slitting can be used to improve the downward movement of water. It also helps to relieve soil compaction, improve soil structure and will eventually extend the life of the sward.

The operation is performed by making a series of 6 mm (2 in) wide slits which are cut to a depth of between 250 mm (10 in) and 375 mm (15 in). The trenches are cut at approximately 0·6 m (2 ft) intervals and should run at right-angles to any existing sub-surface drains. Once prepared they should be backfilled with a fine or medium grade sand, and firmed by running a tractor wheel or roller over the slits (Fig. 3.1).

It is important when sand slitting over existing sub-surface drains to prevent the sand from settling between the porous backfill, as this will produce an uneven surface which may reduce the efficiency of the system.

When all the slits have been prepared, the site can be re-seeded. The establishment of the seed can be encouraged by the application of a light top dressing consisting of peat or a mixture of peat, sand and base dressing. The peat is applied to retain moisture, which can be used by the germinating seedlings, whereas the base dressing is incorporated to aid establishment. The sand is added to the dressing to maintain the slits in an open condition and to produce a level surface suitable for use.

Fig. 3.1 Sand slitting. Section of turf removed to show the slits.

Sub-surface drainage (underdrainage)

This consists of producing some form of channel beneath the soil surface to allow excess water to run away. The channels can be produced either by digging trenches and laying cylindrical drains, or by dragging equipment beneath the soil surface to produce a continuous series of holes.

Mole Drainage

This is a method of draining which utilizes the fact that clay particles have a tendency to stick together. The drain is produced by drawing a 'mole plough' (Fig. 3.2) through the soil. As the plough passes

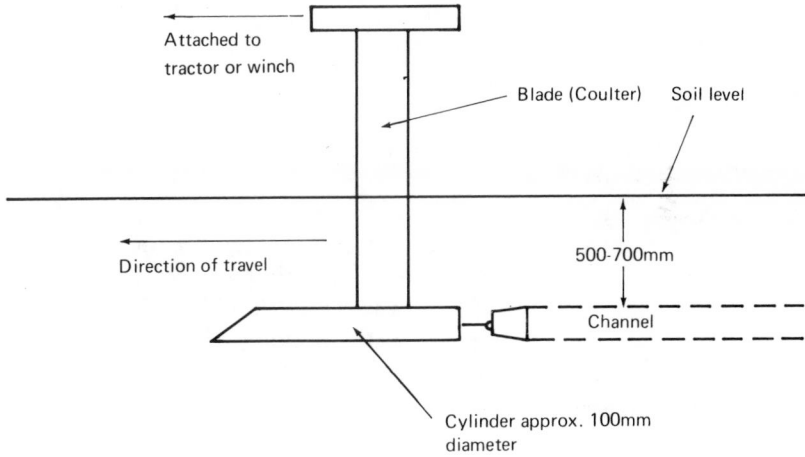

Fig. 3.2 A mole plough.

through the soil it compresses the sides of the channel, leaves a cylindrical hole beneath the surface and produces a fissuring effect which extends upwards at about a 45° angle.

Mole drains are drawn through the soil at approximately 3 m (9 ft) intervals and at a depth of between 500 mm (20 in) and 750 mm (30 in). The drains usually last for about 9 to 10 years, but it has been known for them to last many more especially when drawn through ideal clay soils.

If the soil contains pockets of gravel, sand or silt the drainage channels can have a tendency to collapse. It is therefore recommended that mole drainage is only carried out on soils which have a high percentage of clay and are free from such pockets.

Points to remember when mole draining

a) The aim of mole draining is to quickly remove excess moisture;
b) The fall of the drains (gradient) must be even, otherwise silting up or the collapse of the drains may occur;
c) Channels must be deep enough to be in good clay and avoid damage by cultivations;
d) The plough works best when the soil is slightly moist;
e) Moling is carried out in conjunction with tile drainage; care should be taken to ensure that the channels run through the permeable backfill;
f) The permanent underdrains should be large enough to remove the water from the moles;
g) Crawler tractors should be used so as to prevent damage to the soil structure;
h) Mole channels should be at least 75 mm (3 in) diameter with the invert of the mole not less than 300 mm (20 in) below the surface of the ground;
i) If mole drains are run into ditches, 2 m (6½ ft) of continuous tile drain should be laid to prevent the drain from collapsing after heavy rain (see Fig. 3.3) and the outlet should be high enough above the ditch to prevent water backing up the mole drain during flooding, as this will cause the collapse of the channel;
j) Regular maintenance of the outfall channels is necessary to prevent silting up.

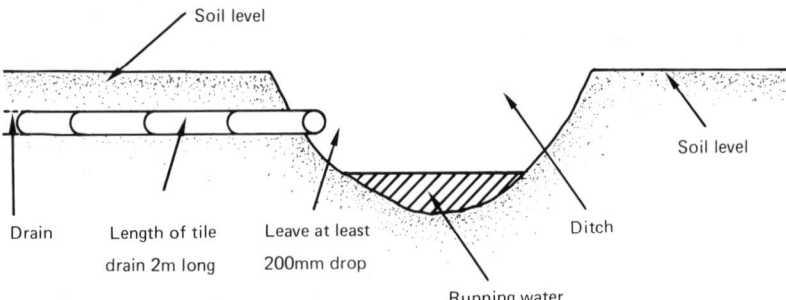

Fig. 3.3   An outfall.

The main use of mole drains is to increase the efficiency of existing tile drain systems. They do this with little movement of the soil surface and at a relatively low cost. However, their main disadvantage is that they are unsuitable for use on land which contains large pockets of sand, silt or gravel or which has a very uneven natural fall.

Tile Drainage Systems

This type of system is produced by laying either plastic or clay drains beneath the soil surface. On large sites this operation is carried out by specialized draining equipment which lay the drains in one of two ways—the 'trenched' method and the 'trenchless' method. The former consists of making a trench wide enough to accept the drain, then backfilling it with permeable material, whereas the latter consists of drawing the pipe through the soil without the necessity of open trenches.

Types of drainage pipe

The traditional type of drain used is the clayware field tile which is commonly called the 'tile drain' (Fig. 3.4). This type of drain has been

Fig. 3.4   Clay drainage pipes.

used for many years and has shown itself to be very efficient. Care should be taken when purchasing tiles to ensure that they are of the correct standard and that no faults are present such as cracks or distortions.

The most common sizes of tile drain used are the 75 mm (3 in), 100 mm (4 in) and the 150 mm (6 in) the diameter, varying with the site and whether the tile is to be used, as a main or a lateral (Fig. 3.8).

Plastic drainage tubes were first used in the early 1960s and since then their popularity has gradually increased. Their most important advantage is that the tubes are capable of removing more water per diameter than the clayware pipes. This means that the tubes can have a relatively smaller diameter and still remain efficient.

The tubes can be purchased in two main forms (Fig 3.5). The corrugated type comes in continuous lengths of approximately 220 m (660 ft) and is suitable for laying by the 'trenchless' method. The smooth rigid type comes in lengths of approximately 7 m (21 ft) and is usually laid by the trenching method.

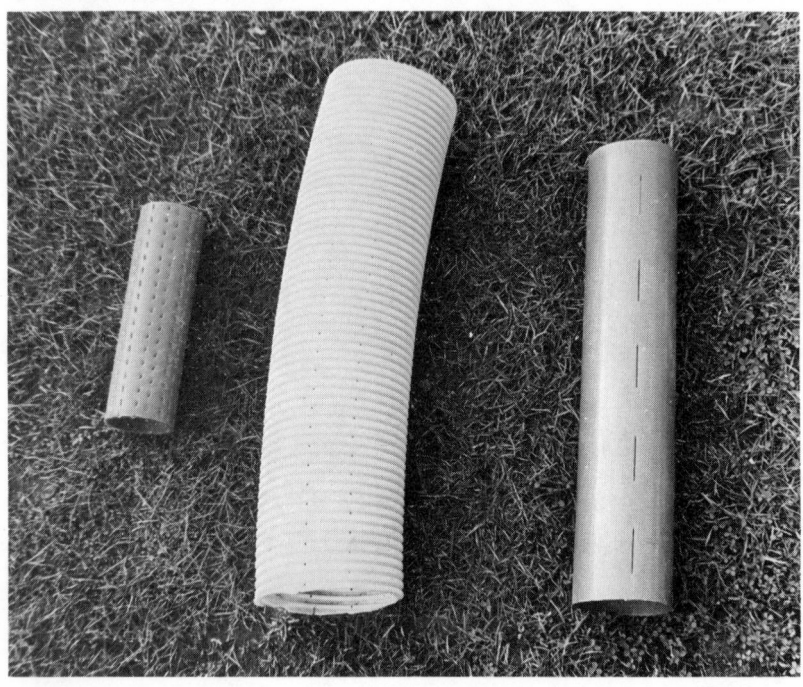

Fig. 3.5   Plastic drainage pipes.

Depths of drains

The depth of a tile drain system will vary depending upon the type of soil; the heavier the soil the nearer the drains will be to the surface. The aim of the system should be to lower the height of the permanent layer of moisture in the soil (water table). On heavy soils this may mean that the drains are at a depth of 0·6 m (2 ft), whereas on lighter soils they may be down to a depth of 1·0 m (3 ft).

The distance between the drains will also be dependant on the type of soil. On heavy soils the drains will have to be somewhere in the region of 3–4 m (9–12 ft) apart but on light soils they may be as far apart as 8–10 m (25–30 ft).

Falls (gradients)

The gradient at which the drains are laid should allow the water to run away as quickly as possible. In most cases, the fall will be regulated by the soil conditions and the size of the site. On small areas a fall of 1 in 100 may be acceptable but, on large areas this can be reduced to 1 in 125 or even 1 in 150 without causing lack of efficiency and silting up.

Backfilling

Unless the trenchless system of drainage is used, some form of backfilling will be necessary. On small sites this can consist of producing various layers of permeable materials (Fig. 3.6), whereas on large

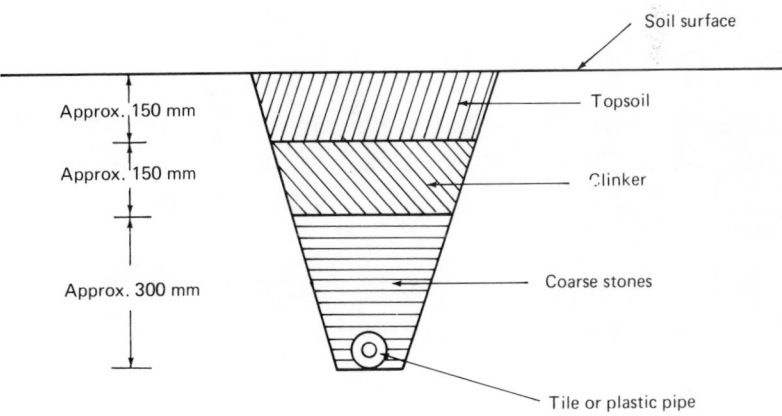

Fig. 3.6   Backfilling a tile drain.

sites only one type of fill will be used. The layer of backfill is used to replace the impervious sub-soil excavated during the trench digging to speed the movement of water into the drains.

Types of drain and system

The system (or pattern) of laying tile or plastic drains will vary with each site. On sites with localised wet areas, it may only be necessary to lay one line of tiles but, on other sites it will be necessary to drain the whole area. As a general recommendation choose the simplest system as this will make laying and maintenance as easy as possible. If a large area is to be drained it will always be worthwhile to employ a qualified drainage expert who has the expertise and equipment to carry out the operation successfully.

Herringbone system of drainage

This is a very popular system of laying drains which is commonly

Fig. 3.7   A drainage machine.

used on large areas and is relatively easy to lay by machines (Fig. 3.7). The tiles are laid in a staggered pattern reminiscent of the bone structure of a fish (Fig. 3.8).

Grid system of drainage

The grid system is a method suitable for large areas and is less complicated to lay and maintain than the herringbone system. When this system is used 'silting up' at the junctions between the main and

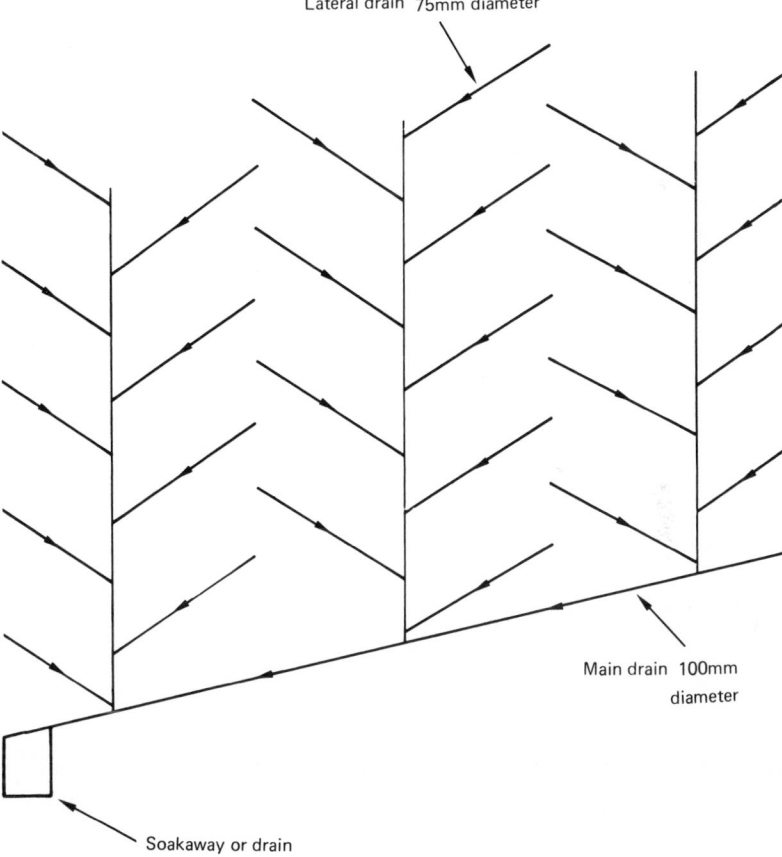

Lateral drain 75mm diameter

Main drain 100mm diameter

Soakaway or drain

Fig. 3.8   The Herringbone system of drainage. The arrows indicate the direction of flow.

lateral tiles can occur. This should be prevented by making the joining angles as wide as possible. (See Fig. 3.9.) Sub-laterals can be incorporated if necessary, the diameter of pipe being slightly less than the laterals.

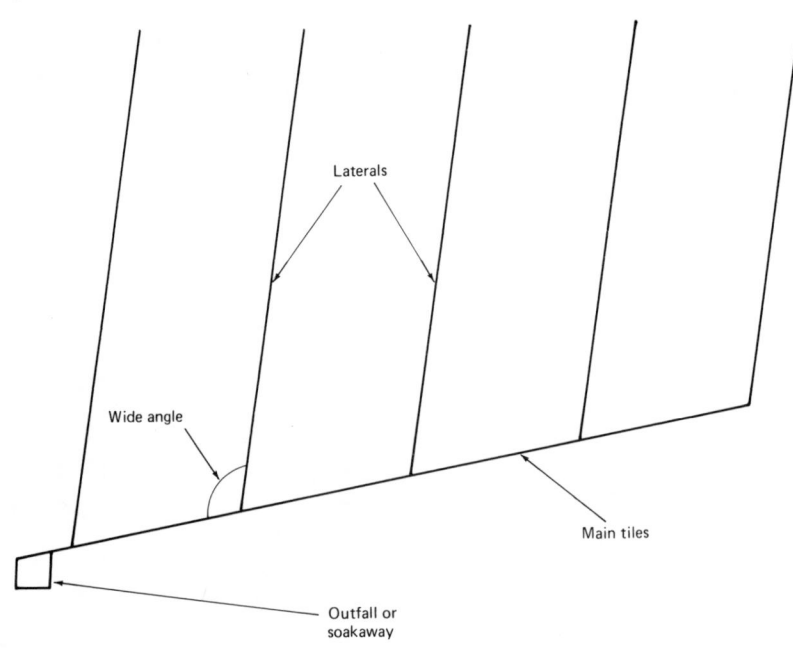

Fig. 3.9   The grid system of drainage. Sublaterals and inspection points can be incorporated if required. Notice the wide angles where the laterals join the mainline. This prevents silting up.

Fan system of drainage

This is a very simple system which is mainly used on sites which have localised wet spots. It is easy to lay and maintain but is unsuitable for large areas. (See Fig. 3·10.)

Note the acute angles produced between the pipes at the soakaway (Fig. 3.10). This can lead to problems in laying and in subsequent maintenance.

46

Whatever system is used, it is advisable to incorporate some form of inspection point which will give easy access for maintenance work.

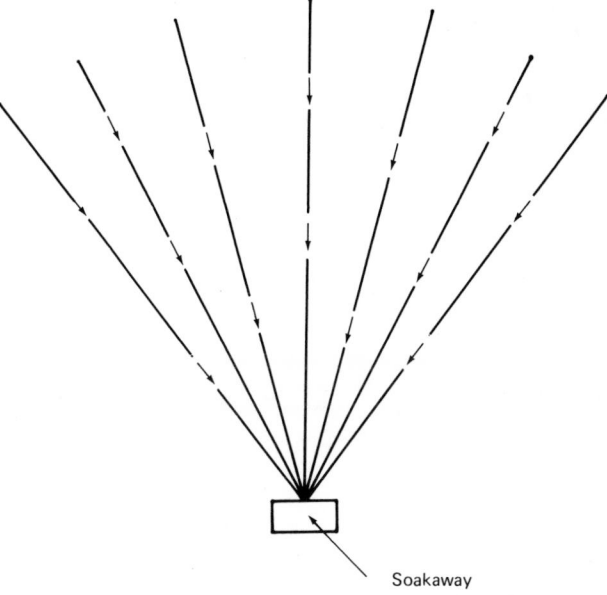

Soakaway

Fig. 3.10   The fan system of drainage. The arrows indicate the direction of flow.

4 Basic Grass Structure

All grasses belong to the family Gramineae. This is a family of mono-cotyledonous plants (producing one seed leaf or cotyledon) which consists of over 600 genera and over 10,000 species. Examples of the family can be found in all regions of the world and in almost every type of habitat.

At first glance, the structure of the individuals appears to be very complex. However, if a closer look is taken it will be seen that all the species have a typical basic structure. Differences in structure and habit do occur and it is these variations which give the grasses their individual characteristics.

The stems of grasses are really long narrow cylinders or tubes which are blocked at intervals by swollen joints or 'nodes'. During normal growth the plant produces vegetative stems but, during the period of flowering (late spring to summer in most species) special inflorescence stems (culms) are produced. These culms are modified so as to hold the floral organs in an ideal position for pollination (Fig. 4.1).

In some species of grass, underground stems or rhizomes are produced, whereas in others overground creeping stems, called runners or stolons, can be found. These structures provide the plant with a rapid means of development and during certain circumstances can provide an ideal means of overwintering (Figs 4.2 and 4.3).

When a new shoot or stem is produced, it can develop in one of two ways. If it grows up within the enveloping sheath, a tufted type of growth is produced and the shoot is said to have been produced *intravaginally*. If however the developing shoot bursts through the base of the sheath a spreading type of growth is produced and the shoot is said to have developed *extravaginally*.

The leaves of grasses are characteristically narrow structures which are arranged alternately on either side of the stem. Each leaf consists

48

Smooth stalked
Meadow Grass

Poa pratensis

Perrenial
Rye Grass

Lolium perenne

Fig. 4.1   Grass structure.

49

of a leaf 'blade' which is free from the stem and a leaf sheath which clings closely to the stem. On some grasses, small claw-like structures or outgrowths can be found clasping the stem at the point where the sheath joins the leaf blade. These structures are called auricles (Fig. 4.4).

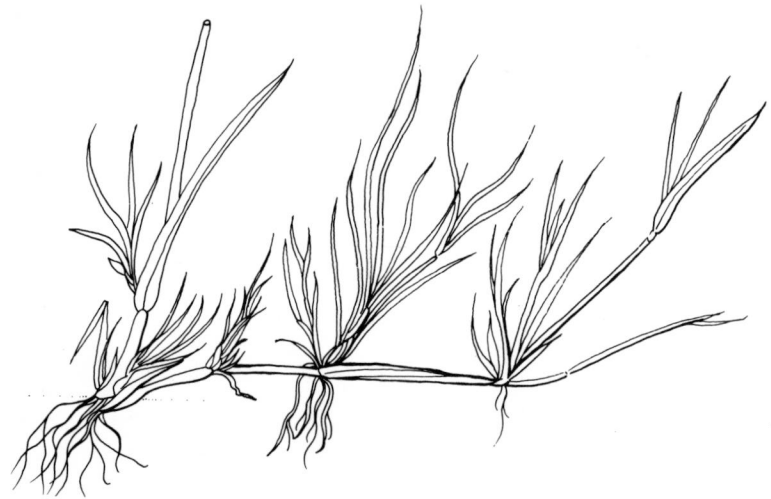

Fig. 4.2   A typical grass stolon.

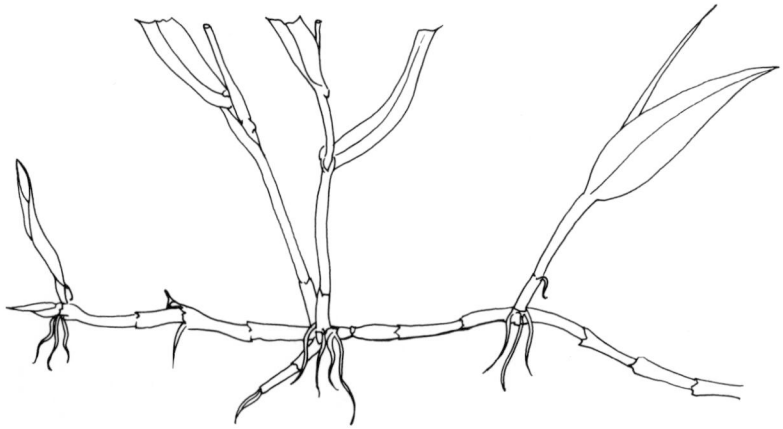

Fig. 4.3   A typical grass rhizome.

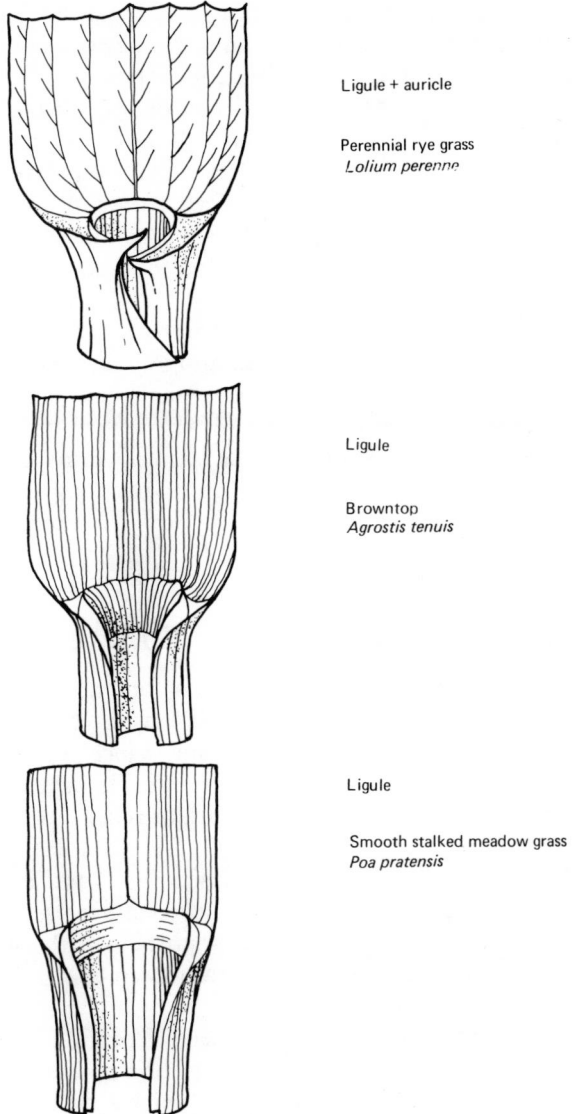

Ligule + auricle

Perennial rye grass
Lolium perenne

Ligule

Browntop
Agrostis tenuis

Ligule

Smooth stalked meadow grass
Poa pratensis

Fig. 4.4   Auricles and ligules.

51

Outgrowths of membranous tissue, or sometimes a row of fine hairs, may also be seen at the point where the leaf blade joins the sheath. These structures are called ligules (Fig. 4.4). Ligules and auricles are important to gardeners and groundsmen as they provide a reliable and fairly rapid means of identification.

Grasses produce flowers during certain periods of the year. Grass flowers are never produced individually, instead they are arranged in the form of 'spikelets'. These spikelets contain the male and female organs which, after pollination and fertilization produce the seed. The inflorescence of a grass can be made up of a number of spikelets and when this occurs they are produced in the form of either panicles or 'spikes'.

The roots of grasses are always of a fibrous nature (Fig. 4.1) and are comprised of large numbers of small individual roots. The roots are only produced at the base of the growing stems and, at the nodes of creeping species. Grasses are one of the few plants whose roots are capable of taking in nitrogen in the form of ammonia gas. This is one of the reasons behind the practice of injecting either gaseous ammonia or anhydrous ammonium hydroxide directly into turf-covered soils.

Principal Grasses used in Turf Culture

There are many different species of grass, but not all of them are suitable for use in fine lawns. Those used must be capable of tolerating the varying site conditions and maintenance techniques which today's turf is subjected to. For example, grasses which are used in the production of ornamental lawns will not require the same ability to withstand hard wear as the species used in the formation of football pitches. Similarly, the species chosen for roadside verges will not be subjected to the same maintenance as those used on bowling greens. The choice of species is most important. If the wrong selection is made the establishment of the sward can be poor and the life of the area may be greatly reduced.

In recent years, plant breeders have been selecting new varieties of grasses which are capable of withstanding the rigours of modern day turf culture. Some of the characteristics which they look for during selection are as follows:

a) Hardwearing;

b) Drought resistance;
c) Tolerance of frequent close mowing;
d) Lack of unsightly flower stalks;
e) Resistance to disease;
f) Capability of tolerating various soil conditions;
g) Tolerance of shade;
h) Production of fine leaves;
i) Ability to blend with other grasses;
j) Ability to re-establish after hard wear;
k) Good summer and/or winter colour.

Before actually seeding an area, it may be worthwhile getting in touch with one of the seedhouses who specialise in grass seeds. Most companies employ technical representatives who will be willing to give advice on the selections of varieties suitable for particular sites. The principal grasses used in turf culture are described below.

The bents

These grasses belong to the family Agrostis. The family is made up of over 100 species but, only a few of these are suitable for use in ornamental lawns or sports fields. The bents show a considerable diversity in habit, ranging from closely tufted species to types which spread widely by the production of stolons or rhizomes. Bents can be found growing in many types of soil but, the majority prefer slightly acid conditions.

BROWNTOP BENT (*Agrostis tenuis* Sibth.)

This is one of the most widely used species for fine lawns. It is used for lawn production in many countries and in the U.S.A. it is known as Colonial Bent Grass and Rhode Island Bent Grass.

Browntop is a fine-leaved, tufted perennial plant (Fig. 4.5) which spreads by short underground rhizomes or over ground stolons. It can be found growing in poor acidic soils, in meadows and moorlands, but does not flourish in very light soils.

Browntop produces a tough, hard-wearing, uniform sward which is suitable for use in very fine lawns such as bowling greens. For this type of lawn it is usually mixed with Chewings Fescue. The seed of Browntop is very small and when used in mixtures with fescues it is

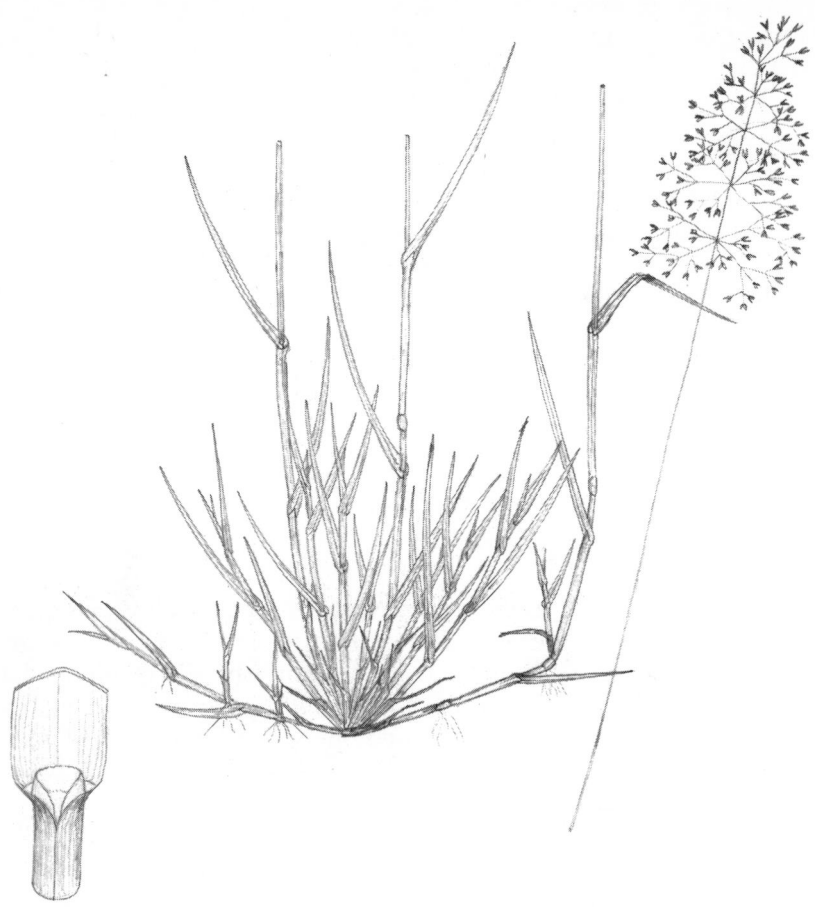

Fig. 4.5 *Agrostis tenuis*—Browntop.

advisable to sow the species separately, preferably the fescue first, followed by the bent.

Once Browntop is established it can become very aggressive and if the site conditions are favourable the growth of other species will be restricted. Numerous commercial strains are available each having their own specific characteristics; examples of these are the 'Highland' strain, 'Tracenta,' 'Boral,' 'Holfior' and 'Brabantia.'

VELVET BENT (*Agrostis canina*)

Velvet Bent is a long-lived perennial with finer leaves than those of

54

creeping bent grass. It is a native of Europe but is used for lawns in many parts of the world. The best growth is produced on damp soils, but it does show some resistance to drought.

Velvet Bent spreads by the production of stolons and because of this feature the grass is sometimes used to produce lawns by vegetative means. The stolons produced by Velvet Bent are finer and less aggressive than those found on Creeping Bent. However, they are more aggressive than the stolons which are occasionally produced by Browntop.

Velvet Bent can produce high-quality, close-knit swards which are suitable for fine lawns. Unfortunately, the turf can become very spongy. Some commercially available strains are 'Norobent,' 'Acme,' 'Piper' and 'Raritan.'

CREEPING BENT (*Agrostis stolonifera*)

Creeping Bent is a tufted perennial which spreads by the production of large stoloniferous growths. It is an aggressive species but can have a very variable habit. The Marsh Bentgrass (*Agrostis stolonifera* var *palustris* Huds.) is frequently used in the U.S.A. for the production of lawns by vegetative means; its use in the U.K. is very limited.

The swards which are produced by Creeping Bent are loose and are unsuitable for use in fine lawns. However, they are suitable for some utility sports areas.

The fescues

These grasses belong to the genus *Festuca* which consists of over 100 species and in common with the bents covers a wide variation in growth habit. The fescues can be divided into two main types—the Sheep Fescues and the Red Fescues. The difference between the two lies in the nature of the leaf sheath; in the Sheep fescues the sheath is split, whilst in the Red Fescues the sheath is entire.

CHEWINGS FESCUE (*Festuca rubra commutata* Goud.)

This species of grass is also known as *Festuca rubra* var 'Fallax'. The species is a non-rhizomatous, densely tufted perennial which can produce both intra- and extravaginal growth (Fig. 4.6). It blends well with other grasses and is often used in mixtures with Browntop Bent. It is quick to establish but is not as aggressive as Browntop. In

Fig. 4.6 *Festuca rubra* ssp. *commutata*—Chewings Fescue.

established lawns, the Chewings Fescue may deteriorate allowing the Browntop to become dominant.

A feature of Chewings Fescue is that it can suffer from 'bleeding' of the leaf tips after mowing. This bleeding can cause the tips of the grass to turn yellow and in certain circumstances can make the sward look untidy. An advantage of Chewings Fescue over other grass species is its ability to withstand periods of drought. Commercial varieties of Chewings Fescue are available which produce excellent swards. Some examples are 'Highlight', 'Flora', 'Waldorf' and 'Koket'.

CREEPING RED FESCUE (*Festuca rubra rubra*)

This is a very variable grass with numerous 'types' that are suitable for lawn production (see Fig. 4.7). The plant spreads by underground

56

Fig. 4.7   *Festuca rubra* ssp. *rubra*—Creeping Red Fescue.

creeping rhizomes, which when established can produce very fine swards. It will grow on most sites but the best swards are produced on light soils. As with Chewings Fescue, creeping red fescue has the ability to withstand periods of drought and cold weather.

A type which is sometimes sold as a distinct form of Creeping Red Fescue is *Festuca rubra genuina*, or Genuine Red Fescue. This is a vigorous grass which is quick to establish. It is a creeping form which produces loose turf of good colour which is capable of standing periods of drought. Its main use is in the formation of golf greens and putting greens. One of the best commercially available strains is S59 which is a selection originating from Aberystwth in Wales. Other available varieties are 'Oasis' and 'Dawson'.

Another type of Red Fescue which is sometimes used is given the name Cumberland Marsh Fescue (*Festuca rubra genuina* var. glaucescens). This is a species of grass which is found in sea-washed turf. It has a blue appearance and produces a very high quality sward which is highly rated for bowling greens and golf greens. If Cumberland Marsh Fescue is used in fine seed mixtures, it is usual to substitute it for some of the Chewings Fescue.

SHEEPS FESCUE (*Festuca ovina*)

This is a species which is widely distributed throughout Europe. It is a very hardy, densely tufted perennial plant which prefers light soils and moorland conditions (Fig. 4.8). Sheeps Fescue shows some resistance to drought and is also capable of withstanding close mowing. The best type for ornamental lawns is the Fine-leaved Sheeps Fescue.

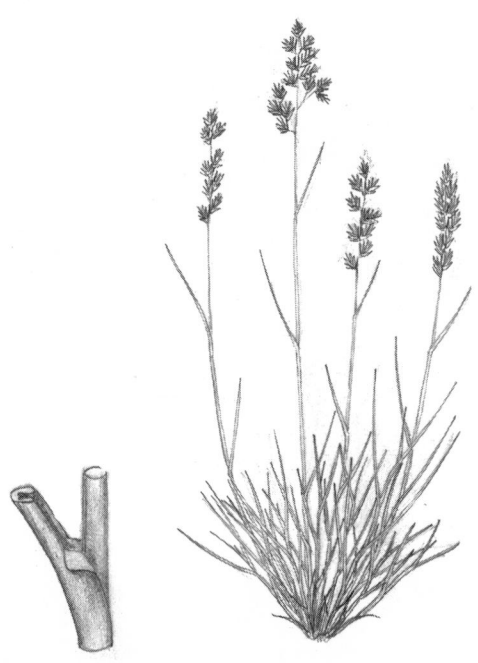

Fig. 4.8 *Festuca ovina*—Sheeps Fescue.

FINE-LEAVED SHEEPS FESCUE (*Festuca ovina tenuifolia* Sibth.)

This is a densely tufted perennial plant which produces very narrow leaves resistant to drought. It is a species which will produce a good sward on all but heavy or damp soils. This grass is sometimes used in fine mixtures, but it is not recommended to be sown by itself. It is sometimes added to mixtures to reduce the cost. An example of a commercially available variety is 'Novina'.

The meadow grasses

This group of grasses belong to the genus *Poa*. This is a large group of grasses but only three species are used to any extent in Europe. These are: *Poa pratensis, Poa trivialis* and *Poa nemoralis*. A fourth species called Annual Meadow Grass (*Poa annua*) is found in the majority of lawns but seed of this species is not commercially available to any extent.

ANNUAL MEADOW GRASS (*Poa annua*)

This is a loosely tufted annual plant which has a very variable habit (see Fig. 4.9). The grass is distributed and grows on a wide variety of soils. Annual Meadow Grass can reproduce itself all the year round by seed, but the main period of reproduction is during the late spring. It can be found in almost all areas of turf, except on sites which become very dry. When this does occur, the grass turns yellow and dies. It is because of this and its propensity for producing seed that annual meadow grass is considered a weed in fine turf.

SMOOTH STALKED MEADOW GRASS, KENTUCKY BLUE GRASS (*Poa pratensis*)

This grass is commonly used in turf areas in both Britain and U.S.A. and the American name Kentucky Blue Grass is often the one commonly used. It is a species which spreads by short, underground, creeping rhizomes, but occasionally stolons are produced which give the turf a ragged appearance. This is a species which will grow on a wide range of sites ranging from moist light loams to clays, but the best growth is produced on moist light soils of medium texture.

Kentucky Blue Grass will not tolerate frequent close mowing and for this reason it is not recommended for use on very fine lawns. However, it will withstand drought and hard wear and is ideally

59

Fig. 4.9   *Poa annua*—Annual Meadow Grass.

suited for use on golf fairways, cricket outfields and football pitches. Examples of commercially available cultivars are 'Prato', 'Baron', 'Modena' and 'Monopoly'.

ROUGH STALKED MEADOW GRASS (*Poa trivialis*)

This is a tufted creeping perennial which spreads by means of over-ground stolons or short runners (see Fig. 4.10). It grows best on rich moist soils and when established develops faster than Kentucky Blue Grass. On dry soils the grass growth is greatly reduced and the foliage turns a reddy Brown colour.

Rough Stalked Meadow Grass is unsuitable for fine lawns as it will not tolerate frequent close mowing. It should only be used in mixtures with other grasses to produce swards suitable for utility turf.

60

WOOD MEADOW GRASS (*Poa nemoralis*)

This is a very variable species of *Poa* which is ideal for moist shady sites such as woodland parks. It is unsuitable for use in fine seed mixtures and should not be sown on its own.

The Rye grasses

Rye grass is the common name given to grasses which are included in the genus *Lolium*. The only species which is of any importance for

Fig. 4.10 *Poa trivialis*—Rough Stalked Meadow Grass.

turf culture purposes is Perennial Rye Grass. However, Italian Rye Grass is sometimes used on certain specialised areas as a nurse grass.

PERENNIAL RYE GRASS (*Lolium perenne*)

This is a tufted perennial grass which is widely used for the production of second class lawns and sports fields. Perennial Rye prefers moist fertile land which encourages vigorous growth. The leaves of the grass are relatively broad and tough, which enables them to withstand hard wear. They do not however 'blend in' very well with other fine-leaved grasses. Commercially available cultivars include the Aberystwth strain S23 and the varieties 'Stadion', 'Manhattan' and 'Melle'.

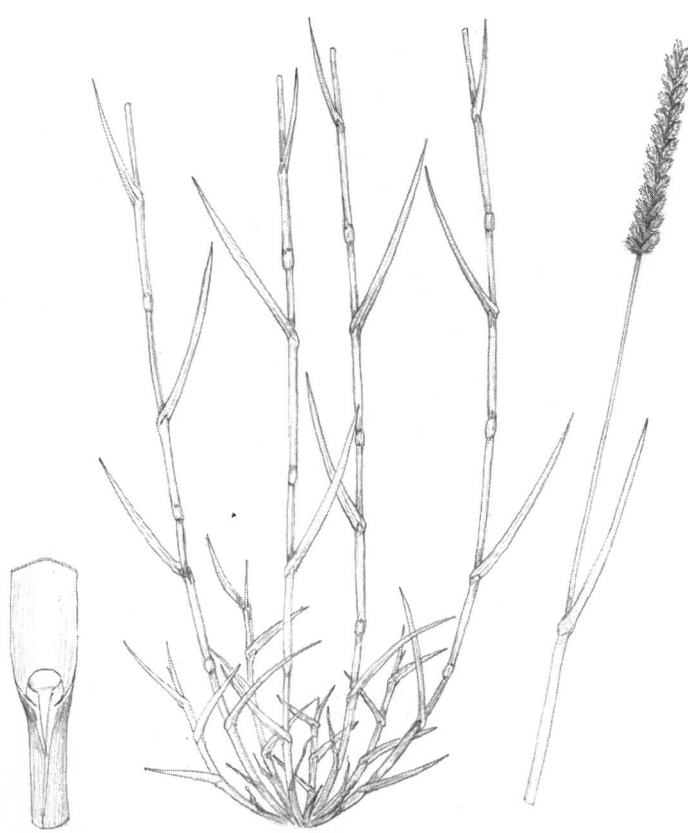

Fig. 4.11 *Cynosurus cristatus*—Crested Dog's Tail.

Dogstails

CRESTED DOGSTAIL (*Cynosurus cristatus*)

Crested Dogstail belongs to the group of plants which make up the genus *Cynosurus*. The grass is found naturally in dry, hilly places and areas of heavy clay. It is slow to develop, but once established it is resistant to low temperatures and periods of drought.

Crested Dogstail produces tough leaves which resist hard wear and tear and because of this feature its main use is in sportsgrounds such as cricket tables where the hard wearing properties are beneficial (Fig. 4.11).

Fig. 4.12 *Phleum pratense*—Timothy.

63

Table 4.1 Characteristics of some of the important grass species

Latin Name	Common Name	Ligules	Auricles	Growth Habit	Type of Foliage	Seed	Soils	Uses
Agrostis tenius	Browntop Bent	Blunt	None	Tufted with rhizomatous or stoloniferous growth	Bright green and hairless	Very small, approx. 0·5 mm	Most, except very dry sites	Fine lawns, e.g. bowling greens
Agrostis canina	Velvet Bent	Pointed, approx. 2–4 mm	None	Tufted with stolons	Bright green to greyish. Blades finely pointed	Very small	Damp sites	Fine lawns and utility turf
Agrostis stolonifera	Creeping Bent	Blunt and membranous	None	Tufted perennial, creeping by stolons	Green to bluish-green. Hairless	Medium (1·5 mm)	Most sites	Some sports turf and utility lawns
Festuca rubra commutata	Chewings Fescue	Blunt and extremely short	Very Small	Densely tufted without rhizomes	Grass green and hairless	Medium (3 mm)	Well drained	Fine lawns, e.g. bowling greens
Festuca rubra	Red Fescue	Blunt round and very short	Small and rounded	Creeping rhizomes	Green to grey green. Bristly	Fairly large (3–5 mm)	Most but grows well on light soils	Sports grounds and some fine lawns

Species	Common name	Ligule	Auricles	Growth habit	Leaf colour	Width	Soils	Uses
Festuca ovina	Sheeps Fescue	Blunt and extremely short	Rounded	Tufted without rhizomes	Grass green or greyish green. Hairless	Fairly large, approx. (3-5 mm)	Acid moorlands and light soils	Utility lawns, e.g. tennis courts
Poa pratensis	Smooth Stalked Meadow Grass	Membranous blunt or hooded tips	None	Very variable spreads by rhizomes	Green or greyish green. Sheaths smooth	Medium (2 mm)	Wide range good on light soils	Sports grounds
Poa trivialis	Rough stalked meadow grass	Pointed. Approx. 4–10 mm	None	Loosely tufted with stolons	Pale green or purplish. Hairless	Medium (2 mm)	Moist soils	Shaded areas and sports grounds
Poa nemoralis	Wood Meadow grass	Membranous. Approx. 0·55 mm	None	Loosely tufted without rhizomes	Leaves green hairless sheaths. Smooth	Medium	Moist soils	Shaded areas
Lolium perenne	Perennial Rye grass	Blunt and large	Small and narrow	Loosely to densely tufted perennial	Green hairless pink at base when young	Large (5 mm)	Moist fertile soils and heavy soils	Sports and lower quality turf
Cynosurus cristatus	Crested Dogstail	Blunt and small	None	Tufted	Dark green	Medium (2 mm)	Moist but grows well on heavy sites	Sports turf
Phleum bertolonii and *P. pratense*	Smaller Catstail or Timothy	Large and ragged	None	Loosely to densely tufted perennials	Green to greyish green. Hairless	Medium (2 mm)	Moist to heavy soils	Sports grounds and utility turf

Cats tails (Timothy)

These grasses belong to the genus *Phleum*. Only one species is commonly used in turf, namely *Phleum pratense* (Fig. 4.12). However, a second species *Phleum bertolonii* has been used occasionally. *P. pratense* produces a much larger plant than *P. bertolonii* and it is for this reason that its use is limited.

The main use of Timothy in lawns is on areas which receive heavy wear. It should never be used by itself and is unsuitable for areas which receive frequent close mowings. An improved selection of Timothy has been produced at Aberystwyth in Wales and has been given the number S50.

* * *

Many other grasses such as Wavy Hair Grass (*Deschampsia flexuosa*) can be used in the production of turf but the ones previously mentioned are the species which occur most commonly in turf culture.

5 Lawn Production

Before the production of a lawn can take place, the soil must be in an ideal condition to encourage the rapid establishment of grasses. The initial preparation of a site for either sowing or turfing is most important as inadequate preparation can lead to both cultural and managerial problems in the later years of the sward's life. The first essential for rapid establishment is the production of a well-structured seedbed. The structure of a soil may be classified as the way in which the particles of sand, silt and clay are joined together to form conglomerates. The term texture, on the other hand, is given to the actual percentages of the above mentioned mineral materials. It is of the utmost importance that the soil should have a good structure, as without this the useful life of the area can be greatly reduced. The major considerations when preparing a seedbed are given below.

Soil Improvements

The ideal soil for the production of turf would be a deep, well-drained, medium-textured loam, with a pH of between 5·5 and 6·5. As all sites are not endowed with such idyllic features, some form of soil improvement is usually necessary. The degree of improvement will vary with each particular site, but the aim should always be to produce a well-structured soil which will remain in good 'heart' during long periods of inclement weather. The method of improvement and the equipment used will depend upon the size and accessibility of the site. On small sites or areas having restricted access, digging by hand or rotary cultivators (Fig. 5.1) may be the only suitable methods, whereas on large accessible sites ploughing (Fig. 5.2) and deep subsoiling may be carried out.

Before digging or ploughing takes place, all large stones, builders' waste and rubbish should be removed. If the site is covered with rough herbage, it will also be beneficial to carry out some form of scything or mowing as grass can be very difficult to dig in.

The best time to carry out digging or ploughing is during dry periods of weather in autumn or winter as this gives a long period of time for the soil to be broken down by frost. During cultivation

Fig. 5.1   A rotary cultivator.

care should be taken to ensure that any compacted layers (pans) should be broken up as these will inhibit soil aeration and drainage. If a pan is present it will be necessary to carry out some form of sub-soiling. On small sites this can be done by double digging, whereas on large sites specialised sub-soiling ploughs can be used.

Before the final preparation of the site takes place it is advisable to carry out a complete soil analysis. This will indicate the nutrient status of the soil as well as the degree of acidity which exists. These analyses cost a small amount of money but they are well worthwhile and can save a lot of hard work in later years.

Weed Control

Weed control during preparation can be obtained by two methods namely, cultural and chemical. The system used will vary with the site, the scale of operation and the weed species present. The main aim should be to eradicate all perennial weeds.

Fig. 5.2   A modern reversible plough.

Cultural control

This consists of killing weeds without the use of chemicals. Cultural control is usually carried out by hand, or by soil moving equipment such as tractor mounted discs (see Fig. 5.3), harrows and hoes. Simple weed control can be obtained by removing weeds during digging, whereas on extensive sites frequent cultivations will be required.

Perennial weeds such as Couch Grass (*Agropyron repens*), which have underground creeping rhizomes, can be difficult to control. With this type of plant all the living parts of the underground organs must be removed or killed. Otherwise, the plants will become re-established.

Fallowing the soil

If the site is to be sown in autumn, an operation called fallowing can take place. Fallowing consists of keeping the site bare for a number

Fig. 5.3   Tractor mounted discs.

of months during the summer and periodically hoeing or discing it to kill any germinating weed seedlings. The period of fallowing should be as long as possible, as this helps to produce a weed free seedbed which is ideal for seed sowing.

The period of fallowing need not be so great if turf laying is to be carried out. Turves cover the soil and prevent annual and biennial weeds from germinating. However, it is important to have a soil free from established perennial weeds as these can easily grow through a thin layer of turf.

During the period of fallowing, pests and diseases can be controlled by the incorporation of a soil insecticide such as H.C.H. (formerly B.H.C.) or a fungicide such as Captan.

Chemical weed control

This consists of applying chemicals to kill weed growth. Residual (soil-acting) and translocated herbicides are not recommended for use during a period of six months prior to sowing, as these chemicals can cause serious damage to young grass growth.

The only chemicals which are recommended for use during the six months prior to sowing are materials which have a contact action such as dimexan or paraquat. These chemicals can be safely used until approximately two days before the grass seedlings emerge.

Whenever chemicals are used, great care should be taken to ensure that they are applied correctly. Always read the manufacturer's instructions and *always* wear the appropriate protective clothing (for further details of weed control see Chapter 7).

Soil sterilisation

It is now possible to incorporate chemicals which act as sterilants into the soil. These chemicals can be used to produce a site free from weeds, pests and diseases which is conducive to healthy grass growth. The best time to apply the chemicals is during the summer months because the soil temperature is high and this encourages the rapid spread of the poisonous gases.

Once the chemical is incorporated, the soil must be 'sealed' so that the gases are retained. There are two main methods of sealing the soil. The first is to cover the site with polythene, the second is to break the surface soil down into a fine tilth and then apply large amounts of water to cap it. Once sealed the site should be left for approximately three to four weeks to allow the chemicals to work. After this period the soil should be opened up to aid the release of any gases that are still present. An example of a chemical sterilant which can be used in this way is 'Basamid'.

Final Preparation of the Seedbed

The final preparation of the seedbed should ideally take place during the summer months as this will enable the soil to be either fallowed or sterilised. The topsoil should be at least 15 cm (6 in) deep and when broken down should provide a firm, well aerated seedbed. On large sites the soil will be broken down by using harrows, spring tines or discs, whereas on smaller sites it will be done by hand raking.

Before the seed can be sown the soil must be firm, as any loose pockets will quickly dry out and lead to poor germination of the seeds. Firming can be carried out in two ways. For large areas Cambridge rollers (Fig. 5.4) are used. These rollers are attached to

Fig. 5.4   A Cambridge roller.

tractors and are drawn over the land in different directions. The shape of the roller ensures that any small pockets of loose soil are removed.

On smaller sites however, firming can be carried out by 'treading'. This consists of putting all ones body weight on ones heels and 'shuffling' over the site. To produce a firm seedbed it may be necessary to tread the soil more than once. If this is the case the soil will benefit from being raked after each treading.

Once the site has been firmed, all that remains to be carried out is the final raking and the application of a base dressing. The raking will ensure the removal of all heel and roller marks whilst the fertiliser will encourage rapid healthy establishment.

Base Dressings

The three most important nutrients which plants obtain from the soil are nitrogen (N) in the form of nitrates, phosphorus (P) in the form of phosphates and potassium (K) in the form of potassium salts.

These nutrients help to produce healthy vigorous growth in plants. However, if for some reason one or more of them are deficient, plant growth will suffer. If a soil analysis has been carried out, the results will indicate which nutrients are lacking.

Fertilisers containing high percentages of phosphorus will encourage healthy root development and ones containing potassium will aid the overwintering of grass seedlings. On the other hand, fertilisers containing large quantities of nitrogen will produce lush, green, leafy growth which will be susceptible to damage by winter frosts.

Mixtures or compounds of these nutrients can be purchased which are suitable as base dressings. The important point to remember is that they should contain a high percentage of phosphorus and potassium and a low percentage of nitrogen.

An example of a compound fertiliser which would be suitable as a base dressing is:

$$5\text{--}10 \text{ g sulphate of ammonia/m}^2$$
$$30 \text{ g superphosphate of lime/m}^2$$
$$15 \text{ g sulphate of potash/m}^2$$

If the lawn is to be produced during the spring months, the higher rate of nitrogen can be applied.

Methods of Lawn Formation

Lawns are produced in three main ways namely, sowing seed and laying turves and by vegetative propagation—a method used more frequently in the U.S.A. Each method has its advantages and disadvantages but the final choice of production will depend to a large degree upon the individual site and personal preference.

The production of turf from seed has the advantage of a low initial cost, good keeping quality, choice of specific species, subsequent ease of management, and if the soil conditions are correct, a low percentage of weeds. However, the major disadvantages are the greater amount of seedbed preparation and the length of time that the sward takes to become established.

Turves on the other hand produce an established sward in a much shorter time than seed and the initial seedbed preparation need not be so involved. Their main disadvantages are their high initial cost, variable composition of grass species, the possibility of a high infestation of weeds and the possible presence of pests and diseases.

Seeding

Before buying grass seed the groundsman should identify the characteristics necessary to produce a suitable sward. Availability of the seed in commercial quantities should be confirmed, ensuring also that it is true to type and contains the minimum amount of other species.

Within the European Economic Community (E.E.C.) regulations exist to standardise the sale of seeds (including grasses). However, the regulations do not as yet cover all grass species, a notable example being Crested Dogstail (*Cynosurus cristatus*). Before a cultivar can now be placed on the national lists it must conform to a number of specified standards. The main points of importance when scheduling seed are:

a) cultivar purity;
b) percentage of other species;
c) total analytical purity;
d) germination percentage.

The regulations governing the percentage of purity and germination do not affect seed mixtures, but each cultivar or species in a mixture must meet its own statutory standards. As long as they meet the standards a seedhouse need not state the percentage of purity or germination. However, most companies will readily supply the information on request.

A comparison between seed samples can be obtained by calculating the 'Real Value' of each mixture in the following way:

$$\text{Real Value of a sample} = \frac{\text{Germination \% } \times \text{ Purity \%}}{100}$$

When formulating a grass seed mixture the choice of the individual species and cultivars will depend to a large extent upon the eventual use of the sward and the soil conditions upon which it is to be grown.

High quality swards

The choice of species for high quality swards such as bowling greens is limited because the species chosen must be fine-leaved and capable of withstanding frequent close mowing whilst still retaining a uniform colour and true surface. It is common practice to produce this type of sward from two or more species, suitable examples are as follows:

a) 70% Chewings Fescue
   30% Browntop Bent

b) 50% Chewings Fescue
   20% Cumberland Marsh Fescue
   30% Browntop Bent

On moisture retentive soils it is possible to reduce the percentage of Browntop and increase the amount of Chewings fescue. This will lead to a more balanced sward as there will be less risk of the Bent becoming dominant. A mixture that could be used is:

80% Chewings Fescue
20% Browntop Bent.

Ornamental lawns

The species chosen for the production of ornamental lawns need not be as fine-leaved as those for bowling greens. This means that the choice of species may be extended and consequently the cost of the mixture can be reduced. This type of sward is often composed of species such as Perennial Rye Grass (*Lolium perenne*) and Rough Stalked Meadow Grass (*Poa trivialis*). However, it is beneficial to incorporate some of the finer grasses such as the Fescues and Bents. Suitable mixtures for this type of area are:

a) 45% Chewings Fescue
   35% Red Fescue
   10% Rough Stalked Meadow Grass
   10% Browntop Bent

b) 40% Hard Fescue
   30% Red Fescue
   20% Chewings Fescue
   10% Browntop Bent

c) 30% Perennial Rye Grass
   30% Red Fescue
   25% Chewings Fescue
   15% Browntop Bent

Sports areas

In addition to bowling greens and ornamental lawns it is sometimes necessary to produce special types of swards for sports areas. These swards must be capable of rapidly establishing themselves, withstanding very hard wear, forming a good strong root system and be tolerant of mowing. Some of the individual types of area are given below.

Cricket wickets must contain fine-leaved species capable of being closely mown whilst not adversely affecting the bounce of the ball. Suitable mixtures for this type of sward are:

a) 75% Chewings Fescue
   10% Browntop Bent
   15% Crested Dogstail

b) 45% Chewings Fescue
   40% Perennial Rye Grass
   15% Browntop Bent

c) 60% Chewings Fescue
   20% Browntop Bent
   20% Crested Dogstail

Winter sports areas need species capable of growing during periods of damp, cold weather. They must also be hard wearing, have a well anchored root system, produce a dense sward and have the ability to quickly re-establish themselves. Mixtures which are used for this type of area are:

a) 50% Perennial Rye Grass
   25% Red Fescue

15% Chewings Fescue
10% Timothy
b) 30% Perennial Rye Grass
30% Red Fescue
20% Chewings Fescue
10% Browntop Bent
5% Crested Dogstail
5% Rough Stalked Meadow Grass

It must be noted that all the above mixtures are only given as guide-lines and that they are in no way meant to cover every type of situation. It is also important to note that in recent years many new cultivars have been introduced which are improved selections of the straight species. For more information on these and advice on mixtures it is recommended to consult a specialist seedhouse.

SEEDING RATES

The rate at which grass seed should be sown will vary with the soil conditions and the composition of the mixture. Attention should also be drawn to the fact that fungal diseases can be encouraged if the seed is sown too thickly, whereas establishment will be very slow if sown too thinly. With this in mind, it will be seen that the amount of seed sown greatly affects the speed of establishment and subsequent ease of management.

As a generalisation, a rate of 60 g/m² (2 oz/sq. yd) would be suitable for mixtures containing large seeded species and 45 g/m² (1½ oz/sq. yd) would be adequate for general purpose swards. However, where the soil conditions are ideal or, where very fine seed is used the rate of sowing can be as low as 20–30 g/m² (¾–1 oz/sq. yd).

In mixtures where species of Bent are used, it is important to ensure that the seeds are mixed correctly as small seeds can very easily settle to the bottom of bags. If settling does occur a poor distribution of grasses may result which in turn can lead to the production of an unbalanced sward. To overcome this problem some groundsmen purchase their seed as 'straights'. This enables them to firstly sow and cover the large seeded species followed by oversowing with the finer types.

SEED SOWING AND GERMINATION

Once the seedbed has been prepared and the mixture chosen, all that

77

remains is for the seed to be sown. Before this is described it will be beneficial to explain some of the factors affecting germination and subsequent establishment of seedlings. Three main environmental conditions must be met before seeds can germinate, these are:

1   The correct amount of moisture;
2   The correct amount of oxygen;
3   An adequate temperature for germination.

Water is important as without it the seeds will be unable to germinate, or they will germinate and then perish. On the other hand, too much water can cause waterlogging of the soil which leads to poor aeration and ideal conditions for fungal attack. The soil moisture status for sowing should be as close to field capacity as is practically possible, as this gives the most suitable conditions for germination.

Oxygen is required by plants and seeds for the process of respiration; it is also a necessary constituent of the soil, as without it both biological and chemical processes are unable to take place. The percentage of air—and consequently the percentage of oxygen—in the soil is controlled by the type of structure and the amount of water held between the particles. It is for these reasons that surface drainage and the maintenance of a good soil structure are essential prerequisites for seed sowing.

In addition to moisture and oxygen, seeds require a certain amount of heat before germination can take place. An adequate temperature is also required to encourage the rapid establishment of the seedlings. The optimum temperature for grass seed germination is between 16°C and 21°C (60°–70°F). However, certain species can become established in cooler situations.

On large sites, sowing can be carried out by machines such as the Brillion seed drill or agricultural type seeding units and harrows. On smaller sites however seeding is usually done by hand, or occasionally hand operated machines (fiddles).

Seeding is usually done at two main times of the year namely, autumn and spring. Autumn is recognised as the best time because the soil is still warm after the summer and the seedlings have time to become established before the winter months. If on the other hand, sowing takes place during the springtime, the soil is still cold after the winter months and consequently seed germination is very slow. The stages in seed sowing can be summarised as follows:

1   Mark out the plot into multiples of 1 m² (about 1 sq. yd);
2   Divide the seed into the correct quantities to cover each of the marked areas;
3   Sow the seed over each area;
4   Lightly rake in the seed.

Under ideal conditions grass seed takes approximately 10–14 days to germinate depending upon the temperature and moisture content of the soil. The process of germination follows a definite sequence, the main stages of which are:

1   Absorption of moisture;
2   Swelling of the seedcoat;
3   Activation of enzymes;
4   Release of energy from stored foods;
5   Splitting of the seedcoat;
6   Elongation and emergence of the young root;
7   Elongation and emergence of the young shoot;
8   Young shoot begins to photosynthesise.

ESTABLISHMENT PRACTICES

After germination but, prior to the initial mowing, it is advantageous to remove any large stones from the site as these can produce an uneven surface and damage the mower blades. Once the grass is approximately 25 mm (1 in) high, a light rolling is beneficial. This will firm the seedbed, aid establishment of the sward and prevent the seedlings being torn out during mowing. If a light roller is unavailable, the same effect can be achieved by using a cylinder mower with its blades in the raised position.

Once rolling has taken place, the young seedlings should be left until they are about 50 mm (2 in) tall. When they reach this height they can be given their first mowing. The best type of machine for this operation is the side-wheel mower but a cylinder mower can be used if necessary. Whatever type of mower is used it should be sharp and set to remove about half the topgrowth (25 mm or 1 in) as this encourages the production of numerous sideshoots, commonly known as tillers. It is these tillers which help to form a dense, close-knit sward. Under no circumstances should the first mowing do anything more than lightly tip the young seedlings, otherwise the establishment of the sward can be greatly impaired. When established, and

79

not before, the height of cut can be gradually reduced until the grass is at its final required length.

Other than stone picking, rolling and mowing, the only other necessities for healthy development are regular fungicidal sprays for the prevention of seedling diseases and hand weeding, or application of ioxynil to control troublesome broad-leaved weeds.

HYDRAULIC SEEDING

Hydraulic seeding has been specifically designed to establish grass swards on semi-inert soils, steep slopes and inaccessible areas. The technique is commonly used on sites such as roadway embankments, reservoirs and river banks but, is suitable for any site where large amounts of earthmoving has taken place.

Before seeding, each site is subjected to a soil analysis from which recommendations on the type of fertiliser, micro-organisms and spreading medium can be obtained. The species of grass are then specifically chosen to suit the soil conditions and location. Examples of grasses used are Perennial Rye Grass, Smooth stalked Meadow Grass, Red Fescue and Crested Dogstail. However, it is also possible to include clover and even hardwood species if required.

The seed and nutrient mixture is applied in the form of slurry, via large spray jets. The composition of the mixture varies with the type of soil and the degree of exposure. On normal banks that are not too exposed a straight seed/water mixture can be used but on sites with little topsoil a sufficient surface must be built up to maintain the young grass. In this situation, a mixture of seed, water, fertilisers, micro-organisms and bulky mediums such as wood pulp, latex, fibre glass or chopped straw would be necessary.

Seed germination varies with the method of application and the time of year. It can take approximately 3 weeks in early spring or late autumn with standard applications, whereas when a mulch is applied it can be in the region of 4 weeks. On difficult sites germination and establishment may be poor or the plants may not survive, if this does occur re-seeding will be necessary.

Turfing

Laying turf (sods) instead of sowing seeds, produces a lawn in a very short period of time. This is because the sods are composed of thin sheets of densely rooted, matted grass which is easily transplanted.

The type of sward achieved in this manner is greatly dependant upon the situation of the proposed lawn, and the source of the sods.

Consideration should always be given to the problem of the degeneration of a sward once removed from its natural environment. When turf is removed from areas such as sea washed marshes, a gradual degeneration of species takes place followed by the establishment of broader-leaved types. This is because the turf no longer receives the environmental conditions of its natural habitat. The main reason behind using sea-washed turf for bowling greens and the like, is that it gives a high quality sward which is a sound basis for cultivation.

The main considerations when selecting turf for lawns are:

a) The species of grass in the turf; this can be very variable ranging from very broad-leaved species to the finest of Bents;

b) Disease problems; this is dependant upon the cultural management, situation of the site and the species present;

c) Weed problems; the number and type of weeds can be variable depending upon the location, soil type and degree of herbicidal control.

The major consideration when producing a fine lawn should be the species of grass that are present in the turf. This is important as the composition of the sward is very difficult to change, whereas weeds and diseases can be controlled by chemicals.

SOURCES OF TURF AVAILABLE FOR LAWN PRODUCTION

Quantities of good quality turf can be very difficult to obtain, mainly due to the fact that transport costs can be prohibitive. This usually means that the selection of turf is restricted to local supplies. As this is the case it is advantageous to go and view the turf before purchase as orders made by telephone can often lead to disappointment.

The main types of turf available commercially are given below.

Parkland turf

Established parkland turf is excellent for producing lawns, although it can be in short supply and expensive. The species of grass present is dependant upon the soil type and cultural management, but a good sample will contain a high percentage of Fescues and Bents.

Meadow turf

Farmers occasionally sell off areas of turf from meadows. This is very variable and often contains many broad-leaved weeds, undesirable grass species and sometimes diseases. It is only recommended for large areas of turf which do not require to be maintained to a high standard.

Sea-washed turf

This turf is obtained from sea washed marshes, e.g. in the U.K. it comes mainly from the Lancashire coastal areas. The turf consists of fine-leaved species and is used mainly for very fine lawns such as bowling greens. Sea-washed turf degenerates when removed from its natural conditions, broader-leaved grasses taking the place of the finer species. This type of turf is very desirable and much sought after, but its cost can be prohibitive due to high transportation costs.

Downland turf

This type of turf is obtained from chalk downlands. It is only used for localised supplies, but when used it can produce a good quality sward. The predominant species of grass found in downland turf are Sheeps fescues, Bents and Crested Dogstail.

Lagoon turf (Tana-grass)

Tana Grass is formed floating on a lagoon of water. It is a type of hydroponics which enables up to 4 crops a year to be produced. The system consists of floating a slurry of Perlite or Hygromull (an artificial peat made by BASF) and wetting agent on water. The slurry is then covered with a thin carrier sheet of polyurethane foam, to act as a platform for the seeds which are sown on top. This also prevents the seeds from sinking. The foam mattress provides a constant level of moisture for the germinating seeds and once established the young roots grow through the foam to bind the slurry together, so that a firm carpet of grass is produced.

The turves are very light and tough, and can be rolled up like pieces of carpet. They are flat, all of the same thickness, easy and light to transport, less liable to damage and easy to lay.

The grass is grown on a sterile medium carrying no weeds or disease and the roots are not cut during lifting, so establishment of newly laid turf starts immediately.

The foam acts as a mulch during establishment and then decomposes to become part of the soil. Tana turves do not shrink in dry weather so they can be laid in almost all conditions. It is claimed that, under the correct conditions, a Tana bowling green could be ready for use in 2–3 months after laying.

Fig. 5.5   A half-moon.

Turf lifting

On a small scale, turf is lifted manually by means of turfing irons or 'floats' as they are sometimes called. The turf should be marked out to the correct size by means of tapes and cut with a half-moon (Fig. 5.5) or turf race. If lines are used it is important that they should be

Fig. 5.6   A turf float.

kept as taught as possible otherwise the sods will not be square. A better system where small amounts are to be cut is to use a plank as a straight edge. It is then a simple operation to stand on the plank and run the half-moon against its edge.

When turf has been marked out and cut, it is ready for lifting. This operation is carried out by pushing the turf float (Fig. 5.6) beneath the sods and lifting the individual pieces. If a large quantity has to be lifted in this manner it is a good idea before starting, to bend the float shaft into a comfortable working position.

On a large scale, purpose built turf lifting machines are used. These machines are designed to cut the turf to the correct size and at the correct depth. They lift turf very quickly and where large quantities are required, their use should always be considered.

SIZES OF TURF

Turf sizes vary depending upon suppliers and soil types. On sandy soils, which will not hold together, the size of a sod will be small, e.g. $0 \cdot 3$ m $\times$ $0 \cdot 3$ m (1 ft $\times$ 1 ft), whereas on fibrous loams the turves can be as large as $0 \cdot 3$ m $\times$ $1 \cdot 0$ m (1 ft $\times$ 3 ft).

Two main sizes are available commercially, these are:

$$0 \cdot 3 \text{ m} \times 0 \cdot 5 \text{ m} (1 \text{ ft} \times 1\tfrac{1}{2} \text{ ft})$$
$$0 \cdot 3 \text{ m} \times 1 \cdot 0 \text{ m} (1 \text{ ft} \times 3 \text{ ft})$$

The standard thickness of turf also varies with suppliers and soil types, the range being between 25 mm and 40 mm (approximately 1–$1\tfrac{1}{2}$ in).

BOXING OF TURF

If turf is lifted by hand, the process of boxing is necessary. Boxing produces turf of even thickness which is easily laid. The method consists of placing turf upside down in a wooden box of the desired depth and removing the excess soil by running a sharp knife, such as a scythe blade, over the top of the box (see Fig. 5.7). It is important to ensure that the box is clean before each new piece of turf is put in otherwise uneven turves will be produced.

STORAGE OF TURF

Once turf has been cut it should be laid in its new position as quickly

Fig. 5.7 Boxing turf.

as possible. Whatever happens the sods should not be allowed to dry out as when this takes place they shrink and their rate of establishment is greatly impaired.

Turf is commonly stored by one of three methods:

a) The sods can be stacked turf to turf and soil to soil;
b) Long sods (0·3 m × 1·0 m) can be rolled;
c) Laying the sods face upwards in a single layer.

The first two methods are only suitable for short periods of storage as if left for any length of time the grass will turn yellow and die. The third method, on the other hand, is suitable for long periods of storage because the sods can obtain the correct quantities of light to enable them to produce healthy growth.

TURF LAYING

The site preparation for turfing need not be as fine as for seeding, but

86

good soil preparation and the incorporation of a base dressing will give a better chance of establishment, with fewer problems in later years.

Turves are laid in brick fashion (staggered) as this ensures an even knitted sward. However, if sods are laid in ideal conditions and top-

Fig. 5.8   Turf laying. Work in the direction of the arrow.

dressing and irrigation are applied, then staggering is not essential. When laying turf (see Fig. 5.8) it is best to work forwards so that the prepared area is not disturbed by foot marks. Each sod should be individually placed in position and levelled. After the first row has been placed, the second row can be laid ensuring that the sods are packed tightly together. This is usually carried out by 'pulling' the turves with a garden fork.

Once the first couple of rows have been laid, it is expedient to work from a plank as this prevents the turves from being damaged whilst gently firming them in position.

After laying, the turf will benefit from a light topdressing of bulky material such as sand, sandy loam—or a peat, sand and seed mixture. It is also advantageous to incorporate a small amount of base dressing, high in phosphorus as this will encourage root growth and establishment.

When the sods have begun to knit together they can be given a light rolling. This will help settle the sward and firm any sods that may have been lifted by frost. It must be remembered, however, that rolling should only take place when the soil is dry enough, otherwise serious damage can be caused to the soil structure. All other establishment practices are the same as for seed sowing.

Vegetative propagation

This method of lawn production is particularly popular in the U.S.A., though it has never really become established in the U.K. It consists of planting small pieces or clumps of creeping grass species. The clumps are planted at approximately 150 mm (6 in) to 300 mm (12 in) apart and once established the plants produce runners or stolons which colonise the site and fill in any bare patches of the soil. The lawns produced in this country by vegetative means have a tendency to be spongy, uneven in growth and are therefore unsuitable for games such as bowls which require a fine playing surface. Species of grass which are suitable for this type of production are Creeping Bent (*Agrostis stolonifera*), Velvet Bent (*Agrostis canina*) and Bermuda Grass (*Cynodon dactylon*).

Generally speaking the species used for vegetative production are the same in most countries, with occasional differences. However, recent selection work means that more cultivars are becoming commercially available.

Examples of cultivars available in the U.S.A. are Creeping Bent ('Cohansey', 'Northland', 'Norbreck'), Velvet Bent ('Acme', 'Piper', Raritan) and Bermuda Grass ('Midway', 'Texturf 10', 'Turfcote').

6 Plant Nutrition

Plants are unique organisms in that they have the ability to produce carbohydrates by utilising the sun's energy to join together carbon dioxide (CO_2) and water (H_2O). This process, known as *photosynthesis*, takes place in all green plants, the main areas of production being the *mesophyll layers* of the leaf. The mesophyll cells possess specialised structures, the chloroplasts, which contain light-sensitive chlorophyll. It is the chlorophyll that absorbs the sun's energy and which imparts the natural green colour to plant tissues. The process of photosynthesis can be expressed as follows:

$$6CO_2 + 6H_2O + 674 \text{ Kcal. energy} \longrightarrow C_6H_{12}O_6 + 6O_2$$

However, it must be realised, that the above equation exhibits a very simplified version of photosynthesis; the actual process consists of very complex chemical reactions.

Once produced, the carbohydrates can be stored and later broken down to produce energy for the plant's metabolic activities. The katabolic process, known as *respiration*, involved in the oxidisation of carbohydrates, with the subsequent release of energy, can take place under two sets of conditions. *Aerobic conditions* exist where the food-store (carbohydrate) is broken down in the presence of oxygen, the reaction being the opposite to photosynthesis, i.e.

$$C_6 H_{12} O_6 + 6O_2 \longrightarrow 6CO_2 + 6H_2O + 674 \text{ Kcal. energy}$$

Anaerobic conditions occur where the foodstore is broken down in the absence of oxygen. The reaction is

$$C_6 H_{12} O_6 \longrightarrow 2CO_2 + 2C_2 H_5OH + 50 \text{ Kcal. energy}$$

Again, both of these equations are over simplifications, the actual processes being very complex.

89

Plants require a number of nutrients to sustain their healthy growth. If, for any reason, a shortage of these nutrients occurs, the photosynthetic and respiratory processes will be reduced with a subsequent decrease in growth.

Grasses in sports areas, are grown under very intensive, unnatural conditions, which are not conducive to healthy growth. This can be exemplified by remembering that the majority of photosynthesis takes place in active green leaves and it is these that the groundsman constantly removes during the process of mowing. Cutting the grass not only removes the actively photosynthetic areas, it also removes large quantities of chemicals. It is these essential chemicals that the groundsman must replace by the applications of fertilisers.

Plant Nutrient Elements

In Chapter 1 we saw that a number of essential elements are required for healthy growth, each of which has its own affect on the plant structure and metabolic processes. Most of these elements are obtained from the soil. The majority of soils contain ample supplies of most essential elements, but certain nutrients can become deficient during cultivation. When this occurs, the deficiency can usually be alleviated by applications of fertilisers in either granular, powder or liquid form.

Fertilisers can be conveniently divided into two main groups— those of organic or inorganic origin. Organic fertilisers are derived from living organisms, i.e. plants and animals, an example being 'hoof and horn'. These constitute the older types of fertilisers. However, they are still widely used. Their main features are that they:

a) Release their nutrients over a long period of time because the nutrients are present in complex organic molecules;
b) Safe to use as they do not scorch roots or leaves;
c) Not easily washed out of the soil;
d) Weight for weight their food value is not as high as inorganics;
e) Can be very expensive;
f) Can be difficult to obtain;
g) Variable in composition;
h) Can carry disease organisms;
i) Can decompose in store.

90

Inorganic fertilisers, on the other hand, may be produced as by-products of industry (sulphate of ammonia), manufactured (ammonium nitrate), or refined from natural raw deposits (rock phosphate). The main features of these chemicals are:

a) Cheaper to buy than organics (for equivalent nutrient value);
b) Quick release of nutrients (usually);
c) Plants respond rapidly to applications;
d) Can be easily leached;
e) Can cause scorching of plant growth (if over applied);
f) Can sometimes reduce establishment of seedlings (nitrogen scorch).

The rapid release of nutrients from fertilisers is not always beneficial and so in recent years manufacturers have produced specially formulated inorganic chemicals (such as Gold N, Enmag and Osmocote) to have a slow release action. This means that the chemicals give an initial quantity of nutrient for plant growth, followed by a gradual release over a longer period of time.

Major plant nutrients

Not all soil nutrients are required by plants in equal quantities. In fact, the majority of elements will normally be supplied without supplementary applications being necessary. However, some nutrients are either easily leached, or are required in such quantities that the soil cannot provide them and therefore, additional nutrients must be given. The following are the major elements required for healthy growth.

NITROGEN

Nitrogen (N) enters the plant in the form of ammonium ions (NH_4^+) or nitrate ions (NO_3^-) and is found in all proteins and amino-acids within the plant. Large amounts of available nitrogen will increase the size of the leaves on a plant and also their intensity of green colouration.

Nitrogen is applied to turf during the growing season to encourage a healthy green sward. However, care should be taken to prevent over application as during the autumn months soft lush growth can be produced, which is easily damaged by frost and infected by diseases.

Table 6.1   Some Inorganic Nitrogenous Fertilisers

Name	Chemical Formula	Percentage of Nutrient	Remarks
Ammonium nitrate	$NH_4\,NO_3$	35% N	High nitrogen level.
Ammonium sulphate	$(NH_4)_2\,SO_4$	21% N	Lowers the pH of the soil.
Aqueous ammonia (ammonium hydroxide)	$NH_4\,OH$	21–29% N	Injected into the soil.
Calcium cynamide	$Ca\,CN_2$	21–22% N	Changed to urea in the soil.
Calcium nitrate	$Ca(NO_3)_2$	17·1% N	Very soluble.
Gold N	S coated $CO(NH_2)_2$	32% N	Slow release.
Nitra Shell	$NH_4NO_3 + CaCO_3$	23% N	Easy and safe to apply
Nitro-Chalk	$NH_4NO_3 + CaCO_3$	25% N	Easy and safe to apply.
Potassium nitrate	KNO_3	13·8% N	Supplies two nutrients.
Sodium nitrate	$NaNO_3$	16% N	Contains some sodium.
Urea	$CO(NH_2)_2$	46% N	Can be easily leached.

PHOSPHORUS

Phosphorus (P) enters the plant in the form of phosphate ions (PO_4^{-}) and is found mainly in the proteins of cell nuclei. It plays a fundamental role in the release of energy in the plant and is therefore important in cell division in the meristems.

Phosphorus is often incorporated into base dressings when the preparation of turf areas is taking place and is one of the major nutrients incorporated into spring and autumn top dressings. Care

Table 6.2 Some Organic Nitrogenous Fertilisers

Name	Percentage of Nutrients	Remarks
Dried blood	Approx. 12% N	High cost but quick acting.
Fish guano	Approx. 8–10% N	By-product of the fish industry.
Guano	Approx. 10–14% N	The true name given to bird droppings from Peru.
Hoof and horn	Approx. 12–14% N	Availability depends on the manufacturing process.
Soot	Approx. 1–6% N	Very soluble—allow to weather before use.

Table 6.3 Inorganic Phosphorus Fertilisers

Name	Chemical Formula	$\%P_2O_5$	$\%P$	Remarks
Basic slag	Variable	8–18·5 insoluble	3·5–8 insoluble	Contains trace elements and has liming properties.
Ground rock phosphate	Variable	25–39 insoluble	11–17 insoluble	Used on moist acid soils.
Mono-ammonium phosphate	$NH_4H_2PO_4$	48–62 soluble	21–26 soluble	Used in concentrated compounds.
Di-ammonium phosphate	$(NH_4)_2 HPO_4$	53 soluble	23 soluble	Used in concentrated compounds.
Super-phosphates	$Ca(H_2PO_4)_2 +CaSO_4$	18 soluble	8 soluble	Good for base dressing.
Triple super-phosphates	$Ca(H_2PO_4)_2$	48 soluble	21 soluble	Good for base dressing.

should always be taken when applying Phosphorus to the soil, as its availability can be reduced by excess acidity and alkalinity.

Fertilisers are now being increasingly expressed in the more logical percentage of nutrient, e.g. % P and % K instead of the old convention of %P_2O_5 and %K_2O. To overcome the problems in the change over both figures are quoted.

Table 6.4   Organic Phosphorus Fertilisers

Name	% P_2O_5	%P	Remarks
Bonemeal	Very variable, 15–32% P_2O_5	6·5–14	Slow release of nutrients valuable for acid soils.
Fish guano	Variable, 4·5–9% P_2O_5	2–4	See nitrogenous fertilisers.
Guano	Variable, 9–11% P_2O_5	4–5	See nitrogenous fertilisers.
Steamed bone flour	Average of 27–28% P_2O_5	12	Finely ground. Quick acting. Easy and safe to apply.

Table 6.5   Inorganic Potassium Fertilisers

Name	Chemical Formula	%K_2O	%K	Remarks
Kainit	KCL	14·5–30	12–25	Can contain other nutrients.
Muriate of potash	KCL	60	50	Contains chlorine and other salts.
Potassium meta-phosphate	KPO_3	38	32	Useful for sandy soils.
Potassium nitrate	KNO_3	47	39	Also provides some nitrogen.
Potassium sulphate	K_2SO_4	48	45	Used where muriate of potash is unsuitable.
Potassium-magnesium sulphate	K_2SO_4–$MgSO_4$	28	23	Helps to balance the potassium/magnesium ratio.

POTASSIUM

Potassium (K) enters the plant via its roots and is found mainly in the meristematic tissues. It affects the flowering process, enzyme production and osmotic pressure of the plant.

Potassium is frequently applied to areas such as sportsfields, where strong disease resistant healthy growth is required. However, applications must always be balanced with the soil Magnesium content, otherwise availability can be affected.

Table 6.6   Organic Potassium Fertilisers

Name	% K_2O	% K	Remarks
Fish guano	1·8–3·0	1·5–2·5	See nitrogenous fertilisers.
Guano	1·8–3·6	1·5–3	See nitrogenous fertilisers.
Seaweed	1·2	1	Can be applied as liquid feeds.
Wood ash	1·2–7·0	1–6	Percentage varies with the type and age of the wood.

MAGNESIUM

Magnesium (Mg) enters the plant via its roots and is found in young, actively growing leaves. However, it can be transported to areas of high need when required. A deficiency of this element prevents the production of chlorophyll, which in turn causes chlorosis of the leaves and poor growth with brilliant colour tints. A potassium/magnesium imbalance can sometimes take place especially when either of the chemicals is in excess.

CALCIUM

Calcium (Ca) enters the plant via its roots and is found in leaves, cell walls and is important in meristematic tissues particularly those in the roots. Calcium in the soil plays a major role in the balance of acidity and alkalinity; large quantities producing alkaline conditions and low percentages encouraging acidity.

95

Table 6.7   Inorganic Magnesium Fertilisers

Name	Chemical Formula	Percentage of Nutrient	Remarks
Epsom salt	$MgSO_4.7H_2O$	7–9% Mg	Soluble, suitable for sprays
Kieserite	$MgSO_4.H_2O$	16% Mg	Dissolves slowly
Magnesite	$MgCO_3$	27% Mg	Used on acid soils
Magnesium limestone	$CaCO_3MgCO_3$	3–12% Mg	Used on acid soils
Sulphate of potash magnesium	$K_2SO_4MgSO_4$	6·5% Mg	Used on acid soils, potassium/magnesium balance

Table 6.8   Examples of Materials containing Calcium

Common Name	Chemical Name	Chemical Formula	Remarks
Quicklime	Calcium oxide	CaO	Concentrated form but is not used much. Can scorch foliage.
Ground limestone	Calcium carbonate	$CaCO_3$	Very cheap form of lime. Slow acting and is best when finely ground.
Hydrated or slaked lime	Calcium hydroxide	$Ca(OH)_2$	Made by burning chalk in kilns and slaking it with water.
Gypsum	Calcium sulphate	$CaSO_4$	Useful on saline salts.
Dolomitic limestone	Magnesium carbonate	$MgCO_3$	Supply magnesium as well as raising the pH.

96

The chemicals in the table are the commonest forms in which calcium is applied to the soil. However, a number of other materials such as marl, basic slag and some fertilisers also have the capability of raising the pH.

SULPHUR

Sulphur (S) enters the roots of plants as sulphate ions (SO_4) and is found in proteins, amino-acids and actively growing shoots. It also functions in enzyme activity and is associated with nitrogen fixation. Fortunately, sulphur deficiency is rather rare, but where problems do occur they can be remedied by applications of flowers of sulphur, or fertilisers such as 'Gold N'.

Micro-nutrients

In addition to the major elements nitrogen, phosphorus, potassium and to a lesser extent magnesium, calcium and sulphur, the plant requires small amounts of other nutrients, known as micro-nutrients. These are iron (Fe), boron (B), manganese (Mn), copper (Cu), zinc (Zn) and Molybdenum (Mo).

The natural levels of these elements are usually adequately maintained, but under certain soil conditions deficiencies can occur. Where problems do arise they can be alleviated by applications of specially formulated chemicals, known as sequestrenes or fritted trace elements. However, it is important to remember that plants only require *minute* quantities of these materials and that over-applications can lead to serious toxicity problems.

Method of Calculating the Nutrient Percentage of a Fertiliser

If the inorganic chemical fertilisers listed in the tables are studied, it will be seen that each has its own percentage of nutrient. This means that for every 50-kg bag purchased, a definite quantity of plant food will be supplied. The method by which the percentage of nutrient is calculated can be described in the following manner.

Taking the example of urea in Table 6.1, it will be seen that the fertiliser contains 46% nitrogen, the other 54% being materials not directly required, but which are essential if the nitrogen is to be utilised. The reason for this is that urea is a compound containing

97

carbon, oxygen, hydrogen and nitrogen, all of which are chemically bonded together.

The chemical formula for urea is $CO(NH_2)_2$. This actually means that each molecule contains:

1 atom of carbon
1 atom of oxygen
4 atoms of hydrogen
2 atoms of nitrogen

It is then a straight forward calculation to work out the total molecular weight of the fertiliser:

	Atomic weight (each atom)	× No. of atoms	= Total
Carbon	12	× 1	12
Oxygen	16	× 1	16
Hydrogen	1	× 4	4
Nitrogen	14	× 2	28

Grand total—the molecular weight = 60

Once the total molecular weight is known, the percentage of nitrogen can be calculated using the following equation:

$$\text{Percentage of nitrogen in urea} = \frac{28 \times 100}{60} = 46$$

(The reason why the calculation does not work out exactly is because the atomic weights of the elements have been rounded up to the nearest whole number.)

Fortunately in practice, these calculations are not necessary as individual fertiliser manufacturers must state the percentage of nutrients in each bag. The actual percentage of nutrient is very important because it is used when calculating fertiliser requirements.

Within the E.E.C., the old system of recommending fertilisers in 'units' of nutrient per acre has been superceded. The new convention is based on kilogrammes of nutrient per hectare (kg/ha).

The easiest means of explaining the system is by using examples concerning the three major plant nutrients, e.g.

a) 100 kg of sulphate of ammonia (21% N) contains 21 kg of nitrogen (i.e. the percentage of that nutrient). This means that if one hectare of turf requires 84 kg of nitrogen, then the amount of fertiliser to apply can be calculated as follows:

$$\frac{\text{Amount of nutrient/ha}}{\% \text{ nutrient in fertiliser}} \times 100 = \text{Quantity of fertiliser required.}$$

$$\text{i.e.} \frac{84}{21} \times 100 = 400 \text{ kg.}$$

The only complication with this system is that fertilisers are sold in 50-kg bags, which means that the above example would require the application of 8 bags of sulphate of ammonia, i.e. $\frac{400}{50} = 8$.

b) 100 kg of superphosphate of lime (18% P_2O_5) contains 18 kg of phosphorus. If 1 ha of turf required 54 kg of phosphorus, the amount of fertiliser to apply can be calculated as follows:

$$\frac{54}{18} \times 100 = 300 \text{ kg.}$$

Remembering that fertilisers are sold in 50-kg bags, the number of bags required would be $\frac{300}{50} = 6$.

c) 100 kg of sulphate of potash (48% K_2O) contains 48 kg of potassium. If 1 ha of turf requires 120 kg of potassium, the amount of fertiliser to apply can be calculated as follows:

$$\frac{120}{48} \times 100 = 250 \text{ kg.}$$

A total of 5 bags being required, i.e. $\frac{250}{50} = 5$.

Compounds

Not all fertilisers are applied as 'straights'. In fact, the majority are now sold as compounds, or mixtures, supplying two or more of the major plant nutrients. The reasons for their popularity can be listed as follows:

99

1 A saving of time, labour and cost can be achieved because less material is applied than with straights;
2 Mixing is unnecessary;
3 Less area is required for storage purposes;
4 Application is made easy because the materials are often produced in granular form.

It is a statutory regulation that the amounts of individual nutrients in a compound are shown on the bag. This usually takes the form of 3 sets of numbers, e.g. 15 : 10 : 10, the numbers indicating the percentage of nitrogen, phosphorus and potassium, respectively. This means that the above compound would contain 15% N, 10% P_2O_5 and 10% K_2O. However, the situation is further complicated by the fact that the percentage of soluble and insoluble phosphorus must be shown. For example, the nutrients in a 6 : 15 : 15 compound may consist of 6% N, 1·25% insoluble P_2O_5, 13·75% soluble P_2O_5 and 15% K_2O. Again, this is further complicated by the change-over to %P and %K, so, care must be exercised when checking the percentage of nutrient in a fertiliser because it may be expressed as % P_2O_5 or % P, etc.

Plant Food Ratios

The plant food ratio is used to indicate the balance between the nutrients in a compound. It is not a statutory requirement, but most manufacturers supply the information on each bag. The ratio is obtained by making the lowest percentage of nutrient declared to 1 and showing the ratio of the other nutrients to it. For example, a plant food ratio of a 15 : 10 : 10 fertiliser would be 1½ : 1 : 1, found by dividing the three figures by 10. Similarly, a 6 : 15 : 15 compound would have a ratio of 1 : 2½ : 2½, obtained by dividing the three numbers by 6.

It will be seen from these examples that it is possible to obtain two fertilisers with different nutrient percentages, but having the same plant food ratio, e.g. a 7 : 14 : 14 compound would have the same plant food ratio as a 10 : 20 : 20 compound, i.e. a 1 : 2 : 2, obtained by dividing the former by 7 and the latter by 10. When this is the case, it is usually best to select the compound which supplies the correct quantity of nutrients in the cheapest and most easily applied form.

100

Timing of Applications

The application of fertiliser to a sward is largely dependant upon the soil type, what the area is used for (e.g. ornamental or sports), the type of season, whether wet or dry and the amount of topgrowth removed by mowing. A large percentage of fertiliser is applied to turf without adequate prior knowledge of the soil nutrient status. It is a serious and costly mistake to follow general recommendations about applications unless some form of analysis is carried out, or unless the groundsman has gained a wide practical knowledge of his site.

Fertilisers are usually applied during three periods of the year—spring, summer and autumn. As the growth rate of a sward varies with these periods and the incidence of disease is greater at certain times of the year than others, the chemicals chosen should give the maximum benefit with the least amount of damage.

Dressings

Dressings used during the springtime should contain a relatively high percentage of nitrogen to encourage healthy leaf growth, balanced quantities of phosphorus for healthy root growth and potassium for overall sturdiness. These chemicals can be applied as 'straights' but, it is now common place to use proprietory brands.

Applications during the summer months usually consist of straight nitrogen, either in a slow release form such as 'Gold N', or faster acting types such as sulphate of ammonia or ammonium nitrate. The former of these chemicals can be applied at monthly intervals in small quantities of about 30 g/m² (1oz/sq. yd.). However, after the chemical has been applied, a serious risk of scorching may exist. This can be prevented by the application of some form of irrigation.

Autumnal topdressings of fertilisers predominantly consist of high percentages of phosphorus to encourage healthy root growth and potassium to produce sturdy tissues capable of withstanding periods of frost. It is not generally recommended to incorporate high percentages of nitrogen in these applications, because this chemical produces soft, lush, easily damaged top-growth. The chemicals can again be applied in either straight or compound form and can conveniently be incorporated into bulky topdressings for application after aeration has taken place.

Bulky topdressings

Bulky topdressings are made up from mixtures of organic and inorganic materials and when applied to lawns their main functions are to improve the soil structure and extend the playing life of the sward. However, it must be remembered that they are used as soil conditioners and not as major sources of plant nutrients. Where nutrients are required, they can be incorporated as inorganic or organic fertilisers. The benefits of applying topdressings are as listed below.

The producion of level surfaces These can be obtained by 'rubbing in' small quantities of topdressing during the growing season.

Increase of the soil organic matter content Improving the organic matter content of the soil increases micro-organism activity, improves the structure and increases the moisture holding capcaity.

Increases the playing life of a sward Improved soil structure and micro-organism activity leads to better aeration and increased surface drainage, which in turn produces a sward capable of withstanding long, hard wear without being seriously damaged.

The return of nutrients removed by mowing During the process of mowing, large quantities of nutrients can be removed, however, these can usually be returned by the incorporation of fertilisers into the top dressing.

Control of moss Empirical evidence has shown that moss is encouraged by poor surface aeration, excess soil moisture and starved soil conditions. As the application of topdressings improve these conditions a reduction in moss can be achieved.

Topdressings to lawns are mainly applied during the autumn after play has finished. However, where necessary, they can be applied throughout the season. The method of applying these materials varies depending upon the size of the site and the amount to be applied, the commonest systems being those of hand or mechanical spreaders.

Hand applications of topdressings consist of distributing the material with a shovel and working it in with equipment such as stiff brushes or 'Tru-lutes' (Fig. 6.1). Mechanical applications on the other hand, consist of spreading materials using rotating belt type distributors followed by 'luting' in with either hand or mechanical equipment.

102

Fig. 6.1   A 'Tru-lute'.

Whichever method is chosen care should always be taken to prevent over-application as this can smother fine grass species, slow down growth and where fertiliser is incorporated, cause scorching of the sward.

Materials used in topdressings

SOIL

The type of soil used in a topdressing will be dependant upon the make-up of the site. Heavy sites containing a high percentage of clay may require the application of light sandy loams, whereas free-draining hungry soils will require heavier types of topdressing. The choice of the soil will be dependant upon availability and the type of sport to be played—remembering that whilst light sandy loams may be suitable for very heavy sites, they will be quite unsuitable for areas such as cricket wickets. It is also very important to ensure that the soils used in topdressings are free from pests, diseases and perennial weeds; the most expedient means of ensuring this is to carry out some form of soil sterilisation.

SAND

Sand is an inert material which is widely used in topdressings. Its popularity stems from its comparatively large particle size, which helps to confer good surface aeration to heavy soils. It is obtainable from either quarries, river banks or sand dunes, but from whichever source it is procured, care should always be taken to ensure that it is washed, is of the correct grade and calcium-free.

ORGANIC MATTER

Organic matter is available in a large variety of forms, the major types being as follows.

Garden compost This is composed of decaying organic matter collected from kitchens and gardens. It is very variable in consistency and must always be thoroughly composted before use. Good garden compost is a valuable asset to the general horticulturalist, but it has a very limited use for the groundsman.

Grass clippings Large quantities of grass clippings are removed from lawns each year. When correctly composted they can produce an ideal topdressing suitable for most areas.

Peat Either sedge or moss peats are available, the acidity of both varying with the location and conditions under which they were formed. Again, peat, like sand is an inert material and does not, therefore, require sterilising before use. It is light to handle, requires no composting and has the advantage of increasing the water holding capacity of the soil.

Leaf mould Leaf mould, like peat, is produced under varying conditions and from different sources of plant material. However, if correctly composted it can produce a rich, well-structured topdressing.

Spent hops Spent hops are obtained as a by-product from the brewing industry. They have very good moisture retention properties and when composted, make an ideal general topdressing or mulch.

Hollow tine cores The soil removed from lawns during the process of hollow tining (coring) can be broken down by riddling and re-applied as a topdressing. It is, however, beneficial to incorporate some form of fertiliser to this type of topdressing as it can sometimes be deficient in nutrients.

Farm manure Thoroughly decomposed farm manure produces an ideal topdressing for most horticultural situations. It encourages micro-organism activity, improves the soil structure, increases the water holding capacity and nutrient status.

Miscellaneous The above materials are not the only constituents of topdressings. In fact, a number of other substances such as shoddy, animal remains and sewage sludge, are sometimes used. The only problems with these materials are that supplies may be very localised and the components very variable.

Whatever materials are used in topdressings, it is essential that they are non-toxic to plant growth and do not contain pests, diseases or perennial weeds. The mixing and application of the materials will vary depending upon the constituents, use of the sward and the size of the area concerned. On small sites, hand mixing or the use of proprietory topdressings may be quite suitable, whereas for the larger site, shredders, concrete mixers and larger mechanical spreaders may be required.

7 Weeds

When growing crops on agricultural or horticultural land, it is common practice to carry out some form of rotation. This is done to prevent the soil from becoming starved of nutrients, ridden with pests and diseases and smothered with troublesome weeds. Turf is a 'crop', which for various reasons cannot be rotated, and as with any other 'mono-crop' situation, a build up of pests, diseases and weeds can easily occur. When this does happen the species which become established are capable of withstanding the various cultural and chemical treatments that the sward receives.

Before weeds can become established in turf, they must have the ability to survive under conditions of frequent close mowing. Some of the more important features which enable them to become successful are given below.

a) The weeds may be very low growing, often producing a compact rosette type of growth which is unaffected by mowing.

b) They may have the ability to seed very easily under varying conditions.

c) Many weeds such as Dandelion (*Taraxacum officinale*) produce thick, fleshy, underground taproots which are capable of producing new top growth when the plant has been decapitated.

d) Certain species, e.g. the Speedwells (*Veronica* spp), are successful because of their ability to vegetatively reproduce themselves by pieces which are broken off during mowing.

e) A number of species are able to produce long underground or overground creeping stems which enables the plant to spread rapidly over the turf.

f) The weeds may have a waxy layer on their leaves which prevents the retention of herbicides.

106

g) Some members of the grass family (Gramineae) are classed as weeds because of the size of their leaves, or their habit of growth. These are successful as chemical herbicides cannot be used to control them without damaging the turf.

Weed Control in Turf

Weed control in turf can be either by cultural or chemical means. The type of control carried out depends upon the weeds present, the sward and the size of the area.

Chemical control

When spraying chemicals it is important to ensure that an even distribution is achieved and that the correct dosage is retained by each plant. The amount of chemical retained will be influenced by one or more of the following:

a) *The shape of the leaf* Plants with long narrow leaves which point upwards will not receive the same amount of chemical as species with broad horizontally placed leaves;

b) *The type of leaf surface* Leaves which have thick waxy cuticles or large masses of hairs will not retain the same quantity of chemical as plants without these features;

c) *The amount of chemical applied* The amount of chemical applied and the type of formulation will affect retention. It is a waste of money to apply chemicals after the point of 'run-off' unless they have some soil acting properties;

d) Small droplets of chemical will be retained more easily by leaves because the larger droplets will run off and sprays containing wetting agents will be retained to a greater degree than those without.

THE TIMING OF CHEMICAL TREATMENTS

The timing of chemical treatments will vary depending upon the state of the sward. The main treatments are as follows:

'*Pre-sowing*'

This is where a chemical can be applied before the grass seed is sown to achieve a complete weed control. The chemicals that are used are either residual (e.g. simazine), translocated (e.g. 2,4-D), or contact (e.g. dimexan). Whatever chemical is used, it is important to ensure that a long enough period of time can elapse before seed sowing to enable the chemical to become inactivated. Serious damage can occur to grass seedlings if sowing takes place before the chemicals have dissipated. The herbicides simazine, M.C.P.A., and 2,4-D should not be applied to sites intended for seed sowing for at least 6 months prior to seeding, otherwise damage may occur.

Pre-emergence

This is when a chemical is applied to the soil after the crop has been sown but before it has emerged. The main type of chemical used in this way is the contact acting herbicide. However, some residual and translocated types can also be used.

Post-emergence

This is when chemicals are applied after the crop has emerged from the soil. In turf culture the main post-emergent sprays are of the translocated type, e.g. 2,4-D and M.C.P.A. However, the contact herbicide ioxynil can be applied and in practice it is the only chemical which is recommended for use on newly sown turf.

TYPES OF CHEMICAL ACTION

Contact Herbicides

This can be defined as a herbicide which kills those plant parts with which it comes into contact. Examples being paraquat and dimexan.

Translocated Herbicides

Translocated herbicides are chemicals, which when absorbed into the plant via the leaves or roots, moves within it, finally killing it, e.g. 2,4-D and M.C.P.A.

Residual Herbicides

This is a name given to chemicals which are correctly called 'persistent' herbicides. A persistent (residual) chemical is a material which remains active in the soil for long periods of time after application.

M.C.P.A. (4-chloro-2-methphenoxyacetic acid)
2,4-D (2,4-dichlorophenoxyacetic acid)

M.C.P.A. and 2,4-D belong to the group of chemicals known as the phenoxyacetic acids. They are both translocated herbicides whose properties were discovered about 1942. They can be used to control many broad-leaved annual and perennial weeds post-emergence in grass seed crops and in turf. Both are absorbed by roots and shoots and are readily translocated around the plant.

Once absorbed, they stimulate the rapid production of new cells which in turn causes excessive weak growth, typical epinastic bending and eventual death of the plant.

These chemicals are commonly called 'selective herbicides' because when applied to turf they cause little or no damage to the grass species, but extensive damage to broad-leaved weeds. This selectivity is due mainly to the shape of the plant's leaves, the grasses having narrow upright blades which do not retain the chemical, whereas the weeds have broad horizontal leaves which retain large quantities.

2,4,5-T (2,4,5-trichlorophenoxyacetic acid)

This is another translocated herbicide belonging to the phenoxyacetic acid group. It is used mainly to control woody weeds but can occasionally be mixed with 2,4-D and M.C.P.A. to control certain broad leaved weeds in turf.

Mecoprop (2-(4-chloro-2-methylphenoxy) proprionic acid)

Mecoprop is a translocated herbicide which is available either alone or in mixtures with ioxynil, dichlorprop and dicamba, although it can also be used in mixtures with 2,4-D and M.C.P.A. In the U.K. it was introduced by the Boots company as a complementary herbicide to M.C.P.A. and 2,4-D because of its ability to control difficult weeds such as *Gallium* spp. and *Stellaria* spp. However, it is now used to control a wide range of weeds which grow in turf.

Dichlorprop (2-(2,4-dichlorophenoxy) proprionic acid)

Dichlorprop is a translocated herbicide which belongs to the same group of chemicals as mecoprop and fenoprop—the phenoxyproprionic acids. This is a chemical which is sometimes used to control broad-leaved weeds in turf. It is available either alone or in mixtures

109

with 2,4-D, M.C.P.A. and mecoprop, the formulations being either potassium, amines, sodium salts or esters. Like other phenoxy herbicides, dichlorprop has a low mammalian toxicity.

Fenoprop (2-(2,4,5-trichlorophenoxy) proprionic acid)

This is a translocated, growth regulating herbicide which was developed in the U.S.A. by Dow Chemicals. It is occasionally used in the control of weeds in turf, its main application being in mixtures with mecoprop.

Dicamba (3,6-dichloro-2-methoxybenzoic acid)

Dicamba is a translocated herbicide which belongs to the group of chemicals known as the benzoic and phenylacetic acids. Its main usage in turf culture is in mixtures with M.C.P.A. and mecoprop to control broad-leaved weeds such as clover (*Trifolium* spp.) and Dock (*Rumex* spp.).

Ioxynil (4-hydroxy-3,5-di-iodobensonitrile)

Ioxynil is a contact acting herbicide which belongs to the nitrile group of chemicals. It is available either alone or in mixtures with dichlorprop, M.C.P.A. or mecoprop. Its main use being for the control of weeds in newly-sown turf. However, it is also used in mixtures with mecoprop to control difficult broad-leaved species such as Speedwells (*Veronica* spp.) and Rushes (*Luzula* spp.). Ioxynil should not be used where Crested Dogstail is a component of newly-sown turf.

Asulam (methyl N-(4-aminobenzenesalphonyl) carbamate)

This is a translocated herbicide which belongs to the carbamate group of chemicals, however, it has rather different properties from the other carbamate herbicides. It is taken up either via the root system, or foliage, translocated within the plant and then interferes with the growing point, eventually causing chlorosis. Its main use in turf-culture is in the control of Docks (*Rumex* spp.). Care should be taken when applying this chemical as some grasses can be seriously affected.

Maleic Hydrazide (1,2-dihydropyridazine-3,6-dione)

This is a growth-regulating substance which belongs to the diazine group of chemicals. It is available either alone or in mixtures with 2, 4-D for the suppression of grass growth and the control of some weeds in grass verges. It is not recommended for use on fine turf, but is extensively used on roadway embankments, cemeteries, and low quality turf areas.

Cultural controls

Before seed sowing takes place on a new lawn, it is advisable to carry out some form of weed control. This can be done by either applying chemicals such as paraquat or dazomet (basamid), or it can be carried out by cultural means such as fallowing (see preparation of a seedbed). Which ever method is chosen the aim should be to control all perennial and as many biennial and annual weeds as possible.

Even when a long period of fallowing has taken place, it is not possible to control all the annual weeds on a site. Some are inevitably left which will germinate after the grass seed is sown. Annual weeds (Plate 1) in newly sown turf should not pose any real problems as the large majority will be controlled during the first mowings. If, for any reason, weed grasses become a problem during the early days of the sward's life, they will have to be either removed by hand or left until the lawn is established.

SOIL TYPE

The type of soil can appreciably influence the species of weeds which will grow on a site. Poor acid conditions will encourage weeds such as Sorrel (*Rumex* spp.), Rushes (*Luzula* spp.) and Mosses, whereas alkaline soils can encourage the establishment of broad-leaved grasses such as Yorkshire Fog (*Holcus lanatus*).

Many factors such as the condition of drainage channels, fertilizer applications and the incorporation of lime are all important when establishing and maintaining lawns. If any one is incorrect the rapid establishment of weeds may take place.

MOWING

The quality of a sward is largely governed by the height of cut and frequency of mowing. Infrequent close mowing can damage a sward, causing the reduction of fine grasses and the establishment of rosette type weeds.

During normal maintenance, it is the usual practice to remove grass cuttings. However, if the cuttings are allowed to 'fly', weed species such as Annual Meadow Grass (*Poa annua*) may rapidly spread over the lawn.

111

SCARIFICATION (SEE MAINTENANCE OF TURF)

During the normal healthy growth of a lawn, large quantities of dead organic matter such as grass clippings and leaf sheaths are collected at the base of the sward. This collects to form a thick impermeable layer which reduces air and water intake into the soil consequently weakening the turf and producing ideal conditions for the germination of moss spores.

Scarification is used to remove this dead accumulation of 'thatch' which in turn improves the sward and removes suitable sites for weed germination.

AERATION

As was mentioned above, grasses require air and water to function correctly and if these are not obtained in the correct proportions the grasses will become severely affected. During the growing season a lawn can become compacted by the continued use of heavy machines. This compaction coupled with the production of thatch is what prevents the grass roots from obtaining the correct amounts of air and water. Aeration is carried out to relieve this compaction which in turn improves the vigour of the sward.

EARTHWORMS (SEE PEST CONTROL)

A number of earthworms leave casts on the surface of turf. The casts are made up of soil which has passed through the bodies of the worms. These heaps of soil are rich in nutrients and are ideal sites for the germination of weed seeds, some of which are deposited at the same time as the casts. To help prevent the establishment of weeds it is advisable to remove all casting worms from the soil (see worm control).

DISEASE CONTROL

Several fungi attack grasses and in some circumstances they can cause severe damage or death to a sward. When this happens bare patches occur which are ideal sites for weed establishment. If diseases do occur spraying and re-turfing will help to avoid a severe weed infestation.

The Major Weeds of Turf

Although there are a large number of weed species which are successful in turf, the number of families in which these are classified is relatively small. A description of the commonest species listed under their family names is given below.

Compositae

This is a large family of plants consisting of over 900 genera with approximately 14,000 species, a number of which are classed as weeds when found in ornamental turf. The members of the family have a very diverse growth habit, although all the species have a characteristic flower structure and many contain either latex or oil canals.

YARROW (*Achillea millefolium*)

This is a very common weed of turf which can be found growing in pastures, roadside verges and ornamental lawns (Plate 2). It is a strongly-scented perennial which spreads by the production of underground creeping stems. The leaves of the plant are dark green, finely divided and have a fern-like appearance. The flowers are white or pink and are usually formed on erect flower stalks.

Yarrow occurs on all types of soil but thrives under dry, slightly acid conditions. It is often seen growing in association with Woodrush (*Luzula campestris*), or moss and when found in lawns it usually indicates that the soil conditions are poor, or that the sward is being badly managed.

Control Measures

The main method of controlling this weed is by repeated applications of chemicals. However, scarification and correct mowing will help to alleviate the problem. Numerous chemicals are available for weed control in lawns but unfortunately Yarrow shows a marked resistance to the commoner types such as 2,4-D and M.C.P.A.

The recommended means of control is by applying mecoprop-salt at a rate of 2·24 kg/ha, or mixtures of 2,4-D with mecoprop dichlorprop and fenoprop. Applications of lawn sand (see p. 130) have also given an acceptable control.

The chemical 2,4,5-T has been used with success, but care should be taken when using it as it can cause serious damage to certain grass species, especially smooth stalked meadow grass (*Poa pratensis*).

DAISY (*Bellis perennis*)

Bellis perennis is a perennial plant with spirally-arranged, spoon-shaped

113

leaves, which form a dense mat over a lawn surface (Plate 3). It grows best on rich well drained soils, but can be found growing in both wet and dry conditions and on sites which are either acid or alkaline. It can spread rapidly, causing the smothering of fine leaved grasses which can lead to the rapid deterioration of a sward.

Control measures

Daisy is completely unaffected by mowing. The main method of control is by the application of chemicals such as M.C.P.A., mecoprop, 2,4-D and lawn sand.

As Daisy is moderately resistant to M.C.P.A. and mecoprop, it is usually necessary to apply them more than once during the growing season. The most consistent control seems to come from the application of 2,4-D in mixture with mecoprop, dichlorprop or fenoprop.

KNAPWEED (*Centaurea nigra*)

Knapweed is a perennial herb with tough, hard-ribbed, hairy stems and long, narrow hairy leaves. The flowers which are produced during the summer months are purple with blackish bract appendages. It is frequently found growing in soils which are heavy or suffering from poor drainage, but it can also be found growing on soils which have a naturally high pH (chalks).

It is not usually a problem of fine lawns, its main habitat being pasture land and rough turf areas.

Control measures

Knapweed is moderately susceptible to M.C.P.A. and 2,4-D, the best control being achieved by one or two applications during the growing season.

STEMLESS THISTLE (*Cirsium acaule*)

Stemless thistle is a perennial weed which is sometimes seen in turf or pasture land. It is characterised by the absence or reduction of the main stem. The leaves are deeply lobed, prickly and are produced in the form of a rosette.

Control measures

As with knapweed, stemless thistle is moderately susceptible to M.C.P.A. and 2,4-D. Where necessary, adequate control can be obtained by one or two applications during the summer months.

114

CREEPING THISTLE (*Cirsium arvense*)

Creeping thistle is a perennial which spreads by the production of white creeping roots. The leaves are oblanceolate and deeply lobed (Plate 4). A characteristic of this plant is that the male and female flowers are produced on separate plants (dioecious). It is a common plant which is found in waste and cultivated places, but it can also be found in pasture land and low grade turf.

Control measures

The method of control is exactly the same as for stemless thistle namely, one or two applications of 2,4-D or M.C.P.A., however mecoprop and dichlorprop can also achieve an adequate control.

CAT'S EAR (*Hypochaeris radicata*)

Cat's Ear is a plant which is found on a wide range of soils and when established it produces a thick tap root which is reminiscent of a Dandelion root. It is a strong-growing perennial which produces erect stems and sessile leaves, the latter being lobed and hairy on both sides (Plate 5).

Control measures

Control can be achieved by one or two applications of either M.C.P.A., 2,4-D, mecoprop, or 2,4-D in mixtures with dichlorprop or fenoprop.

DANDELION (*Taraxacum officinale* Weber)

This is a plant which is found growing under all soil conditions, although it is most common on moist sites. It is a perennial plant whose leaves are joined directly to its thick, fleshy tap root. The leaves have tooth-like lobes and are produced at, or very close to ground level. The flowers which are produced in early summer are yellow and can be borne on very short flower spikes (Plate 6).

Control measures

On lawns which have a very minor Dandelion problem, it is possible to obtain a total control by 'painting' the individual weeds with 2,4-D. However, on large areas spraying can be carried out using M.C.P.A., 2,4-D or one of the many proprietary mixtures which are on the market. It is also possible to obtain an effective control by applying lawn sand (p. 130).

115

Ranunculaceae

The family Ranunculaceae is made up of a cosmopolitan group of plants consisting of 48 genera and approximately 1,300 species. Although members of the family are found growing all over the world, the majority of species grow in the northern temperate and arctic zones.

CROWFOOT OR MEADOW BUTTERCUP (*Ranunculus acris*)

Crowfoot is a perennial herb which is frequently found in meadows and areas of turf. The stem of the plant is long, erect, hairy and hollow at its base. The leaves are deeply lobed, forming approximately 5 segments, each segment being sub-divided into 3 segments. The flowers which are produced between spring and late summer are yellow and contain sepals which do not reflex (Plate 7).

Control measures

Crowfoot is susceptible to sprays of M.C.P.A., but is only moderately susceptible to 2,4-D and mecoprop. The best control can therefore be achieved by one or two applications of M.C.P.A. during the growing season.

BULBOUS BUTTERCUP (*Ranunculus bulbosus*)

Ranunculus bulbosus is a very variable species, especially in the size of the corm and the number of stems arising from it. It is a perennial plant which produces swollen stems at its base, the basal leaves being long stalked, broad and trilobed, whereas the stem leaves have shorter stalks and are divided into narrow lobes. The flowers are yellow and have sepals which do reflex.

Control measures

This species has been found to be moderately resistant to mecoprop and other chemicals, although some control is possible with repeated applications of M.C.P.A., 2,4-D and 2,4-D in mixtures with 2,4,5-T.

LESSER CELANDINE (*Ranunculus ficaria*)

Lesser Celandine is a perennial plant which prefers moist shady conditions, but it can be found growing in various types of turf. It spreads by short creeping stems which arise from small root tubers. The leaves are cordate, glossy and long stalked whilst the leaf margins are often wavy. The flowers are glossy yellow in colour.

Lesser Celandine shows a marked resistance to 2,4-D, mecoprop and mixtures of 2,4-D with mecoprop, dichlorprop or fenoprop. However, a successful control can be achieved by repeated high volume sprays of M.C.P.A.-salt.

CREEPING BUTTERCUP (*Ranunculus repens*)

Creeping Buttercup is a creeping perennial which is most commonly found on heavy soils in moist conditions. It spreads by the production of long stolons which are capable of rooting at their nodes. The plant flowers from spring to late summer. The blossoms are yellow in colour with sepals which do not reflex.

Control measures

Creeping Buttercup is very susceptible to applications of M.C.P.A.-salt, 2,4-D amine and ester, 2,4-D in mixtures containing mecoprop, dichlorprop or dicamba, but shows some resistance to mecoprop-salt when used on its own.

Rosaceae

The family Rosaceae is a large group of plants consisting of 90 genera and over 2,000 species. Members of the family can be found in many varied habitats all over the world, especially in temperate regions. The growth habit of the various species can be very diverse but it is usually possible to recognise the natural family by its perigynous or epigynous flowers.

PARSLEY PIERT (*Aphanes arvensis*)

Parsley Piert is a small, rather inconspicuous annual plant with close-growing, short-stalked, fan-shaped leaves, which are carried on hairy stems (Plate 8). The leaves are trilobed whilst the flowers are small and green. It is usually found growing in dry soils and has a preference for acid conditions.

Control measures

Parsley Piert is very resistant to applications of 2,4-D and M.C.P.A. even when maximum doses are used. The best control can be obtained by spraying ioxynil-salt at $0 \cdot 63$ kg/ha with mecoprop-salt at $1 \cdot 89$ kg/ha in early spring or autumn.

Lawn sand can also be used at a rate of 136 g/m² (see p. 130), the application being given at any time during the growing season.

SILVER WEED (*Potentilla anserina*)

Silver Weed is a perennial plant which can be found growing on damp sites, although it is sometimes seen on sand dunes and roadside verges. The plant has a slender rootstock which produces procumbent runners. The leaves are usually produced horizontally and are a silvery white colour on both surfaces. The flowers are yellow in colour and are borne on slender stalks (Plate 9).

Control measures

Silver Weed is moderately susceptible to sprays of M.C.P.A. and 2,4-D. However, it may be necessary to make more than one application to achieve a total control.

COMMON TORMENTIL (*Potentilla erecta*)

This is a perennial plant which is found growing in a wide range of soils, but favouring heathland and dry acid conditions. The leaves are coarsely toothed, have short stalks and are attached to the hairy stems in the axils of oval, leafy stipules. The flowers are yellow and appear in summer.

Control measures

Potentilla erecta is moderately resistant to M.C.P.A., 2,4-D and 2,4,5-T. For complete control repeated applications of the above or 2,4-D with mecoprop are necessary.

CINQUEFOIL (*Potentilla reptans*)

This is another perennial species belonging to the genus *Potentilla*. It is found on a wide range of sites and is capable of growing in both acid and alkaline soils. It spreads by the production of slender, creeping stems which root at their nodes. The leaves are carried on long stalks and are divided into five coarsely toothed oblanceolate sections. The flowers are yellow in colour and each petal is notched at the top.

Control measures

The control for this species is similar to that of *P. erecta*, except that

118

P. reptans is slightly more susceptible to sprays of M.C.P.A. and 2,4-D.

Plantaginaceae

Plantaginaceae is a small family consisting of 3 genera and approximately 200 species. The members of the family are found growing all over the world but they are most numerous in the temperate regions. Although this is a small family, a number of species are commonly found growing in turf.

RIBWORT PLANTAIN (*Plantago lanceolata*)

This is a perennial species which is commonly seen growing in pastureland, golf courses and roadside verges. Its leaves are simple, lanceolate, ribbed and are produced in a type of rosette (Plate 10). The flowers which are produced during the summer months are wind pollinated and are formed on long slender stalks.

Control measures

Ribwort is susceptible to M.C.P.A., 2,4-D and mecoprop. The best control can be achieved by one or two applications of 2,4-D during the growing season. On small sites or on areas where numbers are small, control can be achieved by 'painting' the individual plants with concentrated chemical.

GREAT PLANTAIN (*Plantago major*)

A very common grassland weed which occurs in all types of soil although slightly more prevalent under alkaline conditions, and especially common on compacted land. The leaves are broadly ovate, stalked and lined with five or more longitudinal nerves. The flower spike is long and narrow and is produced during the summer months.

Control measures

As for *Plantago lanceolata*.

HOARY PLANTAIN (*Plantago media*)

Hoary Plaintain is the only other major turf weed in this family. It is most common on alkaline soils although it can be found in a wide range of soil types. It is a perennial plant with leaves in the form of a rosette. The leaves are broad and sessile, or have a short petiole. The flowers are whitish with purple stamens and are produced on long stalks.

Control measures

As for *Plantago lanceolata*.

Polygonaceae

A family of plants consisting of approximately 30 genera with over 800 species distributed throughout the world but, mainly in temperate regions. The family exhibits a wide range of growth habit ranging from herbs to large trees. A number of the herbs can be very troublesome when found in fine turf.

SORREL (*Rumex acetosa*)

Common Sorrel is a semi-creeping perennial plant which prefers acid conditions. When seen in turf it indicates that the soil pH is low. The leaves are hastate (arrow shaped) with downward pointing lobes (Plate 11). The flowers are unisexual, brick red in colour and are produced in early summer.

Control measures

Sorrel is a plant which is resistant to mecoprop-salt but is moderately susceptible to 2,4-D, M.C.P.A. and mixtures of 2,4-D with 2,4,5-T. Control can be achieved by one or two applications of the above chemicals during the growing season.

SHEEPS SORREL (*Rumex acetosella*)

Sheeps Sorrel is a creeping, perennial plant which occurs under acid conditions—of which it is a good indicator. It is usually found on poor dry soils but, can also be seen growing on sites which suffer from bad drainage. The plant produces slender, greenish-red stems which bear stalked arrow shaped leaves, the lobes of which are spread out.

Control measures

As for *Rumex acetosa*.

BROAD-LEAVED DOCK (*Rumex obtusifolius*)

Broad-leaved Dock is an erect, branching perennial which is common

120

in pasture land, amenity lawns and sportsfields. It will grow on a wide range of soils, but seems to prefer slightly acid conditions. The lower leaves of the plant are ovate—oblong and are very broad (Plate 12).

A number of other species do occur in turf but they generally prefer the same soil conditions as the above and are controlled in the same manner.

Control measures

Control can be obtained by sprays of M.C.P.A., 2,4-D and asulam. The best control being achieved by one or two applications of asulam ('Asulox') during the growing season.

Caryophyllaceae

A family of approximately 70 genera containing approximately 1,450 species a number of which are classed as weeds when growing in fine lawns. The largest number of species are found in the temperate regions of the northern hemisphere.

MOUSE-EARED CHICKWEED (*Cerastium holosteoides* Fr. syn *C. vulgatum*)

A slender perennial plant which grows on all types of soil, except the most acid. It is most serious as a problem on dry soils which have a high pH. The plant is produced in the form of a dense clump, consisting of closely growing hairy stems with white flowers which are produced between spring and late summer (Plate 13).

Control measures

Mouse-eared Chickweed is susceptible to mecoprop and 2,4-D in mixtures with dichlorprop, fenoprop or dicamba. It is, however, moderately resistant to 2,4-D when applied by itself. Topdressings of lawn sand containing ammonium sulphate and calcined ferrous sulphate will also give some control.

CHICKWEED (*Stellaria media*)

Chickweed is an annual plant which can be found growing under a wide range of soil conditions. It is only a problem when found growing in newly sown turf, as it can not survive under conditions of frequent close mowing. The stems of the plant are slender, smooth and contain a single line of hairs along one side. The leaves are ovate

121

and the flowers, which can be produced all the year round, are small and white.

Control measures

As mentioned above, Chickweed is unable to persist on areas which receive frequent close mowing. If, however, chemicals are required, then one or two applications of ioxynil should give a complete control.

PEARLWORT (*Sagina procumbens*)

This is a small, tufted perennial which is a common weed of turf, especially under conditions of close mowing. The plant produces dense patches which spread by the production of slender stolons. The leaves can be seen in two forms. On small plants they tend to be in rosettes, whereas in established specimens they are produced along the stolons. This plant has the ability to flower nearly all the year round and is able to set seed very easily.

Control measures

Pearlwort can be difficult to control in lawns as it is moderately resistant to both M.C.P.A. and 2,4-D. However, it is susceptible to mecoprop, especially when in mixtures with ioxynil. Lawn sand, when applied under the correct conditions, will also give some control.

Scrophulariaceae

Scrophulariaceae is a large family consisting of over 200 genera with approximately 2,500 species. It is a cosmopolitan family which is easily distinguishable from other groups by its zygomorphic (irregular) flowers. For example, the majority of species which are troublesome in British turf belong to the genus *Veronica*. This genus consists of approximately 200 species which grow in temperate regions some of which are grown as cultivated plants.

ROUND-LEAVED SPEEDWELL (*Veronica filiformis* Sm)

Veronica filiformis is probably the most troublesome member of the Scrophulariaceae. It is a creeping perennial which was originally grown as a garden plant. However, it is now extensively naturalized in grassed areas such as ornamental lawns. The plant spreads by numerous creeping stems, which have short-stalked, crenate leaves and slightly purplish flowers, which very rarely set seed. Its main method of spreading is vegetatively from small pieces of runners.

Control measures

Speedwells are one of the most difficult weeds to control in turf. They are resistant to M.C.P.A., and 2,4-D and are moderately resistant to mecoprop. The best means of control is by spraying ioxynil-salt at 0·63 kg/ha with mecoprop at 1·89 kg/ha. Applications are best made in early spring before the plant produces its flower heads. Lawn sand can also give some control when applied at the correct stage of growth.

GERMANDER SPEEDWELL (*Veronica chamaedrys*)

This is a creeping perennial which is commonly found in neglected turf but can be found occurring in a wide range of situations and under varying soil conditions. The leaves are opposite, oval, toothed and hairy, whereas the stem is slender with two rows of hairs running in line with the leaves. The flowers, which are produced from the early spring to summer, are blue and form long axillary racemes (Plate 14).

Control measures

As for *Veronica filiformis*.

Papilionaceae

This is a large family consisting of more than 300 genera and 5,000 species which mainly grow in the temperate regions of the world. Papilionaceae is commonly placed with other groups of plants to make up the family Leguminosae. Probably the most striking features of this group of plants is their flower shape (papilionate), fruits (legumes) and the ability of a number of species to fix nitrogen in the soil.

LESSER YELLOW TREFOIL (*Trifolium dubium* Sibth.)

Lesser Yellow Trefoil is a creeping annual plant which is common on most soils, although it does show some preference for dry situations. The leaves consist of three leaflets, the terminal one being short stalked. The flowers which are formed in the summer months are yellow and are produced in small spherical inflorescences.

Control measures

Lesser Yellow Trefoil shows a marked resistance to both M.C.P.A. and 2,4-D and is only moderately susceptible to mecoprop. A partial control can be achieved by applications of mecoprop by itself but, for a more effective control repeated sprays in mixture with dichlor-prop, fenoprop or dicamba will be necessary.

WHITE CLOVER (*Trifolium repens*)

This is a creeping perennial plant which is particularly common on clay soils. It spreads by creeping stems which are capable of rooting at their nodes. The leaves are produced on long stalks and consist of three rounded toothed, leaflets. The flowers are white or rosy in colour and are produced between the spring and autumn (Plate 15).

Control measures

Trifolium repens is resistant to applications of 2,4-D and is moderately resistant to M.C.P.A. However, an adequate control can be achieved by applications of mecoprop in early summer.

BIRDSFOOT TREFOIL (*Lotus corniculatus*)

This is a perennial species which is commonly found in pastures and ornamental turf. It produces a thick fleshy rootstock and occasionally short stoloniferous growths. The leaves consist of 3 segments with two leaf-like stipules at their base. The flowers are yellow but are often streaked or tipped with red.

Control measures

Birdsfoot trefoil is resistant to M.C.P.A. and 2,4-D and is moderately resistant to mecoprop. To obtain a complete control repeated appli-tions of mecoprop-salt will be necessary.

BLACK MEDICK (*Medicago lupulina*)

Black medick is an annual or short lived perennial plant which occurs commonly in a wide range of soils. The shoots are slender, downy, and are produced from the base of the plant. The leaves consist of 3 segments which are obovate and finely serrated in the upper half, whereas the stipules are lanceolate and shortly toothed. The flowers are yellow and are produced in small oval spikes, the pods are green when young but turn black when ripe.

Control measures
As for *Trifolium repens*.

Labiatae

Labiatae is a large family consisting of approximately 170 genera and 3,000 species. Members of the family are usually easy to recognise because of their square stems, opposite exstipulate leaves and characteristic flowers. They are frequently aromatic and many are grown as cultivated plants.

SELF-HEAL (*Prunella vulgaris*)

This is a perennial plant which produces slender creeping rhizomes. It is a common plant which is found growing under conditions of poor drainage, mainly on basic and neutral soils. The stems of the plant are square and slightly hairy whilst the leaves are ovate and petioled.

Control measures

Prunella is moderately resistant to M.C.P.A. and 2,4-D, but can be controlled by repeated applications of mecoprop or 2,4-D in mixtures with dichlorprop, fenoprop or dicamba.

Geraniaceae

This is a relatively small family consisting of approximately 11 genera and about 700 species which are mainly found in temperate regions. The family contains numerous species which are grown for their ornamental effect. However, a number are classed as weeds when found growing in turf. Three species which are occasionally found in lawns are:

Common Storksbill (*Erodium circutarium* agg.)
Musk Storksbill (*Erodium moschatum*)
Dovesfoot Cranesbill (*Geranium molle*)

Control measures

Where necessary the two species of *Erodium* can be controlled by applications of M.C.P.A. or 2,4-D. However, *Geranium molle* shows a marked resistance to both of the above chemicals and is also moderately resistant to mecoprop. Some degree of control can be achieved by repeated applications of mecoprop in mixture with ioxynil.

125

Juncaceae

This is a natural family of wind-pollinated plants consisting of 8 genera and about 350 species. It is a cosmopolitan family but the majority of species are found growing in temperate or cold climates. A number of species can be found growing in turf, in the British Isles the commonest being field woodrush.

FIELD WOODRUSH (*Luzula campestris* DC)

Field Woodrush is a compact, loosely tufted perennial which occurs most commonly in acid infertile and badly drained conditions. It is quite often seen growing in association with Yarrow (*Achillea millefolium*) and when this does occur it is a good indication that the soil is in poor condition. The leaves of the plant are linear, grass-like and are thinly covered with hairs (Plate 16). The flowers are brown in colour and are borne on slender stalks which are rarely more than 15 cm (6 in) long.

Control measures

Woodrush can be difficult to control in lawns. It is very resistant to applications of M.C.P.A. and 2,4-D, whilst it shows a slight resistance to mecoprop. The best control can be achieved by repeated applications of mecoprop in mixtures with ioxynil. Once controlled, the soil should be improved otherwise the weed could become re-established.

Gramineae

Not all grasses are used in the production of lawns. Some such as Yorkshire Fog (*Holcus lanatus*) and Creeping Soft Grass (*Holcus mollis*) are classed as weeds when found in turf. This is because they have broad leaf blades, light coloured leaves, and a vigorous habit of growth which can smother fine leaved grasses.

YORKSHIRE FOG (*Holcus lanatus*)

Yorkshire Fog is a loosely tufted perennial grass which grows on a wide range of soils and under varying climatic conditions. The leaf blades are flat, acute and covered with hairs on both surfaces. It is easily distinguished from *Holcus mollis* by the absence of creeping rhizomes.

Control measures

It is not possible to control this weed with herbicides without causing severe damage or death to the other grass species in the sward. Control must be achieved by cultural means, such as removing by hand and re-turfing, frequent 'slashing' with aeration equipment and frequent close mowing.

CREEPING SOFT GRASS (*Holcus mollis*)

This is another perennial grass which spreads by creeping rhizomes. It prefers slightly acid sites but can be found in a wide range of soils. The leaves are flat, rough, acute and very hairy, whilst the basal leaf sheaths can have pink veins.

Control measures

As for *Holcus lanatus*.

8 Moss

Mosses belong to a division of the plant kingdom known as the Bryophyta. They are non-flowering plants which can be found growing in a wide variety of situations. Their growth is usually restricted to approximately 25 mm (1 in) in height, the main body of the plant consisting of slender stems which are soft, fleshy and covered with minute green or brown leaves. The roots, which are like slender filaments, are known as rhizoids. However, they serve the same function as roots in flowering plants, namely to absorb moisture and nutrients and to anchor the plant in the soil.

Common species that are found growing in turf are:

Barbula convoluta Hedw.
Ceratodon purpureus Brid.
Hypnum cupressiforme Hedw.
Polytrichum spp.

Moss is usually found growing in turf when the grass growth is slow, the soil is wet, or during periods of high humidity such as are common in the autumn and winter months. When moss is found on a lawn it usually is a sign that the grasses are not growing to their best advantage. Moss can spread in a number of ways:

a) by pieces breaking off which are carried to new sites;
b) by the production of small detachable buds (called *gemmae*);
c) by the production of microscopic spores.

They have a life cycle which is, in many respects, similar to that of ferns, the main similarity being that they both show typical alternation of generations. This simply means that the plants exhibit two distinct types of growth structure in their life cycle.

Most species produce dust-like spores which are single-celled. When these germinate they produce a fine filamentous structure (called the *protonema*) which quickly turns green and grows in different directions over the soil surface. The protonema is the first stage in the development of the moss plant as we know it. Small buds can be produced on this structure which are capable of forming new moss plants.

When the moss is mature it produces special sexual reproductive organs, the male organs being called the *antheridia*, the female organs being called the *archegonia*. The male sperm cells which are produced in the antheridia are capable of swimming in films of moisture towards the female egg cells. When they meet fertilization takes place and a new structure called the 'capsule' is produced. Once ripe, the capsule splits open to release new spores which are capable of starting the life cycle once more.

Control Measures

Mosses can be controlled by either cultural or chemical means. However, chemicals will not give a permanent control unless all the cultural conditions are correct. Some of the most important cultural factors which can encourage the establishment of moss are:

a) poor aeration;
b) poor drainage;
c) low soil fertility;
d) extremely high or low pH;
e) insufficient topsoil;
f) shaded sites;
g) neglected areas of turf;
h) grasses mown too closely (scalping);
i) deep spongy mat present at the base of stems;
j) presence of large numbers of weeds, pests and diseases.

If a moss-free lawn is required, care should be taken to ensure that none of the above conditions are allowed to develop.

Chemical control of moss

The two main chemicals used in the control of moss are lawn sand and mercurous chloride (calomel).

129

LAWN SAND

Lawn sand consists of the following materials:

>3 parts by bulk ammonium sulphate
>1 part by bulk calcined ferrous sulphate
>10–20 parts of dry inert carrier such as sand.

The mixture is best applied on dewy mornings when the soil is moist and the weather is fine and warm. The most consistent results are obtained when the mixture is applied during the spring months, but applications can be made all the year round if necessary.

Lawn sand should be applied at the rate of 100–170 g/m² (approximately $3\frac{1}{2}$–$5\frac{1}{2}$ oz/sq. yd.) depending upon the season and the amount of moss present. Scorching of the sward can occur if fine weather coincides with the applications, however this can be simply remedied by applying irrigation water.

MERCUROUS CHLORIDE (*Calomel*)

This is another chemical which can be used to control moss in lawns. The best time for application is during the autumn months, but as with lawn sand it can if necessary be applied all the year round. Mercurous chloride be applied in any one of the following ways:

1 applied alone at a rate of 7–12 g/10m² preferably during the autumn*;

2 at a rate of 7 g mixed with 41 g ferrous sulphate applied by watering can in 5 litres of water to 10/m²;

3 at approximately 6 g/10m² in various proprietory mixtures (mercurised lawn sand).

After the application of either lawn sand or mercurous chloride it will be necessary to carry out some form of scarification. This will remove the blackened moss and also allow water and air to enter the soil.

* From the *Weed Control Handbook*, Blackwell Scientific Publications Oxford, 1972.

9 The Safe Use of Chemicals

Much concern is now being shown about the possible dangers of using agricultural and horticultural chemicals. This concern is natural but in practice danger exists with the misuse, rather than the use of chemicals.

Safety is the first consideration when any compound is being developed for commercial use. For example, in the U.K., clearance is required under the Ministry of Agriculture Notification and Clearance Scheme before marketing can commence. Under this scheme the properties of the chemical are thoroughly investigated and if cleared a recommendation sheet is issued for its safe use in the U.K.

These recommendations form the basis of the label which in turn must be agreed with the Ministry. Once accepted the label must appear on every container of the product dispatched by the manufacturer. It is for this reason that the practice of some local authorities and organisations to buy in large packs of chemical which are kept in a central store and broken down into smaller quantities is considered dangerous. With this system there is a definite risk that small quantities will be issued without sufficient information as to their safe and correct use.

The safety recommendations covered by the manufacturer's labels consider the following safety requirements:

a) The protection of operators;
b) The protection of consumers;
c) The protection of livestock, wildlife and others.

The information concerning these points is always included in the manufacturer's label, under the 'Precautions' section. Examples of some recommendations which may be seen on a label are:

1 Wash hands and exposed skin before meals, before smoking and after work;
2 Wear protective gloves when handling the concentrate;
3 Do not gather (harvest) food crops within 7 days of treatment; the interval may be longer or shorter depending upon the chemical;
4 Harmful to bees, do not apply at flowering stage, keep down flowering weeds;
5 Do not contaminate ponds, waterways and ditches with chemical or used containers;
6 Wash out container thoroughly and dispose of safely.

Operators applying these chemicals must therefore read thoroughly the instruction labels on the containers. Spraying should not be commenced until the labels are fully understood and operators are satisfied that the material can be applied in a safe and efficient manner.

Application of Chemicals to Turf and Other Areas

Successful application of these chemicals requires that they are applied as evenly as possible over the surface to be treated. The degree of evenness obtained will depend upon such factors as the quality and suitability of the equipment, the skill of the operator, and the effect of uncontrollable factors such as wind and rain.

Chemicals may be available in various forms and each type will require a slightly different means of application. The most common forms of chemical are as follows.

Liquids Concentrated material to be diluted with water prior to use.
Wettable powders Powders which although not always soluble have been prepared for mixing with water prior to use.
Powder and dusts Materials to be applied in the dry state without dilution.
Granules Solids, some herbicides and occasionally pesticides, of large particle size. Application is without dilution normally to the soil or turf.

Dilution rates

The above formulations of chemicals may require dilution before use, they may also have to be applied at a set rate per hectare (a hectare being approximately 2½ times as large as an acre).

Three basic application methods can occur:

1 The chemicals are used in the neat form (undiluted) and the operator applies sufficient material to cover the foliage to be treated. This generally applies to powders and dusts.

2 The material is concentrated and must first be diluted, but at a given rate. This is then applied as above, ensuring that an adequate coverage of the foliage is obtained. Typical examples of this are insecticides such as nicotine and malathion both of which are diluted with water at set rates and applied as drenches.

It must be remembered that once the point of 'run off' is reached further applications of the chemical are wasted.

3 (i) The material is used neat but applied at a fixed rate per hectare, examples being herbicides and some turf pesticides.

(ii) The material is diluted prior to application but applied at a fixed rate of chemical per hectare. An example is as follows: A selective weedkiller such as 50% 2,4-D must be applied at a rate of 3 to 5 litres of concentrate per hectare. Although the concentrate is diluted prior to spraying, in this case the addition of water is purely as a means of applying a small quantity of concentrate over a large area. In fact the amount of water added may be varied to suit the type of equipment.

Equipment

The type of equipment used to apply chemicals is dependant upon the type of material and on the area to be treated. Each of the four types of chemical is applied as follows.

Liquids and wettable powders Applied in spray form, small areas being treated with a watering can or knapsack sprayer, whilst larger areas are treated by trolley or tractor mounted spraying equipment.

Powder and dusts Applied as dust fogs using hand or power operated blowers.

Granules Granules are broadcast evenly either by hand or mechanical spreaders.

Whatever chemical and equipment is used it is important to adhere to the following recommendations:

a) When filling the equipment always add acidic materials to water and not vice versa;

b) Always use the correct clean protective clothing;

c) Always check nozzles before use;

d) Never spray under very windy conditions as drift can occur;

e) Do not spray in very strong sunlight;

f) Never spray in heavy rain;

g) Do not spray if animals are grazing in the same area;

h) Always thoroughly wash equipment after use.

CALIBRATION OF EQUIPMENT

In the section dealing with dilution, liquids, wettable powders and dusts (p. 133) cases (1) and (2) present no problems, but those of (3) (i) and (ii) require that the exact output of the equipment is known. This information may be available in the manufacturer's data sheets, but if not some form of calibration will be necessary. When applying chemicals two types of machine must be considered, namely sprayers and spreaders.

SPRAYING MACHINES

The rate of application or area covered by a spraying machine will depend upon three factors:

1 *The speed at which the machine travels* The faster the speed, the greater the area covered per filling. In fact, doubling the speed doubles the area covered.

2 *The operating pressure* That is the pressure used to force the spray out of the nozzles. The higher the pressure the greater the rate of application and the smaller the area covered per filling of tank. But, doubling the pressure will not halve the area covered.

3 *Size of nozzle* This controls the volume of the spray outlet and the pattern of the resultant spray.

Calibration

This is basically the operation of the machine at a known forward speed, pressure setting and nozzle size. The operation consists of determining the area covered by the machine when applying a known quantity of water, and from this it is possible to calculate how much area will be covered (under similar conditions) for each filling of the machine. If, after the first calibration, the machine is applying more or less spray per hectare than required, then the procedure can be repeated, altering either the forward speed or nozzle sizes. The pressure setting on most machines is recommended by the manufacturer because if the setting is too low a poor spray pattern can result, whilst excess pressures can encourage spray drift. Alterations to either the forward speed or nozzle size have the following effects.

Increased speed. Reduces the rate of application, but increases the area covered per tank filling.

Decreased speed. Increases the rate of application, but decreases the area covered per tank filling.

Smaller nozzle size. Reduces the rate of application, but increases the area covered per tank filling.

Larger nozzle size. Increases the rate of application, but decreases the area covered per tank filling.

The types of equipment

The type of sprayer used to apply chemicals will depend upon the size of the area to be sprayed and the range of equipment available for use. The types of equipment available are:

Watering can, knapsack-type sprayer, trolley or hand-propelled sprayer, vehicle-mounted sprayer, and hand lances and carry booms fed from either (3) or (4), a trolley, hand-propelled or vehicle-mounted sprayer, the spraying unit however being stationary.

Hand-operated units will have their speed controlled by the walking pace of the operator, and it is therefore very important to walk at a steady pace which can be maintained for long periods.

Calibration procedures

WATERING CAN

a) *Speed of operation*　A constant walking pace.

b) *Pressure*　Not constant, varies as can empties.

c) *Spray width*　Determined by height of nozzle from ground. Should be kept constant.

d) *Spray outlet*　Controlled by type of nozzle, e.g. coarse, fine or dribble bar.

Approach

1 Determine the capacity of the watering can.
2 Fill the can with clean water (a marker dye can be added if required).
3 Choose a suitable site so that the area sprayed can be easily measured.
4 Apply water as an even spray, walking at a steady pace.
5 Measure the area covered.
6 Repeat the operation 3 times and average the results.

$$\text{Application rate per hectare (litre)} = \frac{\text{Capacity of can (litres)} \times 10{,}000}{\text{mean area covered (metres)}}.$$

The area covered per filling can be varied as follows:

a) Increased by using a finer rose or dribble bar.
b) Decreased by using a coarser rose.

KNAPSACK SPRAYERS (Fig. 9.1).

Speed of operation Constant (walking pace).

Pressure Hand pump can be kept constant, especially if a pressure gauge is fitted. Most modern knapsack sprayers have pressure settings so a constant delivery pressure is maintained.

Spray width Determined by height of nozzle from ground and the type of nozzle.

Spray outlet Hand lance fitted with one or several nozzles.

Approach (Method One)

1 Put a measured quantity of water into the sprayer (again marker dye can be added if required).
2 The operator should apply the spray evenly and accurately by maintaining a uniform pressure at the nozzle(s) and by walking at a uniform speed.
3 Continue until the sprayer is empty and measure the total distance travelled.

$$\text{Rate of Application in litre/hectare} = \frac{\text{Amount of liquid used (l)} \times 10{,}000}{\text{Distance travelled (m)} \times \text{width of spray (m)}}$$

Approach (*Method Two*)

1 Measure out 10m².

2 At a normal speed, pressure and spray height apply the water over the area and time the operation.

3 Spray water into a measuring cylinder at the same pressure and for the same time as in (2) above. Then measure the quantity in millilitres.

Fig. 9.1 A knapsack sprayer.

4 *This figure now corresponds to the rate of water applied in litre/hectare,* e.g. 300 ml in x seconds /10m²

To convert to hectare rate multiply by 1000
To convert millilitre to litre divide by 1000
(as there are 1000 ml in 1 litre and 10,000m² in 1 hectare).

Speed Constant for both. In all cases the operator walks behind the machine.

Pressure May be air pressure, petrol driven pump, or a pump system activated when the wheels of the machine are in motion. Pressure gauges are normally fitted to ensure a constant discharge rate.

Spray width Usually constant but can be altered on some machines.

Spray outlet Usually has a spray boom fitted with nozzles at 0·5 m (18 m) centres.

Approach

1 Put a measured quantity of water into the sprayer.
2 Pace or measure 100 m, or a convenient set distance.
3 Set pressure gauge to recommended spraying pressure.
4 Push or drive the sprayer up and down the set distance until the spraytank is empty and estimate the total distance travelled.
5 Measure the width of the spray pattern in metres.

$$\text{Rate of application in litre/hectare} = \frac{\text{Amount of liquid used (l)} \times 10{,}000}{\text{Distance travelled (m)} \times \text{width of boom (m)}}$$

The rate of application in gallons per acre can be calculated:

$$\text{Rate of application in galls/acre} = \frac{\text{Amount of liquid used (galls)} \times 4840}{\text{Distance travelled (yds)} \times \text{width of boom (yds)}}$$

TRACTOR OR LAND ROVER-MOUNTED SPRAYERS (Fig. 9.2)

Speed Variable but often speedometer either not fitted or inaccurate at low speeds. The speed is therefore worked out in terms of gear and throttle settings (see individual sprayer instructions for correct settings).

Pressure A pump system worked off the power take off.

Spray width Dependant on height of boom.

Spray outlet Usually have a spray boom fitted with nozzles at 0·25 m (9 in) or 0·5 m (18 in) centres. The idea behind the 0·25 m centres is to allow for both high volume and low-medium volume spraying. The 0·25 m centre being used for high volume work whilst alternate nozzles can be blanked off for low/medium volume work.

Calibration can be carried out by the method adopted for hand-propelled sprayers, or alternatively the following system can be used:

1 Fill the sprayer to approximately ⅔ its capacity with clear water;
2 Add marker dye if available;
3 Note the quantity of water in the tank using a dipstick or site glass if fitted;

Fig. 9.2   A tractor-mounted sprayer.

4 Mark out a convenient area to provide 0·25 ha for spraying;
5 Set the pressure valve to the recommended figure;
6 Spray over the marked area in both directions at the proposed speed;
7 Re-check the tank contents. The difference of the readings is the amount used to treat 0·5 ha. By doubling this figure the rate of application for 1·0 ha can be obtained.

Although these machines may have been calibrated for normal boom spraying, another check must be made when they are used in a stationary position to feed hand lances and carry booms. This is necessary since the conditions of speed, pressure and nozzle size may have altered. Calibration is easily carried out using the second method suggested for tractor-mounted sprayers.

The task of calibrating spraying equipment is not difficult and although most manufacturers supply a table correlating speed of travel, operating pressure and nozzle size to the quantity of spray liquid applied per hectare (or acre), it is always advisable to check from time to time that the machine is applying liquid at the correct rate.

It must also be remembered that calibration results are only relevant when the machine is operating under the same conditions of speed, pressure, nozzle size and nozzle height above the target, re-calibration being necessary should any of these factors be altered.

SPREADING MACHINES

The calibration of these machines is again similar to that of spraying equipment, but in this case only two variable factors apply, namely the speed of the tractor/operator and the size of the outlet mesh.

Calibration tables are usually available for large types of equipment, but on smaller machines it will be necessary to check the rate of application. This can be achieved by doing a field calibration using some form of inert material, such as dry sand.

The actual means of distribution varies, some machines using a spinning disc (Fig. 9.3), others brush feeds, moving belts, or grooved rollers (Fig. 9.4), but in all cases successful and even application will depend upon:

a) The equipment being well maintained, thorough cleaning after use being essential to prevent corrosion;

b) Calibration tables are accurately followed, or if not available calibration is carried out in the correct manner;

c) That the materials to be distributed are dry and in good condition. Damp or lumpy materials are liable to cause obstructions, blocking up the machines.

Distributors or spreaders vary in capacity, ranging from small, hand-propelled machines to larger tractor- and Land Rover-mounted types. The large types should be calibrated using the correct tables whereas the smaller machines can be set in the following manner.

BELT TYPE SPREADER

The only variable with this type of machine is the gap between the

Fig. 9.3   A moving belt type fertiliser distributor.

hopper and belt. The forward speed is geared to the land wheels, so has no appreciable effect. At the side of the hopper are two setting discs and nuts. These should be adjusted to suit the various requirements.

Approach

1   Measure out a rectangle of a known size, e.g. 2 m² on a clean concrete area.
2   Using the desired material, run the machine evenly over the area.
3   Sweep up and weigh. Divide by two to give the rate in g/m².

4   Adjust the aperture of the machine for the desired application
     rate and repeat the above operation until the correct rate is
     achieved.

SPINNING DISC TYPE SPREADER

The calibration (setting) of this type of machine is similar to that of

Fig. 9.4   A spinning disc type fertiliser distributor.

the belt type distributor, except that the width of spread is greater
than the above type.

*   *   *

To summarise, it can be said that for successful results the correct
application of chemicals is of vital importance and that the following
should always be remembered:

a) That the machine used for distribution should be calibrated
   correctly;

b) That the material is applied evenly;

c) The machine should be adequately maintained;

d) Treatment should not commence until the operator is fully conversant with the machines and chemicals that he is to use;

e) That the operator should wear the correct protective clothing.

10 Pests

A number of insect larvae feed upon the roots of grass and when large populations are present, considerable damage can occur. The damage, in most cases, is caused by the destruction of the plant's underground root system, or by the disruption of the lawn surface.

When grass is growing healthily it takes in water via its roots. If, for any reason, these are damaged, the plant is unable to remain turgid and it therefore wilts. When prolonged, wilting will cause the grass leaves to turn brown in colour, shrivel and eventually die, leaving bare patches in the sward.

Some animals such as earthworms and birds are also regarded as pests of turf because they affect the quality of the sward by their feeding habits. Worms do this by placing small heaps of soil on to the surface of the lawn (castings) and birds by pecking at the soil whilst looking for insect grubs.

Before a complete control of pests can be obtained, the groundsman and gardener must be able to recognise the symptoms and type of damage which a particular insect or animal will produce. He must also have some idea of its life-cycle, as applying chemicals at the wrong time of the year can be very wasteful and expensive.

Leatherjackets (*Tipula* spp.)

Leatherjackets are the larvae or grubs of the insects which are commonly known as Crane Flies. The species which is most commonly found in grass is *Tipula paludosa* Meig. However, various other species can be found: *Tipula oleracea*, *Tipula vernalis* Meig, *Pales flavescens*, *Pales maculata* Meig.

The larvae of the Crane Fly is most commonly found after damp periods in late summer or autumn. The reason for this is probably

144

because they cannot survive under conditions of drought. In fact, large numbers are killed if the autumn months are very dry.

Damage

Leatherjackets feed by eating the roots and underground stems of grasses. Their main area of activity is just beneath the soil, but during warm, damp nights they can feed on the surface. If this type of feeding does occur, the damage to the plants is very similar to that produced by Cutworms (p. 149).

The symptoms of attack appear as areas of turf which wilt during sunny weather. The patches eventually turn a straw-brown colour and die, leaving bare sections of soil. For a positive identification to take place, it is recommended that the larvae should be found in the soil.

Life history

Although there are a number of Crane Fly species which attack the roots of turf, their damage and life-cycles are all very similar. The insect goes through 4 distinct stages during its life cycle—the adult (imago), egg, larvae and pupa. This type of life-cycle is one of complete metamorphosis, as compared to an incomplete metamorphosis where only 3 distinct stages occur i.e. adult, egg and nymph.

The adult Crane Flies are large with long legs, slim bodies and narrow transluscent wings (Plate 19). They emerge from the soil during the summer and autumn months, emergence being later in the warmer regions than in the cooler areas.

Each female can lay in the region of 300 small, black, oval eggs, either directly into the soil or at the base of the grass stems. The eggs hatch after approximately 14 days to give small, grey, legless grubs which move to, and feed upon the grass roots. They feed during moist periods in autumn, winter and spring and when they are fully grown they are about 40 mm ($1\frac{1}{2}$ in) in length, brownish-black in colour and have a tough skin (Plate 18). During the summer months they become fully fed and pupate in the soil emerging as adults from late summer onwards.

Control measures

Leatherjackets can infest areas in large numbers. It has been recorded that up to 1,000 larvae/m² can be found living under ornamental turf.

A good indication of large infestations can be obtained when flocks of birds, such as rooks and starlings are seen feeding on grassed areas. A more scientific method of assessment is to spray a number of small sites with a mixture of ortho-dichlorobenzene and cryslic acid (Jeyes Fluid). This acts as a repellent, bringing the larvae to the surface where they can be counted. If the numbers are greater than about 30/m² (30/sq. yd.), some control will be necessary.

A limited amount of control can be obtained by 'trapping' the larvae beneath sacking or tarpaulins, which are placed over the turf in the evenings. However, the most reliable method of control is by the application of insecticides such as lead arsenate, H.C.H. (formerly B.H.C.) and D.D.T. The uses of D.D.T. have, of course, been limited. It is therefore recommended that it should only be used where there is no other effective or less persistent alternative.

Wireworms (*Agroites* spp.)

Wireworms are very common, soil-inhabiting insects which are capable of causing severe damage to young turf. They are the larvae of the insects which are known as Click Beetles. It is interesting to note, for example, that it has been estimated that approximately 60 species of Click Beetle can be found in Britain. Fortunately, only a small percentage of these are classed as pests of turf. The commonest species found in lawns are *Agroites lineatus*, *A. obscurus* and *A. sputator*.

Damage

Severe symptoms and damage rarely occur in established turf, even though large numbers of feeding larvae may be present. The main problem arises when newly-sown lawns are produced on sites which have previously been covered with grass. If pastureland or areas of old turf are to be used for the establishment of a new lawn, it is essential that the seed is protected before sowing (see below). If this is not possible, then the soil should be treated with chemicals such as H.C.H.

The damage is caused by the Wireworms eating the basal parts of the stem and roots. The symptoms on newly sown turf are similar to those of Leatherjackets, namely wilting of the leaves, browning of tissues and eventual death.

146

Life-cycle

The adult Click Beetles can be found in lawns between the months of April and July. They are approximately 12 mm ($\frac{1}{2}$ in) long and are commonly shiny and very dark brown or black (Plate 19). They lay their eggs either singly or in small clusters just beneath the soil surface in spring. These hatch after approximately one month to produce small transluscent, white larvae.

The larvae are characterized by having distinct brown heads, strong biting jaws and three pairs of jointed legs which are located just behind the head (see Plate 20). They feed sporadically for up to 4 or 5 years during which time they grow and turn a rich golden brown colour. When they are fully fed (July–August) they burrow lower down into the soil, pupate and emerge as adults 3–4 weeks later.

Control measures

Wireworms can be controlled by chemicals in two ways. The first being by seed dressings, the second by the incorporation of chemicals into the soil.

Seed dressings of H.C.H. (formerly B.H.C.) may be applied by seed houses, however it is possible to carry out the operation oneself. It must be remembered that seed is a living thing and if the application is carried out badly the germination rate may be affected. To obtain the best results, only dress high quality seed, always mix the dressing thoroughly and sow the seed as soon as possible after the chemical has been applied.

The second method is probably safer than seed dressing, but more chemical may have to be applied. It consists of working materials such as gamma-H.C.H. into the soil before seed sowing takes place. This treatment is relatively costly and should only be used where heavy infestations are present.

Chafer Grubs

In the British Isles five species of chafer grub are occasionally found living under turf. A sixth species, the Japanese Beetle (*Papillia japonica* Newn.) is occasionally introduced from its normal region of North America. The chafer grubs are the larval stages of the May Bug (*Melolontha melolontha*), Garden Chafer (*Phyllopertha horticola*), Summer Chafer (*Amphimallon solstitiatis*), Welsh Chafer (*Hoplia philanthus fiiess*), Brown Chafer (*Serica brunnea*).

147

Damage

The damage to turf is caused mainly by the larval stages, the adults feeding only on the leaves and stems of plants. It is quite possible to find large numbers of grubs living under neglected turf. When this occurs the roots can be so seriously damaged that the turf can be rolled up like a carpet. Severely damaged areas show clearly defined symptoms ranging from the complete death of small patches to areas which go brown during periods of dry weather. Birds can act as indicators by congregating on sites of high infestation, they can also cause serious damage by ripping up the turf in search for the grubs.

Life-cycle

Chafer beetles (Plate 21) are active during the period of late spring to summer. The females lay their eggs just beneath the soil surface in areas of close plant cover. When the eggs hatch, small grubs are produced which have brown heads with strong biting mouth parts (see Plate 22). The larvae feed on the grass roots at, or just beneath, the soil surface. When fully fed, some of the grubs may reach a length of up to 40 mm ($1\frac{1}{2}$ in). They can stay in the soil from between 9 months to 3 years, depending upon the species, after which they pupate in special cells deep in the soil. The adult beetles can emerge in early autumn, but they usually remain in the soil until the following spring.

The Garden Chafer is the smallest of the above mentioned species, the adult being only about 9 mm long ($\frac{3}{8}$ in). It is the most widespread of the species and is probably the most troublesome. In Britain, the adults are on the wing from May to early July. After mating the females burrow into the soil and lay their eggs. The eggs hatch after approximately 5 weeks and small grubs emerge which feed on the grass roots until the late autumn. When fully fed they burrow into the soil and pupate, the adults emerging the following spring.

The Cockchafer is the largest of the species which attack turf. The adults are approximately 25 mm long (1 in) with a fawn coloured head and redish-brown wing cases. The adults are on the wing from about May to June and after mating the females lay their eggs in the soil. The larvae hatch after 5–6 weeks and start to feed on grass roots. They continue to do so for up to 3 years after which they pupate in specially produced cells deep in the soil surface. The adults usually remain in the soil until the following spring.

148

The Summer, Welsh and Brown Chafers can cause damage to turf but attacks are usually localised and sporadic. However, if large infestations do occur they can be controlled in the same way as the garden chafer.

Control measures

Where necessary chafer grubs can be controlled by applying H.C.H. dust either in early spring or late summer. A satisfactory control can also be achieved by applications of lead arsenate and D.D.T. It should be remembered that birds and other natural enemies will control large quantities of grubs but usually damage the turf in the process.

Cutworms

Cutworms are the larval stages of various moths which belong to the family Noctuidae. This is a very large family which contains a number of pest species. The commonest species which are found in turf are the Turnip Moth (*Agrotis segetum* Schiff.), Heart and Dart Moth (*Agrotis exclamationis*), Large Yellow Underwing Moth (*Noctua pronuba*) and the Garden Dart Moth (*Euxoa nigricans*).

These four species are grouped together because their caterpillars all live in the soil. They hide during the day and come out at night to feed at ground-level on the stems of plants. These are often severed and because of this the caterpillars are referred to as cutworms.

Damage

The commonest species to attack turf is the Turnip Moth (*Agrotis segetum* Schiff.). Where large numbers are found in newly sown lawns it can cause serious damage. The larvae feed by eating the stems and roots of plants at ground level, this causes the plants to wilt and death usually follows. If the soil is disturbed close to the damaged area the culprits will normally be found in a curled up position.

Life-cycle

Three of the four cutworms mentioned above have very similar life-cycles, the fourth (Garden Dart) having a slightly different one. The moths (see Plate 23) appear from the middle of June until the end of July, each species emerging during a slightly different period.

149

After mating, the female moths lay their eggs on the leaves and stems of plants. The eggs hatch approximately 10–14 days later to give caterpillars (Plate 24) which either feed slowly throughout the summer and winter or feed rapidly so as to pupate in late July and August. The rapidly developing group can produce another brood of caterpillars before the winter months whereas the slowly developing group do not emerge as adults until the next year. The caterpillars from both broods become fully fed between the months of February and March, they then pupate and emerge as adult moths in the early summer.

Control measures

Cutworms can be controlled in a number of ways. On small sites it may be possible to locate the caterpillars and remove them by hand whereas on larger areas chemicals will have to be used. The chemicals most commonly used are H.C.H. and D.D.T. However, baits containing 'Paris Green' are also effective.

Fever Fly Larvae

Two species of fly belonging to the family *Bibionidae* are occasionally found living in turf. These are the St. Mark's Fly (*Bibio marci*) and the Fever Fly (*Dilophus febritis*). The adult flies emerge from the soil in early spring and can often be seen visiting the blossoms of Apples, Pears and Cherries. Two generations a year can be produced and in each case the larvae live in large colonies or nests beneath the surface of the turf.

Damage

The main damage is caused by the feeding habits of the larvae. These eat the roots of turf, which subsequently causes the production of thin loose patches that are unsightly and susceptible to drought.

Life-cycle

Adult flies can be seen on the wing during the months of April and May. After mating, each female can lay several hundred eggs on, or just beneath, the surface of the lawn. Large numbers of eggs can also be laid in mounds of grass clippings, compost heaps and leaf mould.

The eggs hatch out to give small greyish-brown larvae which have distinct shiny brown heads. They feed until mid-August and then pupate in earthen cells; the adult flies emerging approximately 1 month later. These flies then mate and produce a second generation which overwinter as larvae and emerge as adults in the following spring.

Control measures

When necessary, control can be achieved by applications of H.C.H., D.D.T. or derris, however lead arsenate applied at the rate of 30 g/m² is also very effective.

Earthworms (Family *Lumbricidae*)

When earthworms are found in garden soils they are usually classed as beneficial organisms. The reasons why they are thought to be so desirable are:

1 They help to break down organic matter which in turn increases the humus content of the soil;
2 They reduce soil compaction;
3 They improve surface drainage;
4 They help to aerate the soil.

Although they are desirable in the flower and vegetable gardens, their presence in lawns is not looked upon with such high esteem because:

a) Their casts may smother fine-leaved grasses;
b) Their casts are unsightly;
c) Their casts may make mowing difficult;
d) Their casts may damage mower blades;
e) Their casts provide ideal sites for the germination of weeds;
f) Their casts produce an uneven playing surface;
g) When they are present in large numbers they can produce a squelchy, slow drying sward.

Species creating the problem

Although there are approximately 25 British species of worm, only

151

two produce large quantities of casts. These are *Allolobophora nocturna* and *Allolobophora terestris f. longa*.

Unfortunately, the control measures which are available at the present time tend to be non-selective. This means that to prevent the production of casts we must kill all the species which are in the soil.

Conditions governing worm activity

The number of worms which are present under turf and the degree of activity which they exhibit is dependant upon the soil type, the cultural techniques which the sward receives and the surrounding climatic conditions.

Generally speaking, earthworm activity is greater in medium-textured soils than it is in heavy clays or light sands. This, however, is not the case with cast-forming species, as they seem to prefer heavier, damp sites which have a high organic matter content and a high pH. Empirical evidence has also shown that these species are more abundant on areas covered with long grass which is infrequently mown than they are on sites which are kept short and frequently cut.

Cultural control measures

Earthworm activity in lawns can be reduced by the following cultural practices:

a) By reducing the applications or organic materials to sites with high worm activity;

b) By carrying out boxing and removal of grass clippings (except in very dry weather);

c) By carrying out mowing at frequent intervals;

d) Applying acidifying fertilisers such as ammonium sulphate;

e) By avoiding the application of lime.

Chemical control measures

Although cultural techniques will reduce worm activity to some extent, it will usually be necessary to carry out some form of chemical control. In the past the best control was achieved by applications of either mowrah meal or derris dust, however, more recently chemicals have been found that are capable of giving a high degree of control without the application problems which can be encountered when applying the above materials.

MOWRAH MEAL

Mowrah meal is applied to turf in a fine powder form at the rate of 170 g/m² (6 oz/sq. yd.); it should then be copiously watered in. The active ingredient (mowrin) acts as an irritant bringing the worms to the surface, where they should be brushed up and removed. To maintain a worm-free sward, applications should be given every 1 or 2 years.

DERRIS

Derris is applied in the form of a dust at the rate of 14 g in 1 litre of water, to cover an area of 1 m² (½ oz/sq. yd.). The active ingredient (rotenone) kills a percentage of the worms below ground level, but the majority are brought to the surface where they die. As derris is more persistent than mowrah meal, it is only necessary to make applications every 2 to 3 years.

LEAD ARSENATE

Lead arsenate is available in either powdered or colloidal form. The rate of application for the powder is 60 g/m² (2 oz/sq.yd.), whereas the rate for the colloidal form is 680 oz/10 m² in 5 litres of water (1½ lbs/10 sq. yd. in 1 gallon of water).

CHLORDANE

Chlordane is a persistent organo-chlorine chemical that controls worms beneath the surface of the soil. It is easy to apply, lasts for 3–4 years, kills a number of other soil-borne pests and can be obtained in liquid or granular form. Applications are best made during early spring or autumn and should be applied at a rate of 60 g/m² (2 oz/sq. yd.) The use of this chemical is being restricted by agreement under the Pesticides Safety Precautions Scheme.

CARBARYL

Carbaryl is a carbamate insecticide and earthworm killer. It is available in the form of a wettable powder and in Britain should be applied to freshly mown turf during the month of September. The best results are obtained when it is applied to moist soils, or to sites where irrigation can be given after application. Where a complete

153

control of worms is required, annual applications may be necessary. Carbaryl is a relatively non-toxic chemical which is taking the place of chlordane as the major means of worm irradication.

Other materials such as copper sulphate, potassium permanganate and mercury-based compounds can also be applied to control worms in turf. Their mode of action takes the form of a repellent, bringing the worms to the surface where they usually die.

Incidental control of worms can be achieved if MBC (benomyl) fungicides are used for disease control.

Moles (*Talpa europea*)

To the Mole, areas of turf are considered as potential sources of easily obtained food and empirical evidence has shown that there is a direct link between the worm population of a soil and the degree of Mole activity. In fact, Moles are now frequently controlled by chemically treating the turf against worms. Damage is mainly caused to playing surfaces although the presence of mole hills apart from being unsightly, does cause damage to turf in the same way as worm casts.

The best time for control of Moles is between autumn and spring as they are active and their workings can be easily detected. Control is carried out in two ways, namely, by the use of traps and chemicals. Trapping consists of placing specially designed and approved metal traps into the mole runs, whereas chemical control consists of placing strychnine-covered worms into the runs. In the U.K., the use of strychnine is controlled by the Pharmacy and Poisons Act of 1933, which means that the chemical is only available to persons who obtain authority for its use from the Ministry of Agriculture.

*   *   *

In addition to the above mentioned pest species, it is possible to find localised or minor damage caused by Rabbits, Ants, Aphids, Bees and Midges. However, it must be stated that these pests are usually of minor importance and that in most cases no control measures will be warranted.

154

11 Fungal Diseases

Turf diseases are most commonly caused by the group of plants known as fungi. These are lowly plant organisms which are unable to produce their own food supplies because they are devoid of chlorophyll. The vast majority of fungi are saprophytic organisms which live on dead organic matter, however, a number of 'parasitic' types occur which are capable of feeding on healthy plant tissues. It is these parasites which cause the most trouble in turf.

The Structure of Fungi

The main body of a fungus usually consists of a number of branching threads called *hyphae*, collectively termed *mycelium*. The hyphae are only one-cell in thickness but often have numerous cross walls (septa) so that they become, in fact, chains of cells. In certain members of the higher fungi, parts of the mycelium can become densely aggregated to form resting bodies or *sclerotia* which may enable a fungus to survive long periods of stress. In other fungi, the mycelium can aggregate into strands, often with a hard resistant covering. These strands which are known as *rhizomorphs* are frequently produced to enable the fungus to grow from place to place.

The vegetative part of a fungus is usually embedded in the tissues of its host, the only parts visible being those of the fruiting body. With this type of growth the mycelium either enters the plant cells (intracellular), or grows between them (intercellular) producing special structures called *haustoria* which penetrate the cells to enable the fungus to extract nourishment from them.

In general, fungi reproduce themselves by minute unicellular or multicellular spores. Both sexual and asexual types can be produced, the sexual being formed after the joining together of two cells,

155

whereas the asexual type is produced as a result of mitosis in a cell nucleus.

The classification of fungi is based to a large extent on the nature of the fruiting body in or on which the spores are produced, and on the form of the spores themselves. The commonest classification is as follows

Phycomycetes   characterized by having aseptate hyphae.

Ascomycetes   characterized by having septate hyphae and sexual spores which are borne in 'Asci'.

Basidiomycetes   characterized by having septate hyphae and sexual spores borne on 'Basidia'.

Fungi imperfecti   characterized by having septate hyphae but as yet no distinct type of sexual spore.

Numerous fungal diseases can be found which live in or on turf. The various species exhibit a wide range of symptoms and growth habit, but they usually cause their maximum amount of damage at specific periods of the sward's life. For convenience the fungi can be divided into two main groups—those which attack seedlings, and those which damage established swards.

Seedling Diseases of Turf

Seedling diseases can also be divided into two convenient sections, or groups depending upon the time that the seedlings are attacked. Pre-emergent diseases attack seeds and seedlings before any growth emerges above the soil. Post-emergent types, on the other hand, attack seedlings once they have emerged. The incidence of both these types of disease can be very high whenever one or a combination of the following conditions occur:

a)   A poorly produced seedbed;
b)   The soil moisture content is very high;
c)   The soil temperature is low;
d)   When old seed is sown;
e)   When seed with a low germination rate is sown;
f)   Where the seed is sown too thickly;
g)   When the seed is sown too deeply;

156

h) When the seed is sown at the wrong time of the year (during dry periods in summer).

SYMPTOMS OF ATTACK

The pathogens which cause damage to young grass swards are collectively known as 'damping off' diseases, the majority of which are classified as members of the phycomycetes (e.g. *Pythium* spp.) and the *Fungi imperfecti* (e.g. *Fusarium* spp.). Those which cause seed rotting can be very difficult to identify, but it has been confirmed that species of pythium, fusarium, helminthosporium and rhizopus are all concerned.

The main symptoms of damage with this type of disease is the failure of the grasses to emerge above soil level, or if they do emerge, the production of a weak, patchy sward which takes a long time to become established.

The damage caused by the post-emergent seedling diseases shows up as yellowing of the leaf blades, followed by the complete collapse of the infected plants. The most serious damage of this type occurs to the fine-leaved grasses such as *Agrostis* and *Festuca* species. Post emergent disease symptoms have been found to be caused by a wide range of fungi, the most common types being *Fusarium* spp., *Pythium* spp., *Cladochytrium* spp. and *Olpidium* spp.

CONTROL MEASURES

Pre-emergence seed rots and 'damping off' can be controlled by ensuring that the conditions for germination and establishment are ideal. This means that the seedbed must be correctly prepared, the soil well drained and the correct amounts of fertilizers (especially nitrogen and phosphorus) incorporated into the seedbed. Care should also be taken to prevent uneven sowing, sowing too thickly, and the use of poor seed, as these can all encourage the establishment of the diseases.

Chemical treatments are available which will reduce the incidence of attack. They consist of either dressing the seed with thiram or captan, or working these chemicals into the soil before sowing takes place. It has been shown that applications of organo-mercurial compounds can increase the rate of establishment of fine-leaved grass species such as Chewings Fescue.

Post-emergence 'damping off' can also be reduced by ensuring that the above mentioned cultural conditions are ideal. If they are, the

157

diseases should not pose any real problem. However, if some form of control becomes necessary, applications of thiram, captan, Cheshunt compound or inorganic mercury can be applied.

Diseases of Established Turf

Even when a sward is established it can still become susceptible to a number of fungal diseases. It is essential that the groundsman and gardener should know under what conditions these diseases are encouraged and also the most expedient means of controlling them.

Fusarium Patch Disease (*Fusarium nivale* Fr.)

Fusarium patch is probably the commonest disease of fine turf in Britain. It is primarily a winter disease that exhibits its most serious symptoms in the late autumn months. However, when climatic and cultural conditions are favourable, the damage may be seen throughout the year.

Fusarium is often found attacking fine-leaved grasses or areas such as football pitches, bowling greens, tennis courts, golf greens and ornamental lawns. The main species to be attacked are those belonging to the Bents (*Agrostis* spp.), Fescues (*Festuca* spp.) and the Meadow Grasses (*Poa* spp.), however some of the broader-leaved species such as Yorkshire Fog (*Holcus lanatus*) are occasionally infected. A number of species do show a degree of resistance to the disease; a noticeable example being that of Perennial Rye Grass (*Lolium perenne*).

This is a disease which thrives on turf which is either lacking in vigour, or containing soft, rank growth typical of that produced by high applications of nitrogenous fertilizer. It may be found on a wide range of soil types and under a variety of climatic conditions, but it is especially prevalent on soils with poor aeration and sites which are frequently covered in snow.

SYMPTOMS OF ATTACK

The symptoms appear as small, yellow, water-soaked patches that are roughly circular and approximately 25–50 mm (1–2 in) in diameter (Plate 25). Under ideal conditions, the patches increase in size to produce larger areas of infection, often over 300 mm (12 in) in diameter. The larger patches can also coalesce to produce large areas of infection.

158

Once established, the patches turn a yellowish-brown colour and the vigour of the sward is reduced. In severe attacks, the grasses can actually be killed, but it is thought that death is usually caused by winter damage or secondary infections.

During periods of moist dull weather the fungal mycelium may be produced on the surface of the turf. When this happens the disease is capable of producing structures called *conidiophores* which release asexual conidio-spores to aid in the dissemination of the disease. As this is a member of the *Fungi imperfecti*, no sexual spores have yet been observed, the spread of the disease being mainly by sections of mycelium and conidiospores.

CONTROL MEASURES

Cultural control

It must be remembered that fusarium patch thrives under conditions of low vigour and mismanagement. Any cultural operations which encourage vigour will, therefore, go a long way in the prevention of the disease.

Most fungi require some form of moisture to enable them to spread rapidly. If, for any reason, soil moisture is abundant, the dissemination of the disease is greatly accelerated. Care must always be taken to prevent excess moisture from lying on the leaf blades, the best method of preventing this being the judicious use of scarification and 'switching' equipment.

During the autumn months, extreme care should be taken to prevent the over application of nitrogen, as this can produce lush green growth which is susceptible to frost. Applications of balanced fertilizer dressings are useful in the fight against disease, but it is a sound practice to have a soil analysis carried out before the chemicals are applied. This will then give a true indication of the soil nutrient status and provide guidelines on the amount of nutrients required.

Infrequent mowing or 'scalping' of the turf during the autumn and winter months can cause a distinct weakening of the sward. This, in turn, reduces vigour and leaves the plants open to attack. When the grass growth becomes too long it is therefore general good management to reduce the height gradually by a series of cuts.

The correct cultural management of a sward will help to prevent the ingress of fusarium, but some form of chemical treatment will be necessary if it becomes established.

159

Chemical control

On high quality swards, which are either important ornamental features or sportsground facilities, the control of fungal diseases is essential. In these circumstances, instead of waiting for the disease to become established, it is common practice to apply 'preventative' sprays. Chemicals which are often used in this manner are mercurous chloride, mercuric chloride and malachite green.

The mercury based compounds are usually applied at a rate of approximately 42 g/100 m² (1½ oz metallic mercury/100 sq. yd.) however, where the disease has already become established they can be applied at twice the normal rate to act as irradicants (84 g/100 m²).

Malachite green is usually applied in formulations with 'Bordeaux Mixture', which is incorporated as a 'sticker'. The rate of application is approximately 4·5 litres of ready made chemical to 50 m² of turf. (1 gall/50 sq. yd.), 3–4 applications being required between the autumn and spring months.

Quintozene (P.C.N.B.) is a fungicide which can be used to control a number of turf diseases, including fusarium patch. It is available in either dust or wettable powder form and should be applied according to each individual manufacturers recommendations.

Benomyl ('Benlate') and thiophanate-methyl ('Mildothane') are both systemic fungicides which give a good control of fungal diseases in turf, 'Mildothane' giving the added benefit of suppressing worm infestations. Certain strains of fungi may, in the future, become resistant to one or both of these chemicals; if this happens their application should be restricted and other chemicals used in their place.

Red Thread *(Corticium fuciforme* Berk.)

Red thread belongs to the group of fungi known as the Basidiomycetes. It is a widespread disease which can be found growing on golf fairways, cricket outfields and ornamental lawns, although it can be found growing on any site which is lacking in soil fertility. The species that appear to be most susceptible belong to the genus *Festuca*. However, the fungus can also be found attacking species of *Agrostis* (Bents), *Poa* (Meadow grasses) and *Lolium* (Rye Grasses).

SYMPTOMS OF ATTACK

Red thread is most serious after periods of wet weather in the early months of autumn, but symptoms can even appear in early summer on sites which are lacking in fertility. The amount of damage varies with the degree of attack and the prevailing climatic conditions. However, it is uncommon for the grasses to be killed outright.

The first signs of attack appear as small patches of water-soaked turf. These later become bleached and die-back of the leaf tips occurs, causing the turf to turn brown (see Plate 26). Once established, the patches can coalesce to produce large areas of infection. As the disease spreads, the sward can take on a pinkish discolouration. The colouring is caused by two things: firstly, during periods of damp weather, a fine web of pink mycelium can be produced which sticks the leaf blades together; secondly, the fungus can produce hard gelatinous needle-like growths which are composed of compacted red mycelium. It is these red structures that give the disease its common name. They are also the main method by which the fungus is spread.

CONTROL MEASURES

Cultural control

Corticium is primarily a disease of impoverished soils and weak swards, containing high percentages of fescues. Cultural methods of control should be aimed at improving the growing conditions, especially in respect of nutrient availability.

The most expedient method of reducing the incidence of this disease is to apply nitrogenous fertilizers during the summer months, coupled with applications of autumn topdressing containing high percentages of phosphorus and potassium.

Frequent close mowing, lack of moisture and shortage of nutrients put a sward under 'stress'. Any plant which is in this condition is unable to grow vigorously and will eventually become susceptible to the disease. The alleviation of stress will help to encourage healthy growth and reduce the ingress of disease.

Chemical control

If a sward is known to contain a high percentage of fescue species, it is advisable to start applying protective chemical sprays in late spring or early summer. Infection can be prevented by applications of inorganic mercury or malachite green/bordeaux mixtures applied at monthly intervals. On established patches, three applications of the

161

above chemicals at 10 day intervals may be required. The range of chemicals available for use is:

> Malachite green/Bordeaux mixture
> Mercurous/mercuric chlorides
> Thiophanate-methyl ('Mildothane')
> Quintozene (P.C.N.B.)
> Benomyl ('Benlate')
> Thiram.

Dollar Spot (*Sclerotinia homoeocarpa* F. T. Bennett)

Dollar spot is a member of the fungal group known as the Ascomycetes. It is a persistent disease favouring moist conditions and sites that are badly drained and poorly aerated. Damage can occur throughout the year, but is severe during the spring and late summer-to-autumn months. It is commonly found in sea-washed turf, especially when Red Fescue (*Festuca rubra* ssp. rubra) is a major constituent of the sward. In the early stages of attack, dollar spot can easily be confused with the symptoms of *corticium fuciforme*. However, the former can usually be recognised by having a distinct edge to the patches. Because of this confusion it is recommended that suspected infections should be positively identified by experienced personnel.

SYMPTOMS OF ATTACK

The symptoms appear as individual spots about 12 mm ($\frac{1}{2}$ in) in diameter, which give a discoloured yellow appearance to the turf. Once established, the spots can coalesce to form larger areas of approximately 50 mm (2 in) diameter (Plate 27). Seriously infected turf turns a yellowish-brown colour and occasionally fine, whitish mycelium may be seen between the leaf blades. A special type of diffused discolouration can also be observed on sites which have been severely infected the previous year.

Probably the main method of dissemination is by mycelium, as it is doubtful if asco-spores are produced in any quantity in Britain.

CONTROL MEASURES

Cultural control

Dollar spot is a problem on sites that are badly drained and poorly aerated. The incidence of attack can be reduced by improving the

162

surface drainage, relieving compaction and by removing any 'thatch' that may build-up at the base of the sward.

Balanced applications of nitrogenous fertilizers will be of benefit, especially when applied during the early summer months. However, care should always be taken to prevent applications being given in the late summer and autumn as this will stimulate lush growth susceptible to attacks of fusarium patch.

Chemical control

Chemical control of dollar spot should go hand in hand with the above cultural practises. It is recommenced that swards containing a high proportion of Red Fescue should be given protective sprays before the disease symptoms become apparent. The occurrence of dollar spot varies with location and season. This means that the first application of chemical will have to be judged by one's personal experience of each particular site. The sprays can be applied at varying intervals, the timing being dependant upon the chemicals used. An example of a protective programme is to apply three sprays of mercurous chloride at 10-day intervals, starting before the symptoms appear.

Other chemicals available for control are:

> Benomyl ('Benlate')
> Mercurous/mercuric chlorides
> Quintozene (P.C.M.B.)
> Thiram
> Thiophanate methyl ('Mildothane')

Ophiobolus Patch Disease (*Ophiobolus graminis* sacc. var *avenae*)

This is another pathogen which belongs to the group of fungi known as the *Ascomycetes*. The disease is found in a wide range of situations including bowling greens, tennis courts, cricket outfields and golf fairways. However, the species of grass affected is usually limited to Browntop Bent (*Agrostis tenuis*) and Velvet Bent (*Agrostis canina*), with occasional attacks on the Meadow Grasses (*Poa* spp.).

SYMPTOMS OF ATTACK

Symptoms commonly occur on soils that have had their pH raised by the application of lime, but they can also become evident on impoverished sites which are suffering from poor drainage.

Attacks occur during the late summer, autumn and winter months especially when the weather is dry. Mild forms can occasionally go unnoticed, whereas severe attacks in warm winters can persist until the following spring.

The symptoms (see Plate 28) show up as small sunken areas, approximately 50 mm to 100 mm (2–4 in) in diameter which have a bleached or bronzed appearance. Once established the patches spread outwards, often reaching 1 m (approx. 1 yd) or more in diameter. As the fungus develops the central portions die out and are replaced with either weeds or less susceptible grass species.

CONTROL MEASURES

The cultural control of this disease consists mainly of avoiding applications of lime or lime-containing substances to swards containing a high percentage of *Agrostis* species. The incidence of attack may also be limited by improving the surface drainage and applying balanced fertilizer dressings at the correct time of the year.

Chemical control

Chemical control of this disease can be obtained by repeated applications of organo-mercury compounds at 10-day intervals.

Fairy rings

The disorder of turf known as 'fairy rings' is caused by species of fungi belonging to the *Basidiomycetes*. They are found in turf all over the world, especially on sites which are lacking in nutrients. The disease manifests itself in a variety of ways depending upon the species of fungus concerned. Very serious attacks can cause the death or damage of large areas of turf, whereas milder forms only produce stimulated zones, or rings of toadstools. Some of the commoner species concerned in the production of fairy rings are *Marasmius oreades*, *Psalliota arvensis*, *Psalliota campestris*, *Collybia butyracea* and *Tricholoma gambosum*.

SYMPTOMS OF ATTACK

The most serious type of fairy ring damage in temperate climates is caused by the fungus *Marasmius oreades* (Plate 29). It can cause serious disfigurement of golf fairways, bowling greens, cricket outfields and ornamental lawns—especially when the soil is light and sandy.

The fungus grows radially from a single point beneath the turf. As it develops, a ring of affected tissue is produced consisting of a circular, dead zone, which is bounded on either side by a stimulated area of grass (Plate 29). Dead areas or zones are caused by the large mass of mycelium beneath the surface of the turf (Plate 30). This mycelium forms a dense mat of water-repellant tissue which prevents the grass roots from absorbing moisture. It has also been shown that damage can be caused by the release of a toxic substance from the mycelium. As the fungus breaks down the organic matter in the soil, it releases nitrogenous substances which stimulate the grass on either side of the dead zone.

Fruiting bodies that are approximately 25 mm to 50 mm (1–2 in) across and reddish-tan to buff colour, depending upon their age and season are produced in the area of the death zone. It is from these fruiting bodies that white basidio-spores are released to spread the disease.

CONTROL MEASURES

Fairy rings are commonly found on light, sandy sites which have a low soil fertility. A limited amount of control will be obtained if the soil nutrient status is improved by the application of balanced topdressings, coupled with aeration to allow moisture to enter the lower layers.

Chemical control

Complete chemical control can be difficult to achieve as the mycelium has water repellant properties. Whenever chemicals are used it is essential to mix them with a wetting agent, e.g. Agral, and carry out some form of aeration before the materials are applied.

The standard method of control is:

1   Remove an area of turf at least 300 mm (12 in) on either side of the affected ring;
2   Break up the underlying soil;
3   Either remove the soil and replace with sterilized loams or, drench the area with a 2·5% solution of formalin + wetter;
4   Cover the area for 1 week;
5   Expose for 2 weeks to allow gases to escape;

6   Re-turf with disease-free material.

Other controls (such as applying ferrous sulphate after the soil has been aerated) have been tried with varying degrees of success.

In recent years, chemical sterilants have been developed to combat soil borne fungal diseases. To date, their use has been limited to the production of weed, pest and disease free seedbeds. However, the signs are that they might give some control of fairy rings when substituted for formalin in the standard control procedure.

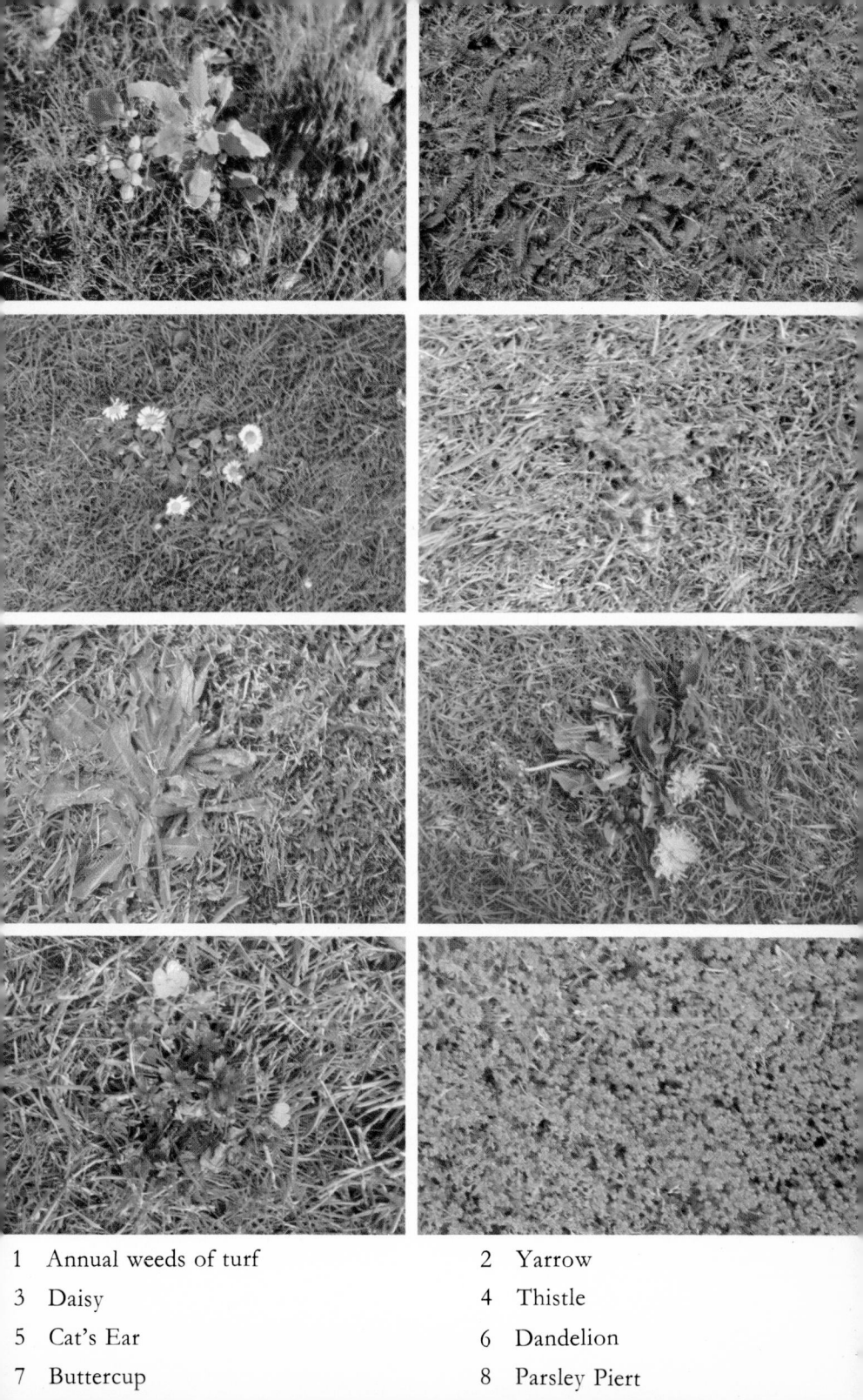

1 Annual weeds of turf	2 Yarrow
3 Daisy	4 Thistle
5 Cat's Ear	6 Dandelion
7 Buttercup	8 Parsley Piert

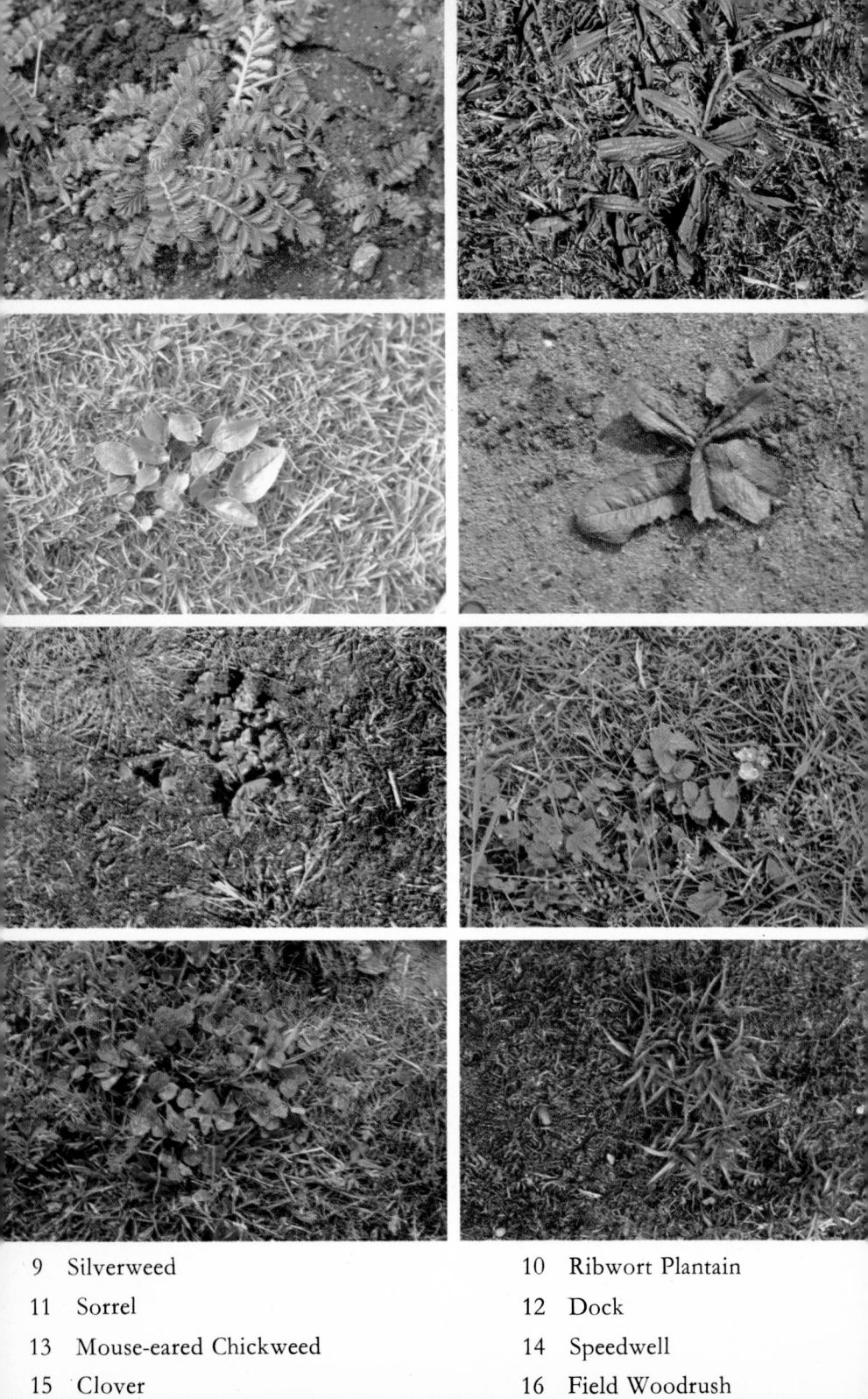

9   Silverweed

11   Sorrel

13   Mouse-eared Chickweed

15   Clover

10   Ribwort Plantain

12   Dock

14   Speedwell

16   Field Woodrush

17 Crane Fly	18 Leatherjacket – Crane Fly larva
19 Click Beetle	20 Wireworm – Click Beetle larva
21 Cockchafer	22 Cockchafer larva
23 Large Yellow Underwing – adult Cutworm	24 Cutworm

25   Fusarium patch disease

27   Dollar Spot disease

29   Fairy rings as they appear
       on the surface

26   Red Thread

28   Ophiobolus patch disease

30   The white fairy ring mycel-
       ium beneath soil revealed
       by cutting and folding
       back a section of turf

12 Machinery

The modern internal combustion engine is widely used for the production of mechanical energy from chemical energy. To achieve this transformation, the fuel must firstly be mixed with a certain volume of air and then burnt under controlled conditions.

The commonest types of power unit used on playing field equipment are the four-stroke and two-stroke petrol (gasoline) engines. The basic difference between the two being in the number of times the crankshaft and piston move to complete one full cycle.

Four-Stroke Engines

The four-stroke petrol engine (Fig. 12.1) consists of a cylinder or tube that is closed at one end and in which the fuel is burnt. A piston is fitted inside the cylinder to compress the fuel/air mixture and to force out the spent gases. In the sides of the cylinder are two close-fitting valves. One is the *inlet valve*, which allows the fuel to enter; and the other is the *exhaust* or *outlet valve*, which enables the spent fuel to be removed after combustion.

As the fuel inside the cylinder burns, it produces heat and expands; this leads to a build up of pressure which forces the piston downwards in the cylinder. The piston is joined to the connecting rod and crankshaft and it is via these that the linear motion of the piston can be converted into rotary motion at the wheels of the machine.

The four-stroke cycle

To complete a full cycle, the crankshaft makes two revolutions and the piston makes 4 strokes—a stroke being one full movement of the piston either up or down the cylinder.

FIRST STROKE (INDUCTION)

As the piston moves down the cylinder, the exhaust valve *closes* and

167

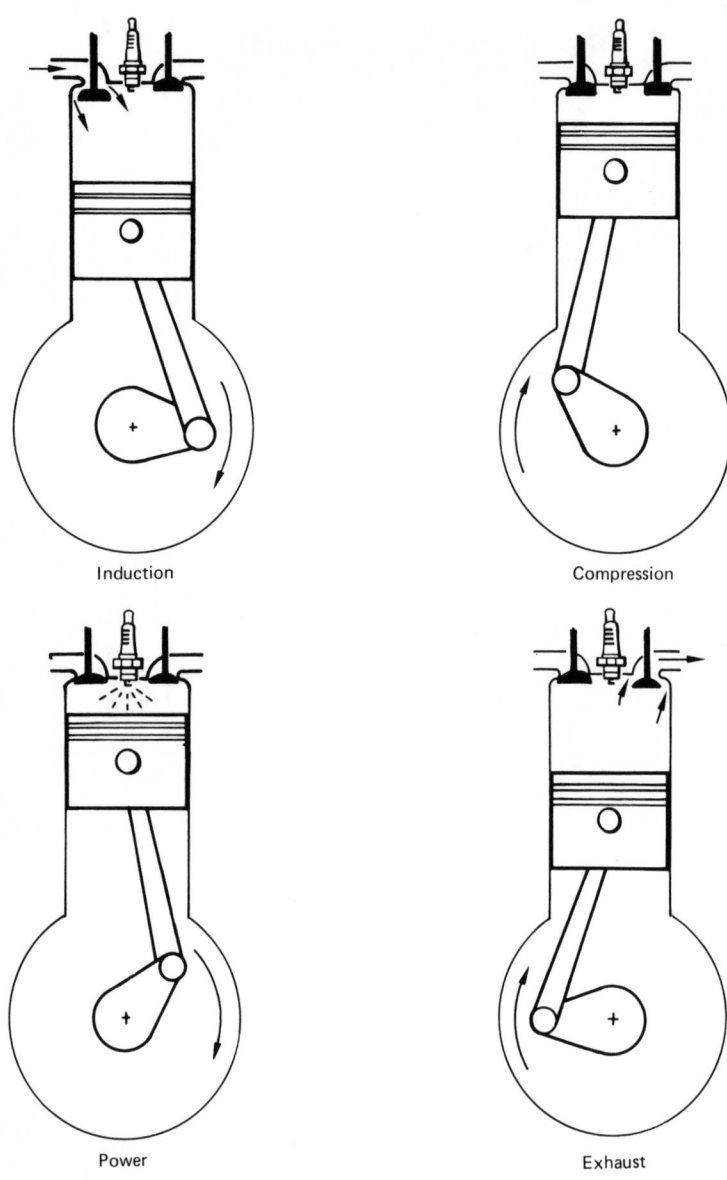

Induction

Compression

Power

Exhaust

Fig. 12.1   A four-stroke cycle petrol engine.

the inlet valve *opens*. The downward movement of the piston causes a partial vacuum in the cylinder which in turn causes the new fuel/air mixture to be drawn in via the inlet valve. As the piston reaches the bottom of the cylinder, the inlet valve closes and the mixture is trapped ready for the compression stroke (see Fig. 12.1).

SECOND STROKE (COMPRESSION)

During this stroke, both the inlet valve and outlet valves are in the *closed* position. The piston moves up the cylinder and compresses the fuel. Just before the piston reaches the top of the cylinder (top dead centre), the fuel is ignited by means of the sparking plug.

THIRD STROKE (POWER OR COMBUSTION)

During this stroke, both valves are *closed* and the piston is at top dead centre. The spark plug ignites the fuel/air mixture and a rise in pressure occurs which forces the piston down the cylinder.

FOURTH STROKE (EXHAUST)

As the piston moves up the cylinder the exhaust valve *opens* but the inlet valve stays *closed*. The upward movement of the piston pushes the burnt gases out of the cylinder via the exhaust valve. The engine is then ready to start a completely new cycle.

Ignition system

This is usually of the flywheel magneto type, incorporating the usual induction circuit. Routine maintenance is limited to the cleaning and adjustment of the contact breaker points. Timing is usually set by altering the position of the flywheel on the crankshaft. It is important that the contact breaker points should be just opening when the piston is at top dead centre.

Two-Stroke Engines

These have a wide application as light power units, and because of their compact construction lend themselves to easy fitment on many classes of playing field equipment. This type of engine also possesses the virtue of having a minimum of working parts, which means that both initial and maintenance costs are low compared with its four-stroke counterpart. Against this it may be said that its overall efficiency and length of life is not so good. The noise of the two-stroke

169

engine may also be somewhat objectionable, particularly when used on school and hospital lawns and surrounds.

The basic principle of the engine bears some resemblance to the four-stroke, but in this case the whole cycle of induction, compression, power and exhaust is carried out with *two* movements of the piston and *one* revolution of the crankshaft.

Valves and cams are eliminated, the induction of fuel/air mixture and expulsion of exhaust gases is achieved by the provision of apertures in the cylinder wall called ports. The piston itself covers and uncovers these as it travels up and down the cylinder. Another important feature of the two-stroke engine is that the crankcase, which is gas tight, acts as a storage space and compression chamber for the fuel/air mixture momentarily before it enters the cylinder.

The two-stroke cycle

This might be more easily understood by referring to Fig. 12.2. Here is a sectional view showing the positions of the parts. The piston shown has a shaped head which acts as a deflector to the fuel mixture which is entering the cylinder from the transfer port at the same time that the exhaust gases pass out of the exhaust port. Some engines do not have a deflector-type piston, but these usually employ twin transfer ports instead.

FIRST STROKE

As the piston travels upwards it covers both exhaust and transfer ports at the same time as it compresses the mixture above the piston. The upward movement of the piston also creates a partial vacuum in the crankcase, so that when the piston nears the top of its stroke and uncovers the inlet port, fuel/air mixture is drawn into the crankcase (crankcase induction). At top dead centre the compressed vapour above the piston is ignited by the sparking plug.

SECOND STROKE

The ignition of the fuel causes the rapid expansion of the gases above the piston which forces the latter down on its power stroke. Its downward movement also compresses the fuel/air mixture in the crankcase and when the crown of the piston has passed the transfer and exhaust ports, the exhaust gases which are still above atmospheric pressure find their way out of the exhaust port; the new mixture

170

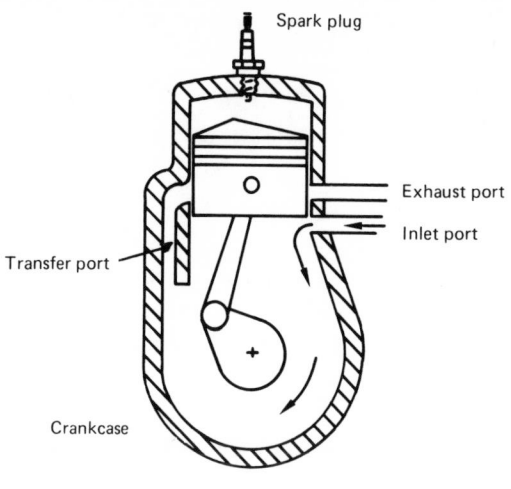

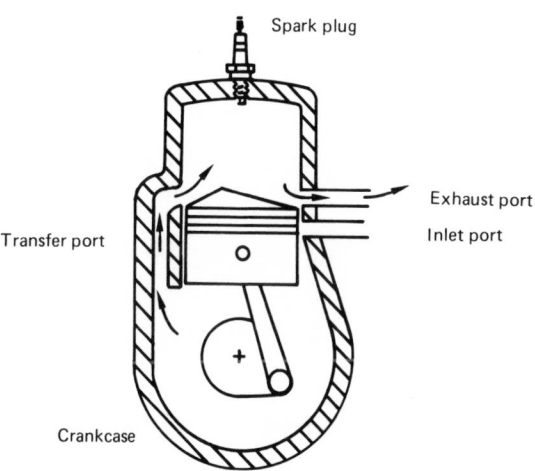

Fig. 12.2   A two-stroke cycle petrol engine.

171

enters the cylinder via the transfer port, thus charging it in preparation for the next upward stroke of the piston.

Ignition system
The ignition system for this type of engine is the same as for the four-stroke engine.

Carburation
A simple jet carburettor is commonly used. If an engine has been standing idle for a long period, it may be necessary to clean out any accumulation of sediment or oil from the float chamber and jet.

Engine Lubrication
However smooth a metal surface may appear to the naked eye, it always has innumerable irregularities which may only be seen under a microscope.

When two metal surfaces are made to slide over each other, these irregularities obstruct free movement and cause 'friction' as the high spots of the surfaces collide.

Friction causes heat, which will result in a further distortion of the surfaces and may even be sufficient to cause them to fuse together, resulting in a 'seizure'.

Friction can be reduced by putting a thin film of oil between the surfaces to keep them apart.

The oil most commonly used is derived from the same crude material as are fuel oils.

Factors affecting the choice of lubricant
Different types of oil are used according to the load on the surfaces, the temperature under which they operate and the speed at which they are moving.

Viscosity is the measure of an oil's resistance to flow, an important characteristic, which together with other factors has a bearing on oil quality. A 'thick' oil that does not run freely has a high viscosity, whereas a 'thin' oil has a low viscosity. The viscosity of an oil varies with the temperature, i.e. as an oil is heated, its viscosity is lowered. This variation in viscosity is much smaller in a good quality oil compared with a poorer oil.

A poor quality oil may break down under load and high temperatures, whereas a good oil will retain its viscosity and film strength and continue to carry the load for which it is designed.

The viscosity of an oil is indicated by its S.A.E. number. The lower the number, the thinner the oil. Engine oils range from S.A.E. 5 to S.A.E. 60 and gear oils from S.A.E. 80 to S.A.E. 250.

All manufacturers specify a certain grade of lubricant for their own particular engine or transmission system, and their advice should always be heeded.

Lubrication systems

Engine oil has three main functions:

1   To act as a lubricant, i.e. to prevent metal to metal contact of moving parts;
2   To act as a coolant to transfer heat from the high temperature regions of the engine;
3   To act as a piston seal; (a) to prevent 'blow-by', i.e. the escape of fuel vapour past the piston rings on the compression stroke; (b) to improve induction.

It must, therefore, be thin enough when cold to circulate freely and yet not lose its viscosity when the engine is hot. A system must be devised to circulate it to all the moving parts of the engine. The systems commonly used in tractors and stationary engines are given below.

SPLASH FEED

With this system, the bulk of the oil is contained in the sump. The lower part of the big end bearings are fitted with scoops which dip into reservoirs which are kept full, either by means of a pump or by the flywheel. The sump must always be full, particularly on hilly ground—otherwise the front or rear bearings may run dry.

SEMI-FORCE FEED

In this case, oil is pumped under pressure from the sump to the main and big end bearings. The small ends and camshaft are splashed with oil issuing from pressure-fed bearings.

FULL-FORCE FEED

All the bearings are pressure fed by a pump, including the small ends, valve gear and camshaft bearings.

With all these systems the cylinder walls are lubricated with oil thrown from the crankshaft or pressure fed bearings.

DRY SUMP

In some single cylinder, four-stroke engines, the oil is contained in a separate reservoir, from where it is pumped to the principal bearings of the engine. An additional pump is necessary to return the oil from the sump to the reservoir. Since the reservoir is remote from the engine, the circulating oil stays cooler—a notable feature of air-cooled engines.

PETROIL SYSTEM

Most two-stroke engines use the 'petroil' system, that is to say the lubricating oil is mixed with the petrol and enters the crankcase and cylinder with the petrol vapour. The usual ratio of the mixture used is 16 parts petrol to 1 part lubricating oil. This 16 : 1 ratio can be varied to some advantage; for instance, in extremely hot weather, engines lubricated this way will remain cooler if a slightly higher proportion of oil is used. On the other hand, in extremely cold weather, engines tend to start easier if slightly less oil is used—although this can be dangerous if carried to excess, and in any case, manufacturer's recommendations must always be followed.

It is imperative, however, that the two following points are remembered:

1   Only use good quality oil of specified viscosity;
2   Be sure the oil and petrol are thoroughly pre-mixed before being poured into the tank.

No doubt most operators will know that there are available some special oils designed specifically for two-stroke engines. These readily mix with petrol and are claimed to require no pre-mixing.

Filters

In all systems, particularly pressure systems, the oil must be clean and free from particles of grit or carbon. Thus, filters are incorporated into most systems. There is usually a coarse filter (to trap relatively large particles of foreign matter from the oil on its way back from the bearings to the sump) and sometimes a second filter at the pump intake.

Almost all tractor engines now have an external cartridge-type filter on the delivery side of the pump. This filter is capable of removing carbon and other extremely small particles of dirt, thus ensuring efficient lubrication.

Whichever type of filter is fitted, it should always be cleaned and renewed according to the manufacturer's instructions.

Pressure Gauges

Nearly all force-feed systems incorporate either a pressure gauge or a 'tell-tale' to indicate the lack of pressure. Any marked drop in pressure shown by the gauge or failure of the tell-tale to operate must be investigated immediately.

SOME CAUSES OF LOSS OF PRESSURE

a) Oil level in sump too low.

b) Blocked or partially blocked filters.

c) Worn bearings.

d) Broken oil pipe or loose union.

e) Worn or damaged pump.

f) Oil pressure relief valve not seating correctly.

g) Heavily diluted oil.

h) Overheated engine.

Sump dilution

The oil in a sump may be diluted in a number of ways.

1 The most serious occurs in vapourising oil (V.O.) engines and is due to unburnt fuel passing down the cylinder walls into the sump. This may result from one of the following reasons:

    a) Running the engine too cold, i.e. by long periods of idling, switching over to V.O. too soon and failure to use radiator blinds. (*Note*   When running on V.O. the engine temperature should not fall below 88 °C (190 °F.));

    b) Excessive use of the choke;

    c) Misfiring.

If these points are not observed, the engine oil may be rapidly diluted to such an extent that it is no longer able to perform its very useful functions.

2   Sump oil may also be diluted and contaminated by other products of combustion—especially water, when the crankcase breather is blocked by particles of carbon, grit, and dust from the atmosphere.

Detergent oils

These are sometimes called heavy duty oils. They are commonly used in diesel engines, where the type of fuel used and the engine's high running temperature give rise to the formation of lacquer deposits causing ring sticking, etc. They consist of ordinary mineral oils with the addition of certain chemicals, which combat the lacquer formation by keeping the particles of carbon and other combustion products suspended in the oil.

Because of the action on carbon deposits, it can be damaging to change from an ordinary straight oil to a detergent oil without giving a thorough cleaning of the oil filters and flushing out of the lubrication system.

Transmission Lubricants

These are available in two grades, namely S.A.E. 90 and S.A.E. 140. They are used for most gear-boxes and rear axles, but for hypoid drives and worm drives in rear axles, special grades are available (some of which contain additives to improve the film strength). Most tractor hydraulic systems utilise the oil in the transmission housing. In this case, the gear oil is relatively light. Regular maintenance of these systems with special attention to the gauze and magnetic filters is of the utmost importance.

Greases

Greases can be regarded as oils made rigid by some kind of base. They are produced in a variety of grades for different purposes, the two most common types for playing field equipment being the ordinary grease for general lubrication and waterproof grease for water pumps. However, gear oil is a better substitute on some machines.

Care should always be taken not to overcharge 'sealed' bearings, as there is always the danger of damaging the seals, allowing the grease to seep out and dirt to enter the bearing.

Rust-preventing Compounds

These products are designed to prevent rust on clean metal surfaces. There are a number of types, the commonest are:

Grease compound   Used on plough mouldboards, tines, blades, etc.;

Liquid compound   Used as a rust preventative on the interior components of engines when they are to remain idle for some months;

Water displacing compound   This can be applied to any clean, wet surface, e.g. a plough after washing off with water, or mowing machine blades and cylinders; it is a remarkable substance which should prove invaluable to groundsmen.

To obtain a complete protection, an even, thin coat of one of these products should be applied. However, it will sometimes be found necessary to remove the substance before putting the machine to work.

Routine Engine Maintenance

Engines demand careful and regular servicing and whilst the following maintenance tasks include the most important points, the operator is well advised to aquaint himself with the advice and recommendations given in the manufacturer's instruction manual. Also, the keeping of a log to record each service is a great asset. Assuming an engine is in every day use, the maintenance can be divided in the manner described below.

(Small power units may have much shorter running periods between services and since there is much variation between different makes the manufacturer's instructions must be followed.)

Daily servicing

Before starting work each day, the following should be carefully checked:

Fuel   Check and top up if necessary.

Radiator   If fitted should be inspected and topped up if necessary.

Air cleaner   Check and clean if necessary.

Sediment bowl   Check and clean if necessary.

Nuts   Tighten any that are loose.

Cooling fins   Remove all dirt preferably with an air line.

Oil level   Check and top up if necessary.

Weekly servicing

The weekly (or 50 hour) service should consist of all the daily checks plus the following (where relevant):

Tyre pressures   Check and inflate if necessary.

Gear box oil level   Check and top up if necessary.

Fan belt   Check tension.

Monthly servicing

Carried out after every 200 hours or so, this consists of all the daily and weekly checks, plus the following:

a) Check engine oil.

b) Clean sparking plugs.

c) Check brakes, clutch and steering (on tractors).

d) Drain radiator and flush out with clean water.

e) Check contact breaker points.

f) Diesel engines should have the fuel filter elements cleaned and renewed at intervals of between 200 and 400 working hours.

Yearly servicing

The yearly servicing should consist of the daily, weekly and monthly checks where applicable, plus the following:

a) Refit new spark plugs.

b) Refit new contact breaker points.

Other operations which should be carried out between the monthly and yearly services are:

Oil filter   (change if forced feed system).

Engine oil   check on larger diesel engines.

Wheel hubs   check and clean.

Diagnosing Engine Faults

When the engine will not start

Causes	Remedies
Tractor vaporising oil (T.V.O.) in carburettor.	Drain carburettor.
Water in fuel.	Drain carburettor and fuel tank. Remove sparking plugs, clean and dry them.
Dirt in carburettor.	Remove carburettor and clean with petrol. Be sure the screen is clean and all jets clear.
No petrol in carburettor.	Check tank; if necessary, clean pipes and filter.
Dirty or broken sparking plugs.	Clean and adjust gaps. (Follow manufacturer's recommendations.) Replace if broken. Sparking plugs should be replaced once a year.
Sparking plug leads wrongly fitted.	Check leads and firing sequence.
Magneto out of time.	Improbable unless magneto has been removed. Check timing gear.
Points dirty or corroded.	Clean and reset.
Dampness on sparking plug leads.	Wipe clean and dry.

Engine Difficult to start

Cause	Remedy
Too much choking.	Do not choke engine excessively. In hot weather or if the engine is hot, very little choking is required.
Too little choking of cold engine in extremely cold weather.	Close choke completely.
Sparking plug cables cracked or broken.	Replace (for temporary repair use insulating tape).

Cause	Remedy
Air leaks in manifold or carburettor connections.	Examine gaskets and replace if torn or broken. Tighten studs. Renew manifold if cracked.
Contact breaker points dirty or not spaced correctly.	Clean points with a fine file, reset points.
Impulse coupling sluggish or broken.	If spring dirty, wash in petrol. If broken renew.
Poor compression. Valves sticking or leaking.	If sticking, loosen up with penetrating oil. Use a lighter and better grade of oil and change regularly.

Irregular Running—Misfiring

Cause	Remedy
Engine too cold for T.V.O.	Switch back to petrol and cover radiator, Check that manifold 'heat control' is set correctly.
Water in fuel.	Clean out fuel tank, strainer, fuel lines and carburettor. Refill with clean fuel.
Irregular flow of fuel to carburettor. Dirt in the system.	Remove and clean out fuel lines, fuel and screen in carburettor. Check that the air vent in the filler cap is not blocked.
Carburettor out of adjustment. Too rich or too weak.	Adjust carburettor. See instruction book.
Choke closed too much.	Open choke and throttle and turn engine.
Air cleaner clogged.	Remove and clean.
Carburettor or manifold gaskets leaking.	Check gaskets for leaks. Replace if torn. Be sure that all studs and cap screws are tight.
Tappets out of adjustment.	Adjust clearances as shown in the instruction book.

180

Cause	Remedy
Valves stuck or leaking.	If stuck, penetrating oil poured around the valve stems will loosen them. Use a good grade of engine oil. Replace any valves so badly burned or warped that they cannot be reseated.
Spark plugs fouled or wrong gap.	Clean plugs and adjust gap.
Contact breaker points pitted or out of adjustment.	Touch up points with a fine ward file. It may be necessary to replace badly pitted points.
Governor sticking or worn.	Clean and oil governor connections. All parts must work freely. Replace worn connections and spring if weak.
Sparking plug cracked.	Replace.
Magneto cables cracked or broken.	Replace, cracked cables can be temporarily wrapped with insulating tape.
Faulty coil or condenser.	Replace.

Excessive Fuel Consumption

Cause	Remedy
Choke partly closed.	Adjust carburettor until engine runs with choke wide open.
Air cleaner clogged.	Remove and clean.
Carburettor or manifold leaking encouraging excessive use of choke.	Check gaskets for leaks. Replace if torn or broken. Be sure that all studs and cap screws are tight.
Incorrect fuel mixture.	Adjust carburettor.
Exhaust heat regulator not set properly—Too much or too little heat.	Set heat-regulating valve to 'hot', 'medium' or 'cold', depending on seasonal temperature changes (see instruction book).
Tappets out of adjustment.	Adjust clearance as shown in instruction book.
Leaks in fuel tank, fuel line or connections.	Repair by fitting 'Olive' type union nipples.
Sparking plug cracked or gap wrong.	Replace if cracked. Adjust gap.
Overloaded engine.	Set governor so that engine runs at recommended speed. Do not overload. Select best gear for job.

Engine Overheating

Cause	Remedy
Water level.	Check. Top up if necessary.
Radiator dirty, inside or outside.	If outside, clean between tubes and fins with high pressure air line. If inside, boil out with a soda solution. If limed up, remove and take to workshop for cleaning.
Fan belt slipping.	Increase tension on belt. If blades are badly bent, replace them.
Faulty thermostat.	Renew.
Weak fuel mixture.	Adjust carburettor.
Poor lubrication.	Change oil if necessary. Use correct grade.
Incorrect engine speed.	Set governor correctly (see instruction book).
Engine overloaded.	Reduce load, operate machine at a lower gear setting.
Tappets out of adjustment.	Adjust (see instruction book).

Pre-Ignition of Fuel

Cause	Remedy
Magneto out of time.	Improbable unless magneto has been removed. Check timing.
Too weak fuel mixture.	Adjust carburettor.
Overheated engine.	Check water in radiator, check fan and belt, also water pump and connections. Clean the outside and inside of the radiator. Check thermostat.
Excessive carbon deposits on heads of pistons, valves and in combustion chamber.	Decarbonise the engine.

Excessive Oil Consumption

Cause	Remedy
Worn cylinder and pistons.	Rebore required.
Oil leaks.	Check engine for oil leaks. Replace defective gaskets or seals.

Loss of Power from Engine

Cause	Remedy
Engine not getting sufficient fuel.	Clean out carburettor and fuel line.
Sparking plugs dirty or wrong gap.	Clean sparking plugs and set gaps.
Poor carburettor adjustment.	Check and adjust carburettor.
Tappets out of adjustment.	Check and adjust to specified clearance.
Carbon in intake manifold.	Clean out.
Air cleaner clogged.	Clean out when necessary.

Faults in Diesel Engines

Since no electrical ignition equipment or carburettor is fitted to a diesel engine, many of the minor causes of poor engine performance are eliminated. However, should they arise they can usually be traced to the fuel injection equipment. When tracing a fault, the diesel engine operator must limit his investigations to the fuel supply lines, filters and injector nozzles. On no account should there be interference with the injection pump itself, other than to carry out the lubrication procedure and bleeding of air when necessary.

183

Injector nozzles

The first symptoms of nozzle trouble usually manifest themselves in one or more of the following ways:

a) Cylinder knock:
b) Engine overheating;
c) Loss of power;
d) Exhaust smoke (black);
e) Increased fuel consumption.

One should not immediately assume that the nozzles are the cause of the trouble. Such features as faulty engine valve timing, badly leaking engine valves, incorrect pump timing, dirty or damaged fuel filters, unsuitable fuel filtration, wrong fuel, water in fuel, defective engine lubrication, or hot bearings may cause similar signs of distress.

Assuming that everything else is in order and the nozzles are still suspect, the particular nozzle causing trouble can often be determined by releasing the pipe union nut on each nozzle-holder in turn, with the engine running, and listening to the idling performance of each of the other cylinders.

In order to test the doubtful nozzle, first remove the nuts from its flange and then withdraw the complete unit (i.e. nozzle holder and nozzle) from the cylinder head. Then turn it round the oil feed pipe so that the nozzle is pointing outwards, away from the engine. Next slacken the unions of the other nozzle-holder oil feed pipes (to prevent fuel being sprayed into their cylinders) and turn the engine until the suspected nozzle sprays into the air, when it will be seen at once if the spray is in order.

If the spray is unduly 'wet' or 'streaky' or obviously to one side, or if the nozzle 'dribbles', the unit should be disconnected and replaced.

Great care should be taken to prevent the hands from getting into contact with the spray as the high pressure will cause the oil to penetrate the skin.

13   Routine Maintenance

Once the lawn has been successfully established the work of regular maintenance must begin. The type and frequency of maintenance, as with most other operations in turf culture, will depend to a large extent upon the size of the area, the availability of machines and labour and the ultimate use of the sward. It will be found that whatever type of turf area is produced, the maintenance will be similar, but the frequency and intensity of work will be different.

Mowing

Mowing is one of the most time-consuming operations in the maintenance of lawns. However, it is necessary if the sward is to be kept neat, vigorous and in a suitable condition for use. On certain areas such as roadway embankments, vigour and suitability for use are minor considerations, but it has now been shown that some previously rare species of wild plants are becoming established in these areas. It is because of this and the cost of maintenance, that many far-sighted local authorities in the U.K. are now leaving sections of motorway embankments unmown.

One of the problems which occur during mowing is that of whether or not to allow the cuttings to 'fly'. In most situations, it is considered beneficial to remove cuttings during mowing. However, during periods of dry weather they can be left to act as a mulch. The benefits of removing clippings can be listed as follows:

a) Discourage worm activity by the removal or organic matter;
b) Prevents formation of dead mat at the base of the sward;
c) Removes flower heads of broad-leaved weeds;
d) Lessens spread of weeds such as Speedwells which are spread by vegetative means;

185

e) Removes suitable germination sites for fungal and moss spores;

f) Avoids the unsightly appearance of the clippings.

Frequency of mowing

The amount of mowing a lawn receives will vary depending upon the function of the sward, the quality of lawn required, the sod status (i.e. its moisture content, fertility and temperature) and the species of grass present.

A lawn should be mown regularly as infrequent cutting weakens the sward and can encourage the ingress of weeds and diseases. When cutting begins in the springtime, the mower should be set 'high' so that the first cuts consist of a light 'tipping' of the topgrowth. After this first mowing the blades can be gradually lowered to their regular cutting height. This is carried out in order to prevent a weakening of the sward and a subsequent yellowing of tissues.

If mowing takes place during the morning, a light brushing or switching will be beneficial. Both of these operations are useful because they aid in the removal of excess moisture from the leaf blades, help in the breakdown of worm casts and raise the grass blades ready to meet the mower.

Where large areas are to be cut, it is important that some form of adequate routine is formulated and adhered to remembering of course to consider the weather conditions, types of machines, breakdowns and holidays.

Height of cut

The height of cut will again be related to various factors each of which have a definite effect on a sward. These factors are:

1   The function of the sward;
2   The grass species present;
3   Trueness of surface required;
4   The season;
5   The soil moisture content.

The function of the sward is probably the most important single factor affecting the height of cut. It is essential that each type of sward is cut to the correct height, otherwise an inferior surface will be produced which is unsuitable for use.

186

The type of grass species is affected by the severity of mowing as areas containing a high percentage of fine leaved grasses such as Chewings Fescue and Browntop Bent are quite capable of withstanding frequent close mowings. However, areas containing broader-leaved species, such as Couch Grass and Yorkshire Fog are discouraged by such actions.

Trueness of the surface is inter-related with the above mentioned factors because broad-leaved grasses and weeds can seriously affect the true movement of cricket balls and bowls. The height of cut will also affect play in these games because the speed of the balls can be markedly reduced when the grass is left long.

Both the season and the moisture content of the soil are important considerations when mowing grass as in dry weather the height of cut can be double that of the normal recommendations.

As a generalisation, it is considered bad practice to excessively close mow a sward. Such close mowing reduces the vigour of the grass and the ingress of moss may be encouraged—in severe cases bare patches may be produced. On the other hand leaving the grass too long can weaken the sward, especially if the grasses are allowed to run to seed, affecting the trueness of the playing surface and give an unsightly appearance.

Some examples of heights of cuts for various situations are:

Bowling greens	4–5 mm long
Fine lawns	5–6 mm long
Golf fairways	10–12 mm long
Ornamental lawns	10–12 mm long
Soccer pitches	25–50 mm long

The quality of cut

The quality of cut is determined by the type of mower used and the condition of the sward at the time of mowing. Even with the use of top quality equipment a high standard of cut is difficult to obtain when the sward is in a poor condition.

When selecting a mower for a specific area care should be taken as each model has its own advantages and disadvantages. For high quality turf it is recommended that cylinder mowers with up to 12 blades are used as these produce the finest cuts. The quality of cut from cylinder mowers is affected by:

a) The number of blades on the cylinder; this varies but the finest cuts come from machines with between 10 to 12 blades;

b) The distance between the front and rear rollers; this should be as small as possible;

c) The speed at which the blades are rotated; the faster the blades are rotated the more cuts per metre will be made and the finer the cut that is produced.

If the number of cuts per metre is reduced, a problem known as 'ribbing' can occur. This is where the grass appears to be composed of small rounded hillocks. It is caused by having too few blades on the mower, the mower being incorrectly set, or when the grass has been allowed to grow too long.

On areas where the cut need not be as fine as for high quality swards, one of the following machines may be used.

Types of mower

CYLINDER MOWERS

Cylinder mowers can be conveniently divided into two groups: those which are sidewheel driven, where the cutting cylinder is linked to the drive wheels by a series of gears or chains; and those that are driven by a large, two-sectioned roller, commonly known as roller-driven mowers. Both types of machine can be purchased in varying widths, ranging from $0 \cdot 3$ m (1 ft) to over $1 \cdot 0$ m (1 yd) and as power driven units, the type of power unit depending upon the size and make of the machine.

Roller-driven mowers have the advantage of being ideally suited to small intricate areas, whilst having the ability to produce a very fine cut. Sidewheel machines, on the other hand, are more suited to large areas, uneven and sloping ground and wet conditions (as less skidding occurs). They are also capable of being jointed together into large cutting units e.g. gang mowers (Fig. 13.1).

The cutting action of a cylinder mower is similar to that of a pair of scissors. As the cylinder revolves, the blades (mounted in a scrolled formation to prevent ribbing) are passed over the sole plate and bottom blade. As this movement takes place, any grass trapped between the blades will be severed. The correct adjustment of the cylinder in relation to the sole plate is for the blades to be set evenly across the bottom blade. This can be easily checked by placing a piece

Fig. 13.1 A set of gang mowers

of paper or grass between the sole plate and blades, followed by the rotation of the cylinder. If the setting is correct, the paper or grass will be cleanly cut over the whole length of the sole plate (see Fig. 13.2).

The height of cut on this type of mower is usually adjusted by moving the small front roller in relation to the driving wheels (side-wheel types) or the sectioned roller (roller driven types). The height is measured by placing a straight edge over the front and back rollers and measuring the distance between the bottom and cylinder blades (see Fig. 13.3).

ROTARY MOWERS

These are very versatile machines that can be used on areas of rough grass or ornamental lawns and are especially suited to roadside embankments and verges.

The cutting unit consists of either a rapidly spinning disc contain-

189

Fig. 13.2   Checking the cutting blades of a cylinder mower.

ing a number of sharpened blades (commonly 4), or a rotating arm with two sharpened edges. The principle behind the cutting action is that of a knife, i.e. a slicing movement (see Fig. 13.4).

Power units for this type of machine vary, the commonest being the 4-stroke petrol engine although electric motors and 2-stroke engines can also be used. The drive from the power unit can also vary with the type of machine, some models being driven by 'V' belts or chains, whilst others have a direct drive from the engine.

Regulating the height of cut of rotary mowers is achieved by a different system than that in cylinder machines. The height is regulated by either moving the wheels outwards on a special linkage (e.g. Atco types) or by lifting and lowering the central spinning disc (e.g. Hayter types). The actual setting usually being a matter of experience and estimation.

The disadvantages of this type of machine are:

a) They are not suitable for very fine lawns such as bowling greens;

190

Fig. 13.3   Measuring the height of cut on a cylinder mower.

b) Blades soon lose their sharp edge which can cause bruising of the grass;

c) Skimming of the surface can occur on uneven sites.

RECIPROCATING BLADE MOWERS

Reciprocating blade (knife) mowers are typified by the 'Allen Scythe'. They are large machines suitable for cutting long grass, rough herbage and the removal of weeds from around buildings. However, they are unsuitable for fine lawns. The major disadvantages of this machine are:

a) They can be very cumbersome to use;

b) The height of cut is very difficult to set;

c) They have a limited sphere of use.

The machine (Fig. 13.5) usually consists of a single cylinder 2-stroke engine mounted on two large land wheels and a series of

191

Fig. 13.4   A rotary mower, showing the positioning of the blades.

Fig. 13.5   A reciprocating blade mower, with details of blade (*lower*).

cutting blades positioned in front of the wheels. The blades, which are driven independently of the land wheels, consist of a 1-m boom holding approximately 12 teeth. The teeth being capable of moving backwards and forwards between a number of horizontally placed 'fingers'.

FLAIL MOWERS

Flail mowers (Fig. 13.6) are machines suitable for cutting areas of

Fig. 13.6 A flail mower.

coarse herbage and grass up to 1 m in height. However, they can also be used on some types of ornamental lawn. The cutting principle of the machine is very similar to that of the rotary mower, except that in this machine 'flails' (instead of discs and arms) are rotated at high speed on a central shaft.

The machines are available as self-propelled or tractor mounted models, the self-propelled types being driven by a 2- or 4-stroke

194

petrol engine, whilst the tractor types are run on the hydraulics and power take off (P.T.O.) shaft.

HOVER-TYPE MOWERS

Hover-type mowers are a relatively new design in grass cutting equipment (see Fig. 13.7). They are light to carry, easy to move when

Fig. 13.7   A hover-type mower.

working and have numerous uses, ranging from cutting ornamental lawns to steep slopes. The principle of their cutting action is identical to that of the rotary mower, but instead of the machine being supported by wheels, it is carried on a cushion of air. The lifting force for this is produced by a fan fitted to the crankshaft of a 2-stroke, single cylinder engine. As the engine runs, the fan revolves causing a build up of pressure beneath the cowling. It is this rise in pressure that lifts the machine from the ground.

The height of cut on this type of mower is regulated by the removal or insertion of 'spacers' between the fan and cutting blade.

195

Aeration

With the ever increasing popularity of outdoor sports and the maximisation of facilities, it is essential that sports areas are available for the longest period of time. This means that the groundsman must maintain his areas to the highest standards. One of the problems which can cause the deterioration of a sward with the subsequent loss of use is that of lack of aeration.

Poor aeration can be caused in a number of ways, the main ones being the build up of surface thatch, the compaction of the soil and the breakdown of soil structure. The methods of alleviating these problems can be conveniently divided into surface and sub-surface aeration.

Surface aeration

During the growing season, a healthy sward will produce a mat of dead and living tissues at the base of the stems. The mat, commonly known as thatch, is made up of the accumulation of living stems roots and leaves, intermingled with decaying or, partially decayed organic matter. The increase of this layer occurs when the accumulation of organic matter is greater than that of decomposition. The factors that affect its production are:

a) Returning of clippings during mowing;
b) Acidic conditions;
c) Poor aeration and compaction;
d) Poor drainage;
e) Vigorous growing cultivars;
f) Excessive applications of nitrogen (produces lush growth).

The problems inherent with the build-up of thatch are those of the formation of a soft, spongy surface capable of seriously affecting sports such as cricket and bowls, the increased incidence of pests and diseases, and in severe cases the production of chlorotic tissue (yellowing of the foliage). However, it must be said that a small amount of thatch in a sward during the summer months will help in the prevention of damage from drought.

Prevention of excess thatch goes a long way in extending the use of a sports area. The most expedient method of reduction being the correction of the factors affecting its formation. Wherever possible,

196

work should be aimed at encouraging the conditions necessary for the activities of micro-organisms, as it is these that breakdown the organic matter into humus. Operations should also be aimed at controlling the growth rate of the sward by balancing the applications of fertilisers, lime and topdressings.

Scarification

Scarification is the name given to the removal of thatch by mechanical means. It consists of raking the surface of the turf with varying forms of equipment, so as to enable the soil to obtain the maximum amounts of oxygen, moisture and nutrients. In addition to these benefits, it also discourages moss and broad-leaved weeds such as Yorkshire Fog (*Holcus lanatus*), as well as removing the sites for germinating fungal spores.

Fig. 13.8   A springbok type rake.

197

Type of equipment

Hand-operated spring-tine rakes, commonly known as 'springboks' are made from high tensile wire in the form of a series of teeth (Fig. 13.8). They are designed specifically for the removal of thatch from turf and not, as a number of people believe, for raking up leaves. The correct way of using this type of equipment is to draw the teeth through the sward whilst applying firm pressure to the shaft.

Types of scarifiers are available (Fig. 13.9) which are designed for use on areas too large for springbok rakes. These machines work on

Fig. 13.9 A sisis type scarifying rake.

exactly the same principle as the above, the only differences being that they are larger and transported by wheels.

SELF-PROPELLED SCARIFIERS

Motorised scarifiers are now available on the market which are

198

Fig. 13.10   A sisis type duo-rake, showing details of blades *(lower)*.

199

suitable for use on large sites (Fig. 13.10). They work on the same basic principle as the springbok rake but, in this case the thatch is removed by the actions of a number of hardened blades, fixed vertically on a revolving shaft. The machines come in various sizes ranging from 35 cm (14 in) to 50 cm (20 in) and the height of cut is usually adjusted by raising or lowering the small front rollers or wheels.

Other types of equipment that can be used for scarification and rejuvenation of swards are chain harrows. However, these pieces of equipment can produce rather drastic results, especially when used on fine swards.

Sub-surface aeration

Lawns receiving a large amount of wear during the season can suffer a considerable deterioration of the sward. This is caused by actual physical wear, coupled with the hidden problem of compaction. The problem of physical damage to the sward can be corrected by re-seeding, turfing, contravating and general good management—but the problem of compaction can be more difficult to overcome.

The degree of compaction that a sward receives will be directly affected by the type of sward and the amount of pedestrian and vehicular traffic that passes over it during the course of a season. This can be considerable, especially on areas such as football pitches, golf greens and cricket wickets. Compaction is also linked to the type of soil and its physical and chemical composition. This causes serious damage to turf as over-compaction adversely affects the soil structure, the water and oxygen holding capacity, the release of noxious gases from the soil, the movement and adsorption of nutrients and the activities of soil organisms.

To improve the condition of the soil and relieve compaction, the groundsmen can carry out some form of sub-surface aeration. This consists of making a series of slits, or removing a number of cores from the upper layers of the soil. It has the advantages of:

a) Relieving compaction;
b) Allowing the correct amounts of air and moisture to enter the soil;
c) Releases unwanted gases;
d) Improves soil structure;
e) Affects the soil texture (coring + topdressing);

f) Allows healthy activities of micro-organisms;

g) Playing surfaces in use for longer periods of time;

h) Improves the rooting capacity of the sward.

Sub-surface aeration is best carried out when the grass is in active growth, such as in early spring or autumn. However, it has also been found to be beneficial just prior to irrigation, as this allows the rapid absorption of moisture. For good results the operation should take place when the soil is moist. If it is too wet the structure will be damaged, whereas if too dry the tines will have difficulty in penetrating the surface.

The types of equipment and the degree of aeration will vary with the sward, size of areas and the soil type, the three most important systems are described below.

SOLID-TINING

Solid-tining consists of perforating the surface of the sward with solid prongs approximately 75–100 mm (3–4 in) in length (Fig. 13.11). The operation is suited to sports areas, such as bowling greens, cricket wickets and golf greens—but is also suitable for lower quality swards like ornamental lawns. This method of aeration is less drastic

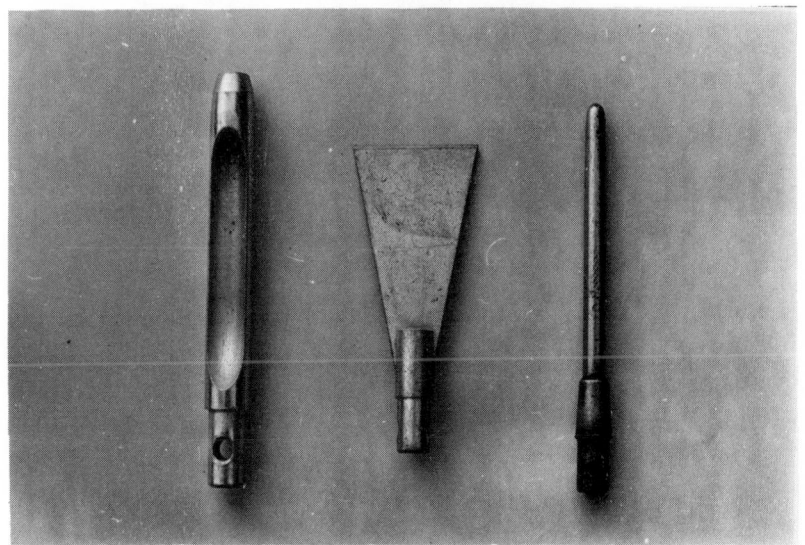

Fig. 13.11   Aeration tines.

Fig. 13.12 A modern tining machine.

than hollow-tining, producing only minor surface disturbances. It is however, very useful in aiding the ingress of water during dry periods in summer and in the temporary alleviation of compacted turf.

The types of machine available for this operation range from garden forks, to specially designed motorised equipment which is capable of being adapted to both slit and hollow-tining (see Fig. 13.12).

Fig. 13.13   Hand-operated hollow tining equipment.

SLIT-TINING

Slit-tining is carried out by inserting triangular shaped blades into the soil to a depth between 75 mm and 100 mm. They can be used in spring, summer or autumn and are suitable for most turf areas. They have the same basic working principle as solid tines, the only difference being in the degree of disturbance.

A less severe form of slit-tining can be achieved by using such machines as the Sisis 'Auto-turfman' with a spiked aerator attachment. This type of equipment slits the sward but only penetrates to a depth of approximately 50 mm.

Hollow–tining is the most drastic form of sub-surface aeration. It consists of inserting tines into the soil which cut and remove cores. The tines (Fig. 13.13) are usually about 100–150 mm (4–6 in) long and about 13 mm ($\frac{1}{2}$ in) in diameter. The cores which are deposited on the lawn surface should be brushed up and removed. If necessary, they can then be stacked or broken down by riddling and later re-applied as a topdressing. The distance between the cores will vary with the degree of amelioration required—the heavier the soil, the closer the cores should be.

The machines available for hollow-tining are exactly the same as for solid-tining, as is the timing of the operations. However, it must be stated that this type of operation is not suited for summer work.

Brushing, Matting and Switching

During the night and early morning, a sward can be affected by a number of environmental phenomena. The most important of these are dew formation and the production of earthworm casts. Dew production does not cause any direct physical symptoms to turf. However, it can have an adverse effect on the efficiency and length of time it takes to mow, as well as producing the ideal conditions for the germination of fungal spores. Worm casts, on the other hand, do produce an unsightly appearance on lawns; but their most serious effects occur from the production of uneven surfaces, as these can adversely affect the playing of ball games.

Brushing (see Fig. 13.14) with whalebone and synthetic fibre brushes is carried out every day on fine lawns before mowing. The actions of the brush encourage the breakdown of worm casts, which in turn prevents damage to mowers, has a slight effect on aeration as it loosens the dead thatch from the base of the sward and finally it raises the grass blades into an ideal position for mowing.

Drag matting and switching are both carried out before mowing and often take the place of brushing. Matting consists of dragging a piece of coconut matting or similar material over the sward. It works on the same principle as brushing but is probably more efficient at removing surface moisture. Switching is carried out by 'flicking' the grass using a long wire, bamboo or glass-fibre cane. This has the same action as the above operations, but is especially useful for removal of dew and worm casts.

Fig. 13.14   Brushing turf.

Rolling

Rolling is one of the most abused cultural operations that turf receives. It is frequently used to try to alleviate problems arising from inadequate initial preparations. However, this is a mistake, as no amount of compaction can overcome these troubles. Where uneven surfaces do exist, the most expedient means of removal is to either lift and re-lay the turf in the vicinity of the trouble, taking away or adding extra soil as is necessary, or to build up the hollows by applications of bulky topdressings.

Frequent heavy rolling should only be given to sites, such as cricket wickets, which require a firm surface for play. Under no circumstances should rolling take place on a soil that is wet or containing a high percentage of clay, as this can result in serious damage to the soil structure. The damage is caused by shattering the soil conglomerates and expelling the soil air. This prevents micro-

205

organisms and plants from carrying out their normal metabolic processes, which in turn produces a weak unusable sward.

It will be seen from the preceding comments that if the correct conditions are to be encouraged, the timing and size of roller is of immense importance. The following recommendations are aimed at providing a basis for the rolling of turf.

Pre-seed sowing

When a sward is initially produced the site preparation should be adequate enough to produce a true surface suitable for seed sowing or turf laying. This can be achieved by the use of a Cambridge roller (Fig. 5.4) remembering that the work should only be carried out during fine weather.

Post-sowing

1 Once the seed has germinated but before the first mowing has taken place it is advantageous to give a light rolling. This settles the seedbed and prevents the seedlings from being ripped out during the initial clippings.

2 Turf produced by sods and vegetative means will also benefit from (1) above, as this will encourage establishment.

3 During the winter months soil is lifted by the actions of frost, and to a lesser degree, by worms. A rolling in springtime will therefore be beneficial to re-settle the soil ready for the start of the new season.

4 A periodic rolling during the summer months will produce a firm surface, however, if a heavy mower is used further rolling will be unnecessary.

5 A number of sports areas such as cricket wickets and bowling greens require a firm surface for the true movement of the ball. In these situations, the frequency and weight of rolling will vary depending upon the area.

Rollers available for sports turf

Rollers that are suitable for use on lawns usually consist of two flat-surfaced, cylindrical drums fitted together on a horizontal shaft. However, spiked rollers which aid in the aeration of turf are also available. A roller is constructed in two pieces so that each section can rotate independently when turning corners and so prevents damage to the grass. They come in a wide range of widths and diameters, the weight of each varying with size and the type of ballast provided. Ballast can be added in a number of ways, the commonest being the addition of water, concrete, sand or cast iron.

The type of roller chosen will depend upon the sward, e.g. a 75–100 kg (1½–2 cwt) roller would be suitable for use on an ornamental lawn, whereas a 1 tonne (1 ton) model would be used on a cricket wicket.

The means by which a roller is propelled also varies with its size and use. Hand-propelled models (Fig. 13.15) are available that are ideally suited for use on small garden and ornamental lawns. However, for large sites, self-driven or even tractor-mounted models should be used.

Fig. 13.15 A hand-operated roller.

Irrigation

As terrestrial plants obtain the majority of their water from the soil, it is important that the soil/plant relationship is clearly understood before any irrigation requirements can be considered.

Plants extract water from the soil via short-lived, single-celled structures called root hairs, which are produced immediately behind the actively growing root tips. As the root hairs grow, they come into contact with the surface film of water around the soil particles and the inward movement of moisture begins. The rate and ease at which this takes place is greatly dependant upon the amount of water in the soil, the soil type and growth rate of the plants; sandy soils release water more readily than clays and the faster the rate of growth the greater the quantity required.

The water enters the roots by a process known as *osmosis*. This is the name given to the movement of water from a weak solution (the soil water) towards a concentrated solution (the cell sap) via a semipermeable membrane (the cell wall). This simply means that the cell wall acts as a sieve preventing the large molecules of cell sap from escaping, but allowing the smaller water molecules to pass through. The effective movement always takes place from the weaker to the stronger solution and although the water actually goes in both directions, more moves from the weak solution to the strong solution. It must also be mentioned here that soil nutrients (i.e. salts) do not enter the plant by osmosis, their entry is an active movement requiring energy, the process being a type of diffusion.

Once the water has entered the plant it moves across the root and up the stem in response to a water-potential gradient. This gradient is caused by the constant loss of water through the leaves of the plant during transpiration. The water is carried from the roots to the leaves in the xylem. Once in the leaves, the water enters the spongy mesophyll and evaporates into the air via small pores in the leaf called stomata; the opening and closing of the stomata is controlled by specialised structures called guard cells. As this water is lost the water-potential gradient is reduced and so more water is drawn up the xylem into the leaf.

The process of losing water from the plant is known as transpiration and the movement of water from the root hairs to the stomata is called the transpiration stream. The factors regulating the rate of transpiration are:

Temperature   The warmer the day the more water lost.

Wind   The stronger the wind the more water lost.

Plant modifications   Plants can modify their growth to minimise water loss, e.g. some plants can reduce the size of their leaves, have sunken stomata or have hairy leaves.

Time of day   The rate of transpiration is decreased or even stopped during the night because the stomata close.

Carbon dioxide content of atmosphere   The CO_2 content of the atmosphere affects the opening and closing of the stomata.

Humidity   Humid atmospheres reduce the amount of evaporation.

Considerations when applying water

When water is lacking in a soil, i.e. when a soil moisture deficit exists, the rate at which plants grow can be adversely affected; the roots are unable to extract sufficient moisture to satisfy the needs of the plant. When this happens the plants become flaccid and wilt. If, for any reason, the wilting is prolonged, then the leaves and stems may turn brown, shrivel and eventually die. To prevent this happening, the groundsman can irrigate the soil. However, when applying water great care must be taken to check that both the infiltration rate and the quantity applied are correct, otherwise the soil can be damaged and water can be wasted.

The infiltration rate, i.e. the speed at which moisture is absorbed into the soil, will vary with the structure and texture of the soil and the type of herbage covering the site. It is very important to ensure that the application rate is equal to, or slightly less than, the infiltration rate; this will prevent the formation of puddles and rivulets on the soil surface. An example of damage caused by incorrect application can frequently be seen on silty soils. On this type of land incorrect use of irrigation can produce a condition, known as 'capping' which consists of the production of a hard surface layer of soil that reduces gaseous exchange and prevents the germination of seeds.

Sources of irrigation water

There are various sources of water available for irrigation, all of which have advantages and disadvantages. The use of individual sources will vary depending upon the amount of water required, the size of the area and the proximity of the source to the site. The commonest sources are set out below.

PUBLIC SUPPLY

The public water supply will probably be the most common source of irrigation. The cost may be high compared to other sources, but if available, the water pressure is usually high enough to work most equipment without the incorporation of expensive pumps. Mains water is also very clean compared to other sources and, therefore, the risk of damage caused by high salt concentrations is minimal. Two problems can occur when using mains supplies:

1 During drought conditions the water authority may restrict the use of irrigation and consequently the plants will suffer;
2 A pump and reservoir are sometimes needed because the authority may only supply irrigation water during the night and not for direct use.

SURFACE WATER

Many lakes, ponds, rivers and streams can be used for irrigation, but before buying expensive equipment a check should be made to verify that the supply will be adequate in times of drought. It is also necessary to check the legalities, as extraction will probably be controlled by legislation.

Rivers and streams which flow through areas such as golf courses, are often the cheapest source of water for irrigation purposes. However, the supply must be adequate enough to supply the required quantity without affecting the 'Riparian Rights' of other users, i.e. you must not drain the stream dry, the stream must have sufficient water flowing below your extraction point to supply any other users.

UNDERGROUND WATER

Any type of well or borehole may be used, provided that it yields water of a satisfactory quality and in sufficient quantity to meet the irrigation demand. This source of irrigation is of lesser importance than mains and surface water, but it may be suitable for isolated positions or sites where the two previous examples are unavailable. It must be remembered that, in general, a licence must be obtained before sinking a borehole.

Fig. 13.16   A large oscillating sprayline (*upper*) and a smaller nozzle (*lower*) for use in a garden or other small area.

Types of irrigation system

Portable systems are very flexible because they make use of transportable pumps, main-lines and spraylines. However, they do require slightly more labour than permanent systems and where labour peaks coincide with the movement of equipment, problems can occur.

Two basic portable irrigation systems exist, namely, spraylines and sprinklers. Spraylines usually consist of interlocking aluminium, galvanised steel, or plastic tubing of 25–50 mm (1–2 in) diameter. A number of evenly spaced nozzles are located along the length (Fig. 13.16). The areas irrigated by these systems are between 10–17 m (30–50 ft) wide, but this will vary depending upon the type of nozzle and the water pressure. It is also usual practice to have

Fig. 13.17   A rotating hammer-type sprinkler.

fitted some form of oscillating mechanism to enable the water to be sprayed on either side of the line. These mechanisms can vary from simple devices utilising the weight of water, to complicated piston-type systems.

On the other hand, sprinklers (Fig. 13.17) apply water in the form of jets. They usually consist of 'hammer reaction' type nozzles capable of distributing water over a circular area, the diameter of which is dependant upon the type of nozzle and water pressure. The rotating mechanisms of sprinklers are commonly composed of a 'riser' with a separately pivoted, spring-loaded, hammer arm which, when at rest, lies against a 'stop' on the nozzle body. Part of the head, known as the 'bucket', lies directly in the path of the jet from the nozzle. The force of water from the nozzle hits the bucket and flings it to one side. However, since it is spring loaded it returns to the rest position against the stop on the nozzle body. As the hammer comes to the rest position, it taps the stop, which in turn rotates the whole spray-head by a few degrees. This continues until the water is turned off.

PERMANENT SYSTEMS

These systems are not as flexible as portable types and are usually very expensive to install. However, once fitted they have a low labour demand. They work by utilising fixed pumps, main lines and nozzles, but certain semi-permanent types with portable sprinklers are also available. Their use is normally limited to large areas such as golf courses, the most typical example for these areas being the 'pop up' sprinkler.

The basic working principles behind permanent systems are very similar to those of the portable types, except that the installation, placement and maintenance are slightly different. The cost of installation, coupled with the water requirement and size of operation, severely restrict the usage of permanent irrigation in the British Isles. However, this type of system is widely used in other countries, notably in the U.S.A.

Whatever system of irrigation is chosen, it must be remembered that the applications should be given at the correct rate and should consist of clean uncontaminated water. This means that regular maintenance is important, especially on systems using water from sources other than the mains supply.

213

Repairs to Damaged Turf

If a high standard of maintenance is required on a lawn, care must be taken to prevent damage to the sward. Damage can occur in many ways, a number of which are beyond the groundsman's control. Some of the more important ways that damage can occur are:

a) People treading on edges of turf;
b) Overplaying of sports areas;
c) Playing on sports areas during inclement weather;
d) Incorrect application of insecticides, herbicides, fungicides and fertilizers;
e) Natural wear;
f) Vandalism.

The two main methods of repairing a damaged sward are seeding and turfing.

If the speed of repair is not critical, then seed can be used, but wherever immediate effect is required, re-turfing will be necessary.

When re-seeding damaged areas it is necessary to loosen the soil surface a little to allow the seeds to be 'rubbed in.' This simply means working the seed into the soil by hand (see Fig. 13.18). Some groundsmen 'pre-chit' their seed before rubbing it into the damaged area. This consists of mixing the required mount of seed with a moist compost and leaving it for a few days, occasionally turning the mixture with a shovel. When the seed begins to germinate it can then be worked into the damaged area. On no account should the mixture be allowed to stand after germination has taken place; this produces long, drawn seedlings that are useless. When using seed it is also very important that the soil should not be allowed to dry out. If this happens and the seeds are just germinating, their growth can be seriously checked if not stopped altogether.

Re-turfing is a slightly more expensive way of repairing damage but it has the advantage of quick establishment. However the amount of work required is greater than for seed. The method is:

1 Mark out the area of damage (see Fig. 13.19);
2 Using a float remove the damaged turf;
3 Fork over the soil (it may be beneficial to incorporate some superphosphate of lime to encourage healthy root growth);

214

Fig. 13.18   Re-seeding a damaged area.

4   Firm the soil by treading;
5   Rake the soil level;
6   Re-lay the area with healthy turf, leaving the sods about 6 mm
    ($\frac{1}{4}$ in) proud, this allows for settling of the soil;
7   Apply a bulky topdressing, e.g. 50/50 peat and sand; this should
    be worked into the gaps between the turf;
8   Ensure that the area does not dry out for a couple of weeks after
    laying;
9   If the area is large, a light rolling just as the sods begin to knit
    together will be beneficial.

Where damage has occurred to the edge of a lawn the repairs can
be done by lifting an area of one sod around the damage and re-laying
with a fresh piece, or by turning the damaged piece round so that
the broken area is away from the edge. If this is done the damaged
area should be filled in with compost and re-sown (see Fig. 13.20).

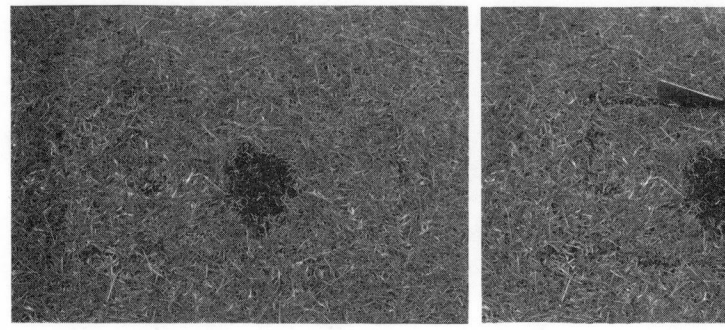

(a) Mark out the area of damage. (c) Cut away the damaged turf.

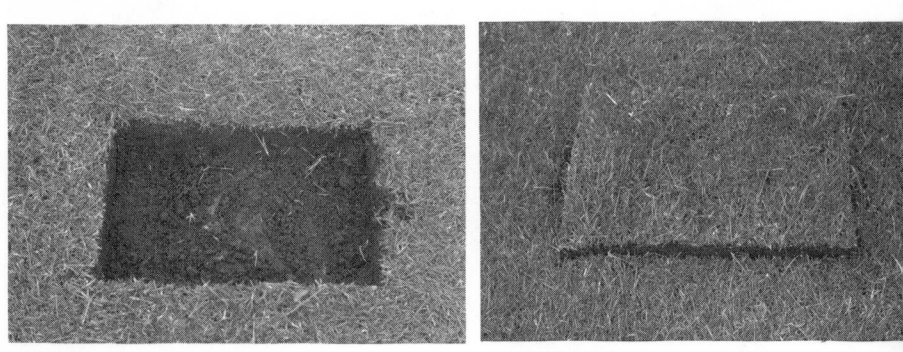

(c) Remove the damaged turf. (d) Re-lay with healthy turf.

(e) and (f) Topdress the whole area.

Fig. 13.19 Repairing a damaged area.

| (a) The damaged area. | (b) Turning the cut turf round. |

| (c) Filling the hole and re-seeding. | (d) Topdressing the whole area. |

Fig. 13.20   Repairing the edge of a lawn.

Brief Notes on Specialised Areas

Cricket squares

AUTUMN MAINTENANCE

Raking

Carried out with a springbok type rake or motorised equipment after the last match has been played. Raking is practised to enable the groundsman to remove any loose stolons and fibrous mat that may have accumulated during the summer months. After raking, the area can be given a mowing with a fine cut mower. This will

217

tidy up the area and remove any loose grass and mat left after the raking.

Spiking

Using either solid fork tines or slit tines to relieve compaction and allow air and moisture to enter the soil. The operation can be carried out by manual or mechanical means.

Brushing

Carry out regular brushing to remove dew and breakdown worm casts.

Fertiliser

Apply a well-balanced autumn fertiliser, low in nitrogen but high in·phosphorus and potassium. This will encourage healthy growth which is capable of withstanding cold weather.

Topdressings

Apply a topdressing of medium-to-heavy loam and work it into the surface. If the square is uneven, give another topdressing later in the season, remembering to work it well into the surface.

Repairs

Re-seed or turf any bare patches, use the correct species of grass seed or fine turf and always ensure that the weather conditions are ideal for rapid establishment.

Diseases

Carry out control measures when and where necessary.

WINTER MAINTENANCE

Do not carry out work on the area until the topdressing is worked in and then only carry out essential operations.

Spiking and Brushing

Carry out spking and brushing when and where necessary.

Mowing

Carry out mowing, maintaining the height of the sward at approxi-

218

mately 12·5–18 mm ($\frac{1}{2}$–$\frac{3}{4}$ in) high. This operation is best carried out with a fine cut, high speed cylinder mower.

SPRING MAINTENANCE

Consolidation

Using a light roller in different directions. Continue weekly from the end of February to the middle of March. Never roll during frosty weather. As the weeks progress, heavier rolling can be given, twice a week.

Spiking

Carried out between rollings to ensure good aeration.

Brushing

Done daily to remove dew and help to discourage fungal diseases.

Mowing

Carry out regular mowing starting in April. The frequency will depend upon the growth rate of the grass. Leave a natural cover to protect against frost. Gradually reduce the height of cut until the required length is obtained.

Fertiliser

Apply in late April to encourage healthy growth. A fertiliser with a ratio of 10 : 8 : 4 would be suitable.

General

Carry out general maintenance when and where necessary, e.g. brushing, mowing and rolling.

WICKET PREPARATIONS

Ten days prior to the first game, start to prepare the wicket.

Brushing

Carry out brushing and raking to remove any fibrous mat that may be present.

Mowing

Use a fine cut mower with a high speed cylinder. To avoid streaks and shades, double mow the area along the same cut.

219

Irrigation

Carry out irrigation ensuring that the water penetrates to a depth of 100–125 mm (4–5 in). Do not irrigate too near the day of the match as this can affect the movement of the ball.

Rolling

Rolling can begin as soon as the surface moisture has evaporated. This will produce a firm level square. Roll on alternate days until the day of the match.

IMPORTANT OPERATIONS

Worm Control

Carry out when and where necessary.

Weed Control

Control weeds during the growing season.

Disease Control

Spray protectant or irradicant sprays as necessary.

Pest Control

Carry out when and where necessary.

Irrigation

Apply irrigation whenever necessary, remembering to balance the application rate with soil infiltration rate.

Repairs

Repair foot holes and other damage as it occurs.

Golf courses

Fairways

The fairways of a golf course are the areas between the tees and the greens. Their maintenance will vary depending upon the type of site and soil conditions.

Scarification

Carried out periodically to aid surface aeration. As with cricket wickets, scarification removes thatch and improves the speed of water absorption into the soil.

Topdressing
Where bare patches arise, topdressing with a suitable medium will be necessary. It will also be beneficial to incorporate some fertiliser into the topdressings as this will encourage rapid re-establishment of the sward.

Weed Control
Carry out weed control during the growing season.

Rolling
In early spring give the areas a rolling. This will firm the soil after the winter months.

General
Carry out the general maintenance of brushing, raking and switching throughout the season.

THE ROUGH
The type of rough can be very variable depending upon the situation of the course. Certain areas of the rough can be left untouched whilst others should be maintained at approximately 50–60 mm (2–2½ in) long.

BUNKERS
Cleaning
Keep the bunkers clean, raked, topped up with sand and weed-free. Care should be taken when using residual herbicides in the bunkers as damage to the sward can occur if sand is splashed on to the greens.

Edging
Cut edges whenever necessary.

TEES
Mowing
Carried out approximately twice per week. Maintain the height of the sward at 10–12·5 mm ($\frac{3}{8}$–$\frac{1}{2}$ in) and always remove the clippings.

Mowing should be carried out on a regular basis as infrequent cutting can lead to a ragged sward.

Scarification

Scarification can be carried out during the summer and autumn months to remove any build up of thatch. It may also be beneficial to carry out hollow-tining and topdressing during the autumn months as these operations relieve compaction and encourage healthy root growth.

Divots

Replace divots and overseed with a mixture of compost and pre-chitted seed.

Fertilisers and Topdressings

To fill in hollows, apply topdressings during the autumn and summer months. Apply balanced fertilisers containing nitrogen, phosphorus and potassium during the spring months; and compounds low in nitrogen but high in phosphorus and potassium in the autumn months.

Moss and Weeds

Control moss and weeds where and when necessary.

GREENS

Mowing

Mowing should be carried out every day, remembering to vary the direction of cut each time. Always use a fine cut mower with a high speed cutting cylinder and always box the clippings.

Scarification

Carried out whenever possible during the season. Scarification will help to remove any dead mat that may build up and will have the added advantage of allowing air and moisture to enter the soil.

Slitting

Carried out during the autumn to winter months. Slitting allows air and moisture to enter the soil, relieves compaction and discourages thatch production.

Topdressing and Fertilisers

Applying topdressing will improve the green surface and help to remove any uneven patches that may be present. Always work the materials into the soil surface. This can be carried out by using hand or mechanically operated machinery.

To encourage healthy growth, fertilisers can be applied 2–3 times during the growing season. The fertilisers used should be relatively high in nitrogen with balanced quantities of phosphorus and potassium.

Rolling

Rolling can take place after frosts to re-settle the surface and give a true level. However, it is important to understand that no amount of rolling will produce level surfaces on uneven sites. All that takes place in these circumstances is that the soil becomes over compacted and a reduction in the amount of air and moisture entering the soil takes place.

Irrigation

If a high standard of maintenance is required, some form of irrigation will be essential. This can be applied by small rotary sprinklers and oscillating spraylines or sophisticated equipment such as the 'pop-up' irrigation system.

General

General maintenance should consist of controlling weeds, pests and diseases, removing leaves, moving the 'pin-holes' and brushing or switching to remove dew and worm casts.

Bowling greens

AUTUMN MAINTENANCE

Repairs

At the end of the season, any bare patches can be re-seeded or re-turfed. It is important to use the correct species when carrying out these operations, otherwise the repaired area will not blend in with the rest of the green.

Scarification

Once play has finished, the green should be scarified to remove any

223

accumulated mat and loose stems, following this, the green will benefit from a close mowing.

Brushing

Brushing should be done in at least two directions. This will again raise loose shoots and dead mat as well as lifting the grass blades ready for cutting.

Aeration

Aeration can be carried out in the autumn months. This will relieve compaction and allow air and moisture to enter the soil. The operation can be carried out using solid or slit tines but, where soil amelioration is needed, hollow-tining can be practiced. When hollow tining it is important to try to maintain as level a surface as possible, so that no major disturbances have to be corrected.

Topdressing and Fertilisers

Autumn fertilisers, low in nitrogen but high in phosphorus and potassium, can be applied at approximately 60 g/m² (2 oz/sq. yd.) after aeration has taken place. Where hollow-tining has been done a sterile topdressing made up of sand and loam with a small amount of peat can be added. After the application of these materials some form of irrigation should be given to prevent scorching of the sward.

Worm Control

Autumn is an ideal time to control worms by the application of chemicals, such as carbaryl.

WINTER MAINTENANCE

Brushing and Switching

Carried out during the morning to remove dew and breakdown worm casts. Drag matting is sometimes practiced for the same reasons.

Topping

If the winter is mild and grass growth occurs a light topping of the sward will be beneficial. Never top the sward during frosty weather or when it is wet, as this can seriously weaken the grass.

224

Ditches and Boardings

During winter all the side ditches or gullies should be cleaned out and topped up with fresh sand. At the beginning of each season any side boarding should be painted white.

SPRING AND SUMMER MAINTENANCE

General

When growth has started, regular brushing, matting or switching to remove dew and worm casts can begin.

Mowing

Once the sward has started to grow, regular mowing can begin, the first few cuts should be used to gradually lower the blades to their final height. During the season, mowing can take place as frequently as 3–4 times per week. Cuttings should always be boxed except in very fine weather.

Rolling

The green should be given a rolling in spring time to settle the soil after the winter frosts. Other than this, no other rolling should be necessary.

Repairs

Repairs should be carried out as and when damage occurs. However, the best time for this kind of work is in spring or early autumn.

Fertilisers

A general fertiliser containing nitrogen, phosphorus and potassium should be given at the beginning of the season. Applications of quick acting fertilisers, such as sulphate of ammonia, can be given at monthly intervals during the season. However, care should be taken to prevent scorching after the materials have been applied. It is now common practice to make one application of a slow-release nitrogenous fertilizer, such as 'Gold N', as these give a steady release of nutrient with less risk or scorch.

Weed Control

Weed control should take place during the growing season using the recommmended herbicides for specific problems.

Worm Control

Control can take place in spring or autumn when the worms are actively feeding near the soil surface.

Football pitches

AUTUMN MAINTENANCE

Soil Structure

All operations carried out during the autumn months should be aimed at producing a well structured soil and a healthy growing sward. This means that work should never be carried out during inclement weather, when the site is waterlogged or when the soil is over compacted.

Fertility

A highly fertile soil will produce a strong healthy sward capable of withstanding prolonged hard wear.

Grass species

The correct composition of the sward is of immense importance. Species such as Perennial Rye Grass should be present, as this type of grass produces a sward capable of growing under adverse conditions such as are found during the winter months.

Weeds, Pests and Diseases

All weeds, pests and diseases should be controlled at the appropriate time.

Repairs

Carry out repairs after each game. Aerate the goal areas with slit or solid tines and carry out regular brushing.

Drainage

If the top-surface becomes easily waterlogged surface drainage such as sand slitting may be required.

Fertilisers and Topdressings

Apply autumn fertilisers low in nitrogen. Apply bulky topdressings, e.g. sand, on to goal areas whenever necessary.

Rolling

Carry out rolling after each game. However, it is essential that this operation is not carried out when the soil is wet as the soil structure can be damaged.

General Maintenance

Carry out the general maintenance of mowing, brushing and spiking during the autumn months.

WINTER MAINTENANCE

All winter operations should be aimed at producing a healthy sward. Maintenance should consist of mowing, rolling after each match, aeration to remove surface water, brushing to remove dew and break down worm casts and the carrying out of repairs whenever necessary.

SPRING AND SUMMER MAINTENANCE

Repairs

Repair damaged turf whenever necessary. In certain circumstances this could mean cultivating sections such as goal areas and re-turfing or seeding with new material.

Scarification and Aeration

Scarify and aerate the area during and after the playing season.

Fertilisers

Maintain the soil fertility by applications of balanced spring and summer fertilisers.

Weed Control

Use selective hormone-type weedkillers to control broad leaved weeds.

General Maintenance

Carry out the general maintenance of mowing and brushing at regular intervals. Remember that frequent cutting causes less damage to a sward then infrequent mowing.

Other winter sports areas

As for football pitches.

Tennis Courts

Repairs

Damage can be repaired soon after play has finished. This can be carried out by laying new turf or sowing grass seed of the correct species.

Weeds

Where weeds are present, control can be achieved by applications of chemicals. However, it may be found that a better control is obtained when applications are made during the early summer months.

Worms

Worms should be controlled by applications of chemicals such as carbaryl.

Fertilisers and Topdressings

Apply slow release autumn fertilisers low in nitrogen. Apply bulky topdressings of medium loam and work them in with a lute.

General Maintenance

Carry out the general maintenance of brushing to loosen thatch and lift the grass blades ready for mowing; scarification to remove any build-up of thatch and aeration to relieve compaction and allow air and water to enter the soil.

WINTER MAINTENANCE

Carry out the essential operations of mowing, maintaining the height of cut to approximately 18 mm ($\frac{3}{4}$ in), brushing to lift the grass ready for mowing and loosening thatch and aeration to relieve compaction.

SPRING AND SUMMER MAINTENANCE

Scarification

To remove any build up of thatch scarify the area in the early spring.

228

Mowing

Begin regular mowing gradually reducing the height of cut to 6 mm ($\frac{1}{4}$ in). In summer, mowing can be done 2–3 times per week.

Rolling

Carry out frequent rolling, remembering not to work on the area when it is wet.

Repairs

If repairs were not carried out during the autumn months they can be done in early spring.

Fertilisers

Apply spring and summer fertilisers as and when required.

Irrigation

Apply irrigation as and when necessary.

General Maintenance

Carry out general maintenance throughout the season.

14 Management in the Sportsground Industry

There are perhaps as many definitions of management as there are organisations, as much depends on a person's point of view, past experience and their role in an organisation. Within the sportsground industry, management can be split into two categories:

Organisational With people and the utilisation of allied resources and
Technical Management of land, sports surfaces and the environment.

Whilst accepting that there are certain factors applicable to both, the *organisational management* is concerned mainly with the running of an organisation for which a person may not necessarily need technical knowledge. In contrast, the *technical management* is concerned with decisions which although perhaps organisational may well have a technical implication. Therefore, the decision maker must have technical knowledge, or access to someone within the organisation to whom he can turn for guidance.

For instance, an organisational manager is concerned mainly with the running of a department, organisation or section. His job is to plan, motivate and control manpower, plant and other sources in order to achieve the overall objective of the organisation or club concerned. On the other hand, the technical manager may well compile programmes, plans, etc. without actually controlling the labour force or the functions of the organisation. In reality, however, one finds that both roles are entwined and sportsground managers have to carry out varying degrees of both functions.

The Manager

A good manager is a person who obtains the maximum effectiveness from the available resources. Mostly, managers are responsible for getting results through other people, they are directors of human activity.

In order to ensure the maximum effectiveness there is a need to define objectives, both for the organisation as a whole and at all levels within an organisation. In this way, all effort is channelled in the 'right' direction.

When an organisation has defined its objectives, policies can be determined and an organisational structure can be formulated, covering each area of activity necessary in order to achieve the overall objective. Each person within the structure should be aware of their responsibilities and the functions for which they will be held accountable.

When an organisation has identified its objectives there is a need to define policies which in this particular context mean the guidelines that top management lay down in general or, specific terms to enable the organisation to reach the target set by the objectives.

Management by objectives

This is a system whereby an individual or group of people define the objective to be achieved within a given period of time. Throughout, progress is monitored against a series of norms and at the end of the time span the person or group compare results to see if they have achieved the objective. At the same time they re-define further objectives. It is an on-going process. All objectives should be recorded clearly and logically in writing they should not represent a pious hope, but an achievable end result.

Management by exception

There is always a danger that certain levels of management may become inundated with control documents, statistics and other information. Therefore, there is a need to minimise the quantity of material arriving at any level of management to a manageable quantity. In this respect, certain levels of management may wish to limit the number of facts and figures being placed before them. 'Management by exception' means that only those facts and figures which differ from the norm and therefore, relate to exceptional circumstances need be referred to them. There is always a danger that if 'management by exception' is practised throughout an organisation structure, complacency may develop and the norm may be being maintained as a result of changing circumstances. It is important to ensure that 'management by exception' is only practised at certain managerial levels and to a limited extent.

Key Activities

In order to produce an end product—whether it be nuts and bolts, a landscape or sports surfaces—all management, individual or collective, has key activity areas. These can be split into a number of different headings.

a) Planning

b) Allocation of Resources

c) Control

d) Motivation

e) Innovation

f) Recruitment

g) Liaison

h) Development and Organisation.

A manager may spend as little as 5% of his total working week on the majority of his key activities. Managerial effectiveness should be judged by the way the manager delegates and controls the roles of the individual within the organisation, in order to produce the end product. His success is, therefore, related to how well he performs in the key activity of his job. Some may spend the majority of their time on innovation. This is fine, provided of course that the other parts of their key activities are being carried out satisfactorily. Managers at different levels spend varying degrees of their time on their key activities. Some will spend most time planning, others on recruitment, but no matter which activity they spend the majority of their time on, all are involved to some extent with most of the activities indicated above.

Management's aim is to effectively utilise the resources under its control with a view to ensuring the organisation's performance and profitability. It is, therefore, advantageous for each manager to define the objectives of their post and then identify each of their key activities. Once these have been established, a framework is provided for improving a manager's performance. It is in such areas that energy should be steered in order to achieve objectives. The measure of success in the key activity areas will determine the effectiveness of the manager within an organisation.

Management Data

Most organisations are split into two parts, the management data side, which collects and analyses data and the operational side. It is, therefore, essential that every organisation has adequate control measures and a feed-back of information, so that the effectiveness of planning and policies can be monitored and adjusted. The majority of managers are reliant on the accurate feed-back of information in order to formulate future programmes. It is important that all organisations have a workable structure in which decisions are made at the appropriate level.

Use of management data

1   Based on management data, a plan is produced.
2 · The relevant section of the operating system takes action.
3   Operating performance is measured against the plan.
4   Results are fed back.
5   If all is proceeding according to plan, further action is taken at operating level.
6   If results are not going to plan, the plan is revised or modified using the information available to management.
7   The cycle continues.

To summarise, the steps are to plan, to take action, to monitor and control performance, feed-back and if need be, to adjust the plan followed by further action.

Decision Making

All too often, managers are not made fully aware of their areas of responsibility and the level at which certain types of decisions can be made. Often problems are taken to a superior when a decision could have been made by the person concerned.

The decision making process is very important. It is imperative that managers are trained in the relevant techniques and they are

233

taught to critically analyse all alternatives. When it comes to making a decision, there are two types of managers:

1 One who refers a problem to his superior, either verbally or in writing and asks for advice or to be told what to do;

2 One who sets out basic facts in a logical order, evaluates the alternatives, makes an intelligent and practical decision, or if need be, refers the information to his superior and, at the same time, recommends a possible course of action.

There should be no need to state which of these is the better course of action for any progressive manager to adopt, and for that matter the more rewarding. Yet, it is surprising how often the easy way out is taken and this in turn tends to throw a further strain on the organisation or structure. Of course, the situation can, work in reverse where a senior manager will not allow his subordinates to make decisions. It is most important that within any sportsground organisation, the level at which a decision can be made is clearly defined so that problems can be sorted out as near to 'grass roots' level as possible. Successful management is about making the right decisions, wrong decisions are expensive.

As already indicated earlier the major activities of management can be summarised as investigating and market research, planning, (short, medium and long term), organising, motivating, controlling, estimating, budgeting, monitoring, co-ordinating and communicating.

To carry out all these functions, a manager has to make many decisions. It is, therefore, important that he develops a systematic approach to problems. Most organisations lay down basic policies which define the parameters within which a manager works. These policies should be the result of careful deliberation and decision, as they may well affect all other decisions made within the organization. It is important that top management has the ability to formulate good policies and make the right decisions.

Often there is indecision because managers do not take the time to weigh up all the facts and information available and they 'pass the buck' to a superior. He in turn becomes inundated with work and is unable to give due consideration to all the relevant facts and information, hence the heart attack and early retirement. Finding the right level for decision making is imperative to the good organisation as it builds the confidence of the various managers so that they feel confident and are able to make decisions based on sound judgment.

The decision making process

In some circumstances, a decision can be made quite easily, the manager drawing on his wide experience. However, on many occasions a detailed investigation is required. What may appear to be the true situation in the first instance, is often proved to the contrary after further investigation. Managers are not born with the ability to make decisions. There are few people so blessed and when they are, they are very lucky! It is important to have a logical method of approach. A suggested approach is described below.

1 Initially define the problem requiring a solution. If it is complex it may be helpful to break the problem down into a number of sections.

2 Look at the problem in total. Do not attempt to find a solution based purely on theoretical information. There is much value in assembling all the relevant facts and setting them down on paper. This way the manager is able to view each aspect of the situation, decide the major element and proceed with a logical pattern of appraisal. The use of diagrams will also help to produce a pictorial view of the problem.

3 In arriving at a solution, the manager must take into account all the possibilities. This requires weighing up the pros and cons of each choice. In many circumstances, in order to find a workable solution, a compromise may be necessary. However, provided all the facts have been taken into consideration such action in itself is not a reflection on the ability to manage. In many organisations major decisions are made on a corporate basis. However, the majority of managers spend most of their working life making independent decisions one way or another. It is important, therefore, that they develop a systematic approach to the business of solving problems.

A useful check list can be defined:

a) Define the problem;
b) Collect all relevant information;
c) Probe the information and isolate major areas of difficulty;

235

d) Identify possible solutions;

e) Weigh up short, medium and long-term effects of each possible solution;

f) Make a decision.

In order for a manager to be effective, decisions must be progressive and for the overall good of the organisation. Careful consideration is most important and the manager must think in positive terms.

Many managers tend to measure their effectiveness by their input, whereas it is their output which is important. In some circumstances, the solution may be to do nothing—in fact, the problem may not be worth solving. This is the decision of the manager. Unfortunately, managers tend to want to do things right rather than do the right thing, i.e. to solve immediate problems rather than produce creative alternatives.

Planning and Control

In managerial terms planning can be divided into three basic categories, i.e. long, medium and short-term.

Long term Referred to in some circles as *broad strategical planning*. Usually the province of top management, dealing with the organisation or company objectives and the adjustment of policies and plans depending on economic, technological and environmental change.

Medium or interim Sometimes known as *tactical planning*; deals with the effective use of available resources within a time-span of approximately one year.

Short term Also called *operational planning*; deals with the day to day running of the organisation and the adjustment of programmes to meet objectives.

In varying degrees, all managers are planners. Success is often determined by their ability to take into consideration the total picture including all possible constraints. Thereafter, building into the plan sufficient flexibility to adjust according to prevailing circumstances. A lack of strategical and tactical planning leads to an abundance of operational decisions, panic measures and 'fire fighting' action.

Controls

In order to ensure a progressive organisation and satisfactory results at all levels, managers must have a feed-back of data on which to base future plans. In this respect an effective control system providing factual data is essential. It is extremely difficult for management to plan if the feed-back of information is poor or inaccurate.

In many organisations, control systems tend to outlive their useful life. They should be reviewed constantly, with a view to dispensing with a system if the information is no longer required. It is important to remember that whilst control systems are essential, they must provide the type of information needed in order to adjust and formulate plans without creating a wealth of useless statistics. There is a need for simplicity within the working environment.

Formulating plans

When designing a plan, all managers should endeavour to build-in sufficient flexibility so as to allow for changes which depend on circumstances. The longer the time-span, the greater the need—a point which cannot be over-emphasised. Consideration must be given to all factors that are likely to occur which will prevent the fulfilment of the plan and hence a failure to achieve objectives.

A systematic approach to planning helps the manager to take into consideration all the facts. In this respect, the following check list may be of assistance.

1 Define the objective.
2 Investigate and collect all the relevant data.
3 Identify the constraints.
4 Ask oneself:
   (i) What tasks or elements are involved?
   (ii) Who is involved?
   (iii) What is the time-span?
   (iv) How is the plan to be implemented and controlled?
   (v) When is the plan to be implemented and completed?
5 Are there other alternatives and have all the facts been taken into consideration?
6 Make decisions and formulate plans, bearing in mind, if required, the importance and need for an effective control system.

Remember, without factual information, good planning cannot take place. No single plan should exist alone. In fact, individual schemes should interlock to form a complete network.

Planning should be seen as a process for improvement, whereas controls are a means to check, guide and manage events towards the objective and to provide information for future planning.

'The aim of all planning is to improve the return the organisation is getting on the capital employed. In the short term it may be necessary to accept a lower rate of return, in order to earn even more in later years. Consequently, the short-term plan should not be prepared in isolation. It should be prepared as an integral part of a long-term plan, although it will probably be in considerably greater detail than will the plans for a few years' time.'*

Recruitment and Selection

The manager must be careful when recruiting and selecting staff. Quite often people endeavour to recruit personnel without relating the requirements of the job to the situation. People consider themselves to be good managers and, therefore, good at recruiting staff. This is very similar to the way most people consider themselves to be either good fathers or mothers—or for that matter good lovers! It is not easy to recruit the right person for the job. Quite often one hears people say such things as:

> 'Joe didn't fit in, he didn't meet the
> requirements of the firm.'

It is not always the individual's fault. In the first place, was Joe the right person for the job? It is the manager's responsibility to ensure that he has the right person in the correct job.

There are four stages of recruitment.

1 Specify the job and the requirements needed.
2 Prepare a job description and a man specification.
3 Attract the right kind of applicant and during the interview assess him against the man specification. In some instances it may also be pertinent to introduce some form of test as part of the selection process.

* Extract from a planning document prepared by the Management Unit of the Trent Polytechnic and reproduced with permission.

238

4 Place the candidate within the job and thereafter monitor his performance. It is important to remember that selection involves prediction which means that the following are necessary:

(i) knowledge of the exact duties to be performed;

(ii) knowledge of the attributes needed.

These can be determined by the man specification and thereafter measured objectively. In preparing the specification, either a seven or five point plan as indicated below can be used.

Seven Point Plan	*Five Point Plan*
1 Physical make-up	1 Impact on other people
2 Attainments	2 Qualifications
3 Intelligence	3 Brains
4 Special attributes	4 Motivation
5 Interest	5 Adjustments
6 Disposition	
7 Circumstances.	

The manager must decide which of the above plans is the most desirable for the post in question.

Advertising

The job advertisement is important. People do not come to work just for money, they come for many other things—including job satisfaction, status, responsibility, companionship, etc. People come to work for money and fun—yes, *fun*—if they are bored, the money must recompense for the boredom, otherwise they will leave. Alternatively, if they enjoy what they are doing and the money is adequate for their needs they will stay with the organisation concerned. The manager must bear in mind the organisation's image. It is absolutely imperative to produce a suitable advertisement for the job in question. The job must, therefore, be sold. If you are looking for a person to fill a specific post, the right kind of advertisement is absolutely imperative, as the type of person you may be seeking may not be looking for a job. Most people tend to glance through trade journals and newspaper situations vacant ('want ads') not because they want to leave, but because they are interested in what is available. People looking for jobs will see the advertisement but it is not necessarily these people you wish to attract. The person you are looking for may be employed already. Advertising a job is, therefore, very important. One must decide *the aim* to recruit at an economical cost and *the function* to communicate with a selected group and a number of replies.

There are many kinds of advertisements. Prestige advertisements in blocks, bold head-lines, gimmick advertisements, etc. The most important thing is to tell people about the job, not the job description or extracts from it, as these will not sell the post in question. Make sure people understand what the job is all about and the type of person you require. It is also important to match the qualification to the job in order to obtain the right person. If you are having trouble filling a post, it may be you need to change the job and the image.

A lot of people do not like writing letters and it may be necessary to provide other means of applying for a post, either a simple application form or a 'telephone in' service. Such a service would be there to explain the job to the type of people you are wishing to attract. Do not let the system fall down, make sure the person answering the telephone is properly briefed and they know what they have to put over to the prospective applicant.

When people apply for a job, do not forget to acknowledge their application. Let the person concerned know what is happening. All too often companies miss good candidates by not replying promptly.

The interview

Preparation prior to the interview is important. Some people have a natural flair for interviewing and social skills come automatically, whereas for the majority of people such skills have to be acquired. Not only is there the professional interviewer, but also the professional interviewee—the type of person that applies for a job every two years. Such people become efficient in the techniques of interviews. It is most important that the interviewer should be able to extract such information from the candidate.

The policy of getting candidates together prior to the interview is good in certain circumstances. There are, however, limitations. The main point to remember is that in the process of assessing there is an inter-action between people. It has been stated by many eminent

240

authorities that there should be a 20–80% ratio between the interviewer and the candidate, respectively. The need is to establish verbal intercourse between both parties. Interviewing, for the interviewer, is the art of listening. 'Nerves' of both parties play an important part in determining the true facts. The aims of the interview are to ascertain facts, feelings, judge and to arrive at conclusions. In fact, the process of transmit and receive by both parties. There are a number of types of interview:

a) The one-to-one interview where the candidate is interviewed by one person.
b) The small panel interview where the candidate is interviewed by two or three people.
c) The large panel interview where the candidate is interviewed by a large number of people, in some cases an entire committee.
d) The concentrated interview whereby the candidate is in the presence of the interviewer or panel for half a day or in some circumstances a day or longer. In this type of interview the environment may well be changed from time to time, either by visiting different places within the organisation, or alternatively, outside the organisation, whereby the candidate can be placed in a relaxed atmosphere and the interviewers get to know the candidate better.
e) A series of interviews either one-to-one or a small or large panel. These may take place on the same day or over a number of days.

The interview should be planned and the interviewer should obtain sufficient background information, decide what the organisation wants and how it is to be obtained. At all times it is important to be objective. In preparing the interview, the following points should be observed:

1 Obtain as much information as possible;
2 Ensure that the interview room is free from noise and other interruptions during the interview;
3 In order to give the candidate a fair opportunity allow adequate time;
4 Make sure that the candidate is positioned in the right place, i.e. do not have the sun shining directly in his eyes.

Throughout the interview, the interviewer should try to achieve the following:

a) State the purpose of the interview;
b) Achieve rapport;
c) Explain, confirm and clarify;
d) Gently lead into areas of question;
e) Stimulate the interviewee to respond;
f) Listen to what is said and observe;
g) Encourage;
h) Take notes;
i) Judge;
j) Bring the interview to a close.

Throughout, the interviewer should endeavour to keep calm and transmit his calmness to the interviewee.

Do not use closed questions unless there are exceptional circumstances. In the main use open ended, reflecting, building, supporting, objective and probing questions and do not prejudge the situation or the outcome. Phrase all questions around what, where, when, who, why and how.

Examples

'When did you commence your present post?'
'Why are you interested in this particular post?'
'What attracts you to the post as advertised?'

There are many examples. Your questions have to give the candidates the opportunity to express themselves.

When interviewing many people have the horn and halo effect on each other. For instance, the chap that comes in with long hair, or wears suede shoes or, alternatively the chap with the halo effect may well be the man who comes in smartly dressed, wearing a tie, hair cut short, etc. If one is to recruit the right staff for the right job, it is important not to prejudge the situation. The interviewer must be prepared to listen and give the candidate his complete attention. That is why it is most important that the candidate does the majority of talking and, as indicated previously, this will amount to 80% of the interview time—whereas the interviewer will only talk for the remaining 20%. The interviewer's job is to obtain information from the interviewee on which he can make a judgment. Wrong selection can be very costly.

The interviewer must close the interview at the appropriate time making sure that both parties agree that a fair interview has been conducted and that *the whole* area of contention has been sorted out. Ensure that the candidate understands what the next steps will be.

After the candidate has departed summarise all the available information. The use of an appraisal form during the interview is most helpful. Discuss with other members of the interview panel and make a decision which must be the right decision fitting the person to the job. Make sure that the organisation's image is not tarnished and if you have told a candidate that a certain course of action will be taken, ensure that it is.

Recruitment and selection of staff is not easy. It is a difficult and responsible task and every care must be taken to ensure that the right person is selected. Wrong selection is costly to all organisations. Remember a little care in the first instance may save thousands of pounds later. Manpower is a very valuable resource indeed.

Managing People

Productivity, motivation, job satisfaction and incentives are all used, in one way or another, when the subject of managing people is discussed. It is often conveniently forgotten that whilst there are various aids to increasing productivity through either incentives, job satisfaction or other forms of motivation, the main motivator in any organisation is the manager's ability as a leader. There are many facets of leadership and although it is easy to analyse some of the many virtues needed, in practice even the most unexpected person will emerge as a leader of others. In order to be successful, leaders must spend a considerable amount of time dealing with people rather than things. For instance, a special interest must be taken in subordinates career progress. Enthusiasm should be sympathetically kept in check if it appears to be over stepping the mark. A good leader encourages and motivates staff by whatever means is appropriate at a particular point in time. It is recognising the correct motivating force which will determine whether he is successful. Thus, an interest in people is very important.

Extrovert and introvert managers

During recent years there has been an ever-increasing amount of study work into the relevance of personality and the successful manager.

It is a general belief that an *extrovert* is an individual who is extensibly interested in the world and the people in it. Usually he is cheerful, sociable, dynamic and has many friends. Often extroverts are impulsive, excitable and sometimes volatile.

The opposite, the *introvert*, is a person who is apparently most interested in his own thoughts and feelings. Such a person is usually of a retiring disposition, inward-looking, reliable, preferring to do things rather than meet people; a person who tends not to take any chance but tends to work out each action well ahead of time. He lives an ordered life which is taken seriously. There are various schools of thought as to whether the good manager falls into one or other of the foregoing categories. However, it is not quite as simple, as the qualities of both types can be found in many successful managers.

In a management setting, there is room for both types. Successful managers can lead from the front or the rear—the successful leader does not necessarily have to be out in front waving the flag. By careful thought and direction he can channel the efforts of the organisation in the right direction without being seen to do so.

It is most essential that a manager achieves emotional poise. There are at least three ways he can do so:

1 First, he must learn to get the right mental picture of his job and be able to see it in its true perspective. For example, with a great many pressures on hand, he can be forgiven for feeling that everything must be done at once, a feeling that usually leads to panic. At any moment in time, it is only physically or mentally possible to do one job, which should be done quietly and efficiently, leaving the others to take their turn. Interruptions should be used as physical or mental rest periods.

2 He should not make emotional demands on other people, whether above or below, and should not expect thanks or appreciation or feel hurt when such gestures fail to arrive.

3 He should widen his horizons as much as possible, by extending interest outwards, which in turn will help to develop his potential and maturity. This suggests some kind of mid-way point in the two extreme areas we have just considered.

To be a successful leader, a manager should have certain innate and acquired qualities, vision, drive, good judgment, initiative, poise and maturity.

A true leader usually has personal magnetism that commands acceptability, enthusiasm, loyalty, co-operation, natural sincerity, tact, courtesy and a sense of humility. To be effective, a manager should radiate confidence and show ability to dominate circumstances when necessary and he should keep up morale and exercise control through inspiration rather than command. Few managers possess all these qualities but personal assets can be capitalised to the full and person liabilities overhauled and improved. Occasionally, a leader is found with completely opposite traits and yet is seen to succeed— perhaps riding 'rough shod' over the rank and file. Such people, however, are few and far between.

It is management's job to create the right atmosphere within an organisation and to this end a manager's relationship with the personnel with whom he is in regular contact is most important.

Motivation is linked very closely with morale. Given a well-motivated management, the right kind of working atmosphere, effective communication and good leadership it is likely that the rank and file will be well motivated and morale will be high. Bad management will tend to breed disharmony, discontent, frustration and other negative aspects which lead to poor output, both quantitive and qualitive.

Behavioural scientists talk of theory 'X' and theory 'Y', the first suggesting that the average worker dislikes work and must be persuaded to make the required effort, the second being the positive integration of the hopes, fears and conditions of responsible workers with the objectives of the firm. Theory 'Y' further suggests that the intellectual potentialities of the human-being are only partially utilised, thus presenting a challenge to management to make better use of its available manpower resources.

Monetary Incentives and Security

Most people will agree that an individual should obtain an adequate financial reward for a fair day's work, possibly with extra reward for extra effort. This latter imposes the thorny problem of evaluation, but less so perhaps as related to quantifiable items such as production bonuses and commission on sales. There must be a recognisable

245

salary or wage scale structure, including bonus or responsibility payments where applicable.

Coupled with salary or wages, the organisation may have other monetary attractions such as pension rights, sickness benefits, extra holidays with pay, welfare facilities when in financial difficulty and perhaps, in some circumstances, housing. Taken together they all add up to increased security for the individual concerned. With this thought in mind, it seems clear that more effective work will be forthcoming, given freedom from financial worry. Whilst some people welcome risk and change, the majority prefer to know where they are going and what the future is likely to hold in store for them.

Job Satisfaction

Security also comes from knowing the job will be properly done, given existing knowledge or special training, and that the work is acceptable to those above. Most people work better if their job is pleasant and is carried out in a cheerful setting. If the end product is worthwhile, either in the form of a commodity or a service to the community, the individual will have personal pride. In addition, there is pride in the individual's creative ability, craftsmanship, etc.

During the past twenty years the work environment has tended to be steered towards increasing automation with the result that many jobs are standardised, monotonous and perhaps menial. It is when such circumstances exist that the monetary gains must be high to relieve the increased boredom. At all times it is important to reassure the individual that his particular contribution to the organisation is both significant and appreciated.

Whilst many workers prefer a routine to promotion, and security to taking a risk, they still want to feel important and acceptable. Where there are 'square pegs in round holes', or the job is too easy or too hard, there is a need for re-arrangement as there may well be disharmony and low output.

Productivity

In order to improve, an organisation must be capable of increasing the number of commodities produced or improve the level of service at the same or a lower cost. All too often, managers relate increased productivity with either extra financial payment to the work-force

246

or the purchase of new plant and equipment. Little thought is given to the working environment and the personal motivating forces of a good leader.

Good planning, selection and recruitment of personnel and plant, all contribute to the stability and profitability of the organisation. Obtaining the right balance at the appropriate time is the responsibility of the manager and he will be judged by the results. Types of managers vary. They can be described as autocratic, benevolent, bureaucratic, charismatic, democratic and dictatorial. Whichever category, success will be judged on ability as a leader.

Communications

The meaning of communication changes depending on whether the person concerned is the speaker or the listener. Every firm or similar organisation depends for its daily functioning upon an intricate communication network which has developed over the years. The bigger the organisation the more elaborate the system must be and the greater the likelihood of expensive and time-wasting mistakes caused through misunderstanding.

There are two kinds of communication, namely internal and external, which break down into:

a) Conversations, direct or by telephone;
b) Memoranda, letters and reports.

The first decision a manager has to make is whether a communication needs to be written or verbal, face to face, or telephoned, taped, etc. It is important to remember that even though the telephone is fast and comparatively cheap, there is no written record of information and poor telephone lines, noisy offices or other interruptions can distort the communication.

For both writing and speaking there are four stages to be borne in mind when communicating:

1 Think clearly;
2 Arrange logically;
3 Express clearly;
4 Use the appropriate language, i.e. express concisely; never obtain conciseness at the expense of clarity.

The first step towards clear communication is to have the material to be communicated clearly in your own mind. Until you are sure that you know what it is that you want to say there is no point in starting to say it.

In spoken communication we are often called upon to think under circumstances that do not permit more than a hasty organisation of our ideas on the subject, but when we start to write we should have time for preparation and planning.

Preparation

Preparation involves the gathering together of material from documents, personal interviews, telephone conversations, from our own knowledge of the subject and from tests and experiments that we may devise, or it may be merely a matter of sitting down for a moment and trying to sharpen the focus of what is in one's mind. Always bear in mind the purpose of the communication.

Every document will have a purpose, this may be to supply or request information, to produce action or reaction, to persuade. It is advantageous to state the purpose of the communication to yourself, i.e.:

a) I am writing this letter so that this employee will not have a lasting grudge against the organisation.
b) I am preparing this report so that Mr. Jones can explain exactly what his section has been working on when he attends the annual conference.

Without this purpose being brought into the open you risk producing a pompous piece of empire building which only bores the conference by its irrelevance and unnecessary length. Try to bring to life the person who is going to read what you write.

Planning is essential with every piece of communication of any length or complexity. It consists of two stages:

1 Devising a system of organisation for the material;
2 Deciding the most effective order of presentation.

Sometimes it may be written down; often the experienced communicator will carry the plan in his head, however, even then he may well have a format laid down on paper outlining the principle sections, divisions and proposed order of presentation.

Most business communications start with an introduction and end with a conclusion. The main body in between needs to be arranged into logical groups, this frequently reveals itself as a succession of steps or stages which inevitably lead to each other, i.e. the reader must grasp 'A' before he can understand 'B' and 'C' makes no sense unless he knows about 'B' and so on.

Five main methods are used for deciding the order of presentation:

Chronological order Refers to the order in which events took place or in which they were observed.

Spatial order Prevents repetition by referring to the organisation on the basis of north and south, inside to outside, back to front, left to right.

Descending order of importance A useful device to combine with 1 and 2.

Ascending order of importance Used to build up suspense and a sense of climax. It could be a method of presenting a succession of arguments.

Ascending order of complexity Particularly useful for explaining something which is unfamiliar. Obviously you start with the simplest and proceed to the more complex.

Clear wording

When we use words, we are using symbols. Just as pictures bring to mind, so words form pictures in the mind. If you are writing or speaking to a colleague you can use words and phrases which are only understood from someone else within this 'special' line of business; but when you are expressing yourself to the rest of the community, you must use words which make your meaning immediately clear to the layman.

Remember that when communicating with men or women whose vocabulary is more limited than our own, breakdown or misunderstanding may occur. You can guard against this by improving your own vocabulary. This can be done by reading and listening, referring to a dictionary when you come across a word that you are not sure about, never be satisfied with material already within your range. To read the same newspaper, magazine, type of novel, or look at the same television show cripples development.

A good dictionary not only supplies definitions but indicates the origins of words, shows their plurals and tenses and is a guide to pronunciation. It is not really worthwhile to buy a cheap dictionary that has only brief entries when for a little more you can have a pocket edition of a major dictionary which is crammed with information. Always make your meaning clear. Remember, clear communication, whether it be verbal, written or pictorial, is most important to the manager.

Requirements of a Sportsground Technical Manager

What knowledge does a sportsground technical manager need in order to carry out the job satisfactorily? A loaded question perhaps. However, an effort should be made to briefly itemise the specialist knowledge required in order to carry out the duties expected of the average technical manager responsible for outdoor sports facilities. The job, can be split into site surveying, development and construction, landscape/sportsground management and management of specialist sports and recreation facilities. Let us consider each section in turn.

Site surveying

In the main, the manager should be capable of carrying out initial investigations into the suitability of sites which are being considered for outdoor recreational and sporting facilities. Managers should be fully conversant and capable of using surveying equipment; know how to read plans and the recording of levels; have detailed knowledge of soil structure and texture, drainage capabilities (including hydraulic conductivity), critical tension and water tables; knowledge of procedures and methods for investigating essential services in order to meet future needs and planning requirements.

Development and construction

There is a need to be able to integrate existing natural features into future plans. The manager must have an appreciation of landscape design within a recreational/sportsground complex. Development costs including earth movement, drainage, grading, cultivations and seeding plus other specialist facilities like the construction of cricket squares, tennis court, athletics tracks, etc. whether they be grass, hard porous or synthetic. In certain types of posts, the manager may have to spend much of his time on surveying sites, preparing drawings, specifications, estimates and bills of quantities, etc. prior to initiating the work. Managers should also be capable of preparing a comprehensive specification, together with the necessary drawings, in order to request tender applications.

A sportsground manager controlling a constructional labour force, whether direct or contract, must have the ability to control both the work and expenditure and, at the same time, ensure that the labour force is carrying out a satisfactory job to an acceptable standard in order to fulfil the ultimate requirements of the client.

Landscape/Sportsground management

In order to manage sports facilities and the landscape successfully, a technical manager must have:

a) Knowledge of turf husbandry, horticultural practice, hard porous and synthetic materials, imaginative and adventure playgrounds, environmental areas, hard and soft landscape, the maintenance and propagation of trees and shrubs and the maintenance of aquatic areas;

b) The ability to compile management programmes, maintenance specifications for manpower, materials and equipment.

Management of specialist sports and recreational facilities

The technical manager should have detailed knowledge of the maintenance and preparation of specialist games areas such as hockey, soccer, rugby, cricket pitches, tennis courts, bowling greens, golf courses, hard porous surfaces, synthetic surfaces, athletics tracks, hard tennis courts, athletics throwing areas, athletics field event run-ups.

The technical sportsground manager has a complex job and he will be judged on his ability to compile a management programme which provides acceptable sports or recreational facilities in an attractive environment. The selection of the appropriate treatment at the right time often determines the ability of the manager.

Managing sports facilities is not easy and many managers have to compile broad programmes for long periods of time. Implementation is usually the responsibility of the person on the job. A good programme will thus take into consideration the need for sufficient flexibility and manoeuvrability by the person who implements the work—depending, of course, on prevailing circumstances and weather conditions. Technical sportsground managers can usually specialise in one or more of the categories indicated. In most large sportsground organisations, the persons with overall responsibility or function usually spends the majority of their time on organisational management and the technical decisions are made by a person in greater contact with 'grass roots' level.

Oct.12,00
Section 2

Jessica Paetz
Rm.137 Gr. White

1. C
2. D
3. A
4. E
5. B
6. A
7. C
8. A

10. A

Appendix 1

Glossary of Botanical Terms

ACHENE   A dry fruit that is indehiscent and contains one seed.

ACICULAR   Needle shaped.

ACULEATE   Having prickles.

ACUTE   The apex of a leaf is described as acute when it forms an acute angle or tapers to a point.

ALTERNATE   Branches, or leaves, are alternate when one proceeds from each node; one on one side and the next above or below on the opposite side of the stem.

AMPLEXICAULE   Leaves are described when the sessile base of the blades clasps the stem.

ANTHER   Part of a stamen which contains the pollen. It is borne on a filament and divided into two pouches or cells.

AQUATIC   A plant which grows in water.

ARISTATE   Awned, bristle-tipped.

ASCENDING   Stems which spread horizontally at the base and then turn upwards and become erect.

AURICLES   The two lateral lobes at the base of a leaf.

AURICULATE   When the auricles are pointed, a leaf is called auriculate.

AXIL   The angle formed by a leaf and a branch.

BERRY   A pulpy, normally several seeded, indehiscent fruit.

BISEXUAL   Both male and female organs on the same plant.

BLADE   An ordinary leaf consists of a flat blade or lamina, usually green, attached to a stem or stalk called a petiole.

BRACTS   The name given to the upper leaves of a plant in flower, when they differ from the stem leaves in size, shape, colour or arrangement.

BRACTEATE   Having bracts.

BRISTLES   Very stiff erect straight hairs.

CAESPITOSE   Tufted.

CALCIFUGE   A term given to a plant which cannot tolerate calcareous soils.

CALYX   A collective name for the sepals.

253

CAPITATE When several sessile or nearly sessile flowers are collected together into a compact cluster or head.

CAPSULE A dry dehiscent pod.

CARBOHYDRATES Compounds which form the largest part of the body of plants. The chief types being sugars and starches.

CARPEL Parts of the pistil containing one or more seeds.

CARYOPSIS The fruit of the plants belonging to the grass family.

CAULINE Leaves which are borne on a distinct erect stalk.

CHLOROPHYLL The green colouring matter in leaves.

CILIATE When the leaves are bordered with fine hairs or hair-like teeth.

CLONE A group of individuals derived from a single plant.

COMPOUND LEAF When leaves are divided to the midrib or petiole.

COMPRESSED Flattened.

CONFLUENT Anthers occasionally have only one cell. When this results from the disappearance of the partition between two closely contiguous cells, these cells are termed confluent.

CONICAL Cone shaped.

CORDATE Heart shaped.

COROLLA A collective name for the petals.

CORYMB A flat topped flower head where all the branches start from different points but attain the same level.

CORYMBOSE Having flowers in corymbs.

CREEPING When stems emit roots at their nodes.

CRENATE When the teeth on the margin of a leaf are regular and blunt or rounded.

CULM A name given to the stem of grasses and sedges.

CULTIVAR A cultivated plant. A plant found in the wild and maintained by vegetative propagation.

CUNEATE Wedge shaped.

CUSPIDATE Abruptly narrowed at the top forming a sharp point.

CYME A branched flower cluster where the central flower opens first. A flat topped inflorescence.

DECIDUOUS When scales, sepals, petals and leaves fall at the end of a season.

DECUMBENT When stems spread horizontally or nearly so but become upright at the apex.

DECURRENT When the edges of a leaf are continued down the stem to form raised lines or ridges as in the petiole of a thistle.

DECUSSATE When leaves or branches are opposite but each pair at right angles to the pairs above and below.

DEHISCENCE Anthers open to let out pollen and fruits open to discharge seeds.

DELTOID Triangular, like the Greek letter Δ.

254

DENTATE   Toothed with the teeth directed outwards.

DEPRESSED   Leaves are depressed when more or less vertically flattened.

DIADELPHOUS   When the stamens are united into two clusters.

DIANDROUS   Having two stamens.

DICHOTOMOUS   When the branch forks into two, when each branch divides again.

DICOTYLEDONOUS   Having two cotyledons or seedleaves.

DIDYMUS   Formed in pairs, divided into two lobes.

DIDYNAMUS   Having two long and two short stamens.

DIFFUSE   Spreading and loosely branched.

DIGITATE   Like the fingers of a hand. Applied to compound leaves like the Horsechestnut.

DIOECIOUS   When the male and female organs are on separate plants.

DORSAL   On the back or attached thereto.

DUCTS   Tubular vessels marked with lines or dots.

EAR   A form of spike.

EMARGINATE   Notched or decidedly indented at the extremity.

ENSIFORM   Shaped like a broad sword.

ENTIRE   Undivided, with even margin.

EPIDERMIS   The outer skin.

EVERGREEN   Remaining green during the winter.

EXOTIC   Not native.

EXSERTED   Extending beyond, when the stamens are longer than the carolla.

FAMILY   A collection of genera.

FASCILED (or FASCICULATE)   When two or three branches or leaves proceed from the same node or the same side of the stem.

FILAMENT   The stalk of an anther.

FILIFORM   Capillary or hair-like.

FIMBRIATED   Fringed.

FLOCCULENT   Having a woolly or downy covering.

FLORETS   The small flowers collected into a head in composite plants.

FOLIACEOUS   Leaf-like.

FRUCTIFICATION   Fruiting body.

FURCATE   Forked.

GAMO   United or fused.

GENUS   A collection of related species.

GLABROUS   Without hairs.

GLANDULAR   With secreting organs.

GLAUCOUS   Having a bluish or sea-green bloom.

GLOBOSE   Globe shaped, spherical.

GLUMES   The bracts enclosing the flowers of grasses.

GLUTINOUS   Sticky.

GUARD-CELLS   Cells which control the opening and closing of stomata.

HABIT   General characteristics which are apparent to the eye, e.g. size, type of growth etc.

HABITAT   The place where a plant is growing.

HALOPHYTE   A plant adapted to grow in saline conditions.

HARDY   Enduring without protection.

HASTATE   Spear or halberd-like.

HEREDITY   The study of inheritance.

HERMAPHRODITE   Bisexual.

HISPID   Hirsute, with long distinct hairs.

HOARY   Covered with whitish or greyish-white pubescence.

HOST   A plant supporting a parasite.

HYBRID   The progeny of a cross between two different species.

HYDROPONICS   Soil-less cultivation of plants in water to which nutrients have been added.

HYPO-   Below, e.g. hypocotyl, the axis of an embryo below the cotyledons.

IMBRICATE   Overlapping.

IMPERFECT   With certain parts missing.

INDEHISCENT   When the fruits do not open to discharge the seeds.

INDIGENOUS   A native of the country.

INFERIOR   Situated below an organ i.e. an ovary is inferior when the other floral organs are situated above it.

INFLORESCENCE   The flowering part of a plant.

INVOLUCRE   A whorl of bracts surrounding a flower.

INVOLUTE   With the leaf margins rolled inwards.

IRREGULAR   A flower that can only be identically halved in one plane.

KEEL   The ridge or lower surface of the leaf blades of some grasses. Two loosely united petals of a leguminous flower.

LAMINA   The blade of a leaf.

LANCEOLATE   Lance-shaped. Long and tapering to tip.

LATERAL   On or at the side.

LATEX   The milky fluid exuded by certain plants.

LEGUME   A pod.

LEMMA   The outer palea or outer flowering glume of a grass.

LIGULE   A small membranous appendage.

LINEAR   Long and narrow. Several times longer than broad.

LUNEATE   Crescent shaped.

LYRATE   Having small lower lobes but the terminal being large and rounded.

MEMBER   A structure of a plant, i.e. a leaf, sepal, petal or stamen.

MOLLIS   Pubescent or soft.

MONOECIOUS   Male and female flowers separate but on the same plant.

256

MUCRONATE   When the midrib of a leaf is produced beyond the apex to
MULTI-   Many.
MUTANT   A new plant produced by mutation.
    form a small point.
MUTATION   A genetic change in a plant during its life cycle.
MYCELIUM   The vegetative part of a fungus.
MYURUS   Tapering like a rat's tail.
NATIVE   Indigenous.
NATURAL ORDER   A collection of families.
NAVICULAR   Boat-shaped.
NECTARY   A small receptacle holding nectar.
NERVE   A prominent rib or vein.
NODE   A point of the stem or its branches at which leaves or leaf buds are
    given off.
NODULE   A small outgrowth of irregular shape.
NUT   An indehiscent fruit containing one seed.
OB-   A prefix denoting reversed or opposite, e.g. Obovate, inversely egg
    shaped: Ob-cordate: inversely cordate.
OBTUSE   Terminating in a blunt point.
ORBICULAR   Circular.
OSMOSIS   The passage of water from a low concentration to a high con-
    centration via a semi-peremable membrane.
OVARY   The female portion of the flower which after fertilisation becomes
    the seed.
OVATE   Egg shaped.
PALEA   Palea, Pales or Chaff are the inner bracts or scales in Compositae,
    Gramineae and some other orders of plants.
PALMATE   (See digitate) Lobed or divided reminiscent of a hand.
PANICLE   An inflorescence where the axis is divided into branches bearing
    two or more flowers.
PAPPUS   A ring of hairs or scales around the top of a fruit.
PEDICEL   The last branch of an inflorescence supporting a single flower.
PEDICELLATE   On a pedicel.
PEDUNCLE   The main stalk of a raceme or similar inflorescence.
PEDUNCULATE   On a peduncle.
PELTATE   Form of leaf where the stalk is attached to the under-surface of
    the lamina.
PENTA-   Five in composition.
PERENNIAL   A plant which lives for more than two years, flowering, and
    setting seed in most years.
PERIANTH   The Calyx and Corolla together. Also used to describe a
    flower where there is no distinction between the Calyx and Corolla.
PETIOLE   The leaf stalk.

PHYLLODIUM   A flat petiole with no blade.

Pilose   Covered with long simple hairs.

PINNATE   When there are several leaflets succeeding each other on each side of the midrib or petiole compared with the branches of a feather.

PISTIL   The female organ of the flower comprising ovary, stigma and style.

PLUMULE   The embryonic shoot in a seed.

PROLIFEROUS   The production of adventitious buds in the place of flowers or seeds.

PROSTRATE   When the shoot lies very close to the ground.

PULVENATE   Cushion shaped.

PUNCTIFORME   Like a point or dot.

RACE   If a variety is reproduced true from seed it is often called a race.

RACEME   An inflorescence where the flowers are produced on pedicels along a single undivided axis or rachis.

RACHIS   The portion of the peduncle extending from the first ramification to the last, or the axis of the inflorescence.

RADICLE   The embryonic root in a seed.

RECEPTACLE   The extremity of the peduncle upon which the corolla, stamens and ovary are inserted.

RENIFORM   Kidney-shaped.

RETICULATE   When the smaller veins are connected together like the mesh of a net.

RHIZOME   An underground creeping shoot containing buds and scales.

RHOMBOIDAL   Quadrangular with the lateral angles obtuse. Like a rhomboid.

RIBBED   The epidermis is said to be ribbed or costate when marked with distinctly raised parallel lines.

ROSTRATE   Beaked.

SAGITTATE   When the leaf resembles a barbed arrow-head.

SCABROUS   Rough to the touch.

SCALES   Leaves very much reduced in size.

SCAPE   A leafless peduncle proceeding from the stock of the base of the stem.

SCARIOUS   Scariose; very thin, more or less transparent, yet rather stiff.

Scattered   Irregularly arranged leaves or stems.

SEPALS   The outer whorl of a flower collectively known as the calyx.

SERRATE   Serrulate; when the leaf margin is cut and the teeth are regular and pointed like a saw.

SESSILE   Devoid of a stalk.

SETACEOUS   Bristle-like.

SHEATHING   When the blade of a leaf forms a vertical sheath around the stem.

SIMPLE   When a leaf is entire, the blade consisting of a single piece with the margin not indented.

258

SINUATE When the teeth of leaves are broad and irregular. Strongly waved.

SPIKE A simple elongated inflorescence with sessile flowers.

SPIKELET Constituents of a spike.

SPIRIOUS Possessing thorns.

STAMENS The male organs of the flower consisting of the anther and filament.

STELLATE or
ROTATE Star-shaped.

STERILE Barren, not producing seeds.

STIGMA A small head or point at the top of the style or ovary.

STIPE A stalk.

STIPULES Leaf-like appendages at the base of a leaf stalk or at the node of a stem.

STOCK The portion of the stem or root which does not die.

STOLON A shoot at or near ground level which produces a new plant at its tip.

STRIATE Slightly raised, parallel, longitudinal lines.

STYLE Comes from the top of the ovary and supports the stigma.

SUBULATE Resembling an awl.

TERNATE In multiples of three.

TILLERING A common mode of branching in grasses and cereals. The formation of shoots from near the surface of the soil.

TOMENTOSE Cottony, woolly.

TRIBE The genera of an order are collected into groups called tribes.

TRIFID Three lobed.

TRIFOLIATE A leaf with three leaflets.

TRUNCATED When the end is cut off square.

TUBERCULATE Covered with small obtuse warts.

TURBINATE Top-shaped.

UMBEL Flower cluster consisting of several nearly equal branches proceeding from the same point and forming a flat head.

UNCINATE Hooked.

UNILATERAL One-sided.

UTRICLE Thin and rather loose pericarp on an achene.

VALVES The longitudinal splitting of the pericarp in a capsule or pod.

VENATION The arrangement of the veins.

VIRGATE Twiggy.

VIVIPAROUS Adventitious leaf buds, produced in place of flower or seeds are termed viviparous.

WARTED See tuberculate.

WHORLED Verticillate; when several branches or leaves are produced from the same node; arranged regularly around the stem.

Appendix 2

Dimensions of Sports Areas

As dimensions are updated from time to time, it is advisable to check with the appropriate governing body, the Amateur Athletics Association or the International Athletics Federation.

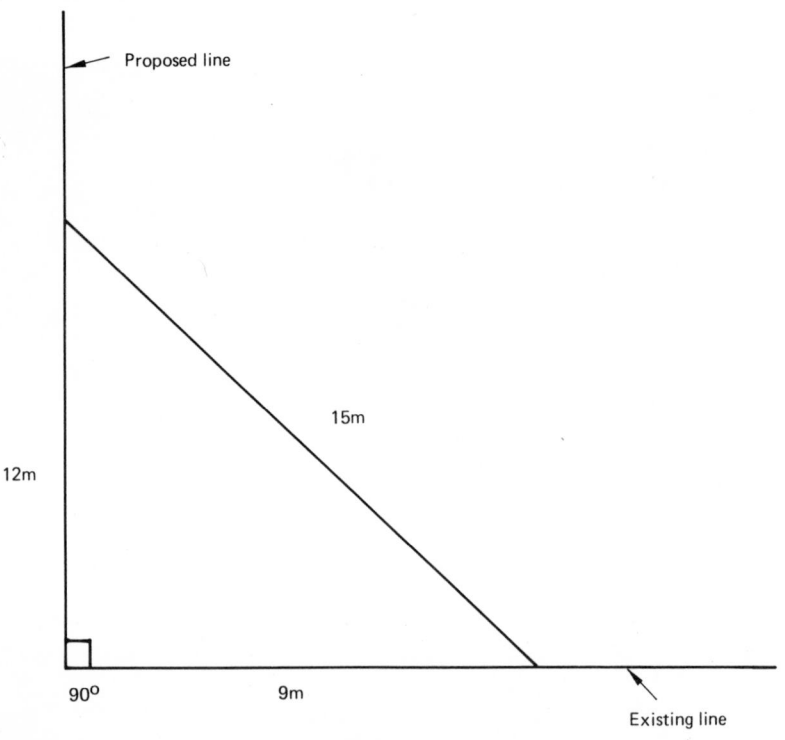

The 3-4-5 triangle.

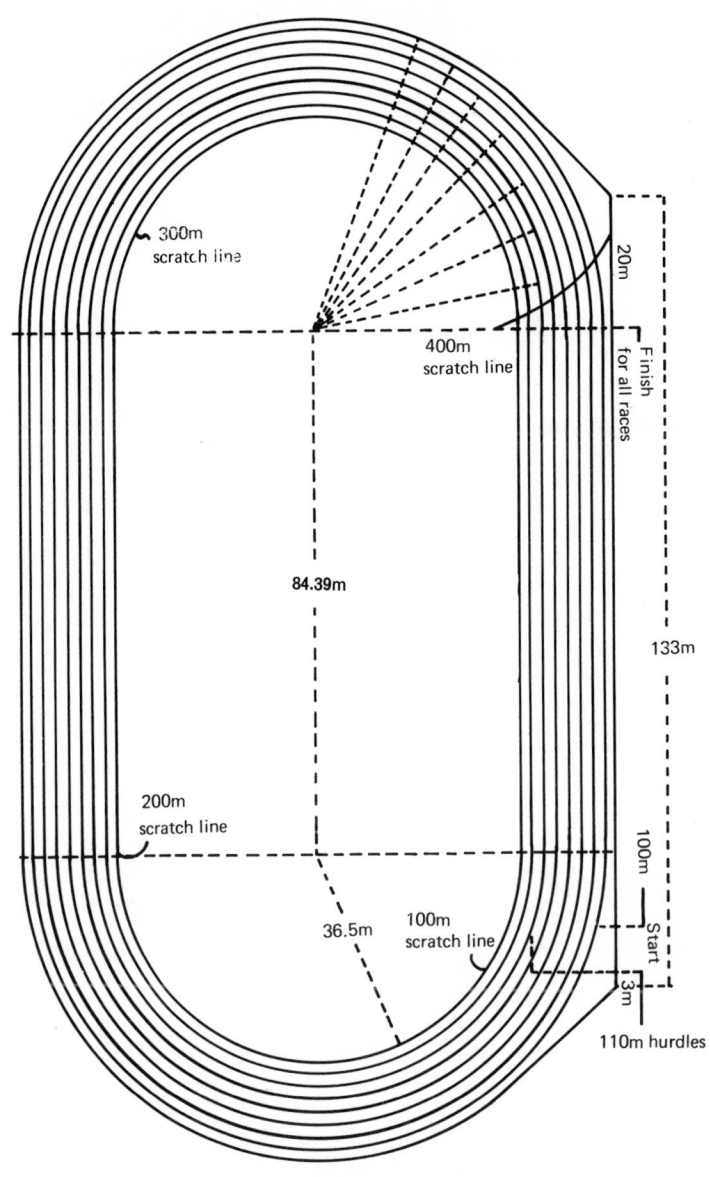

400 m running track.

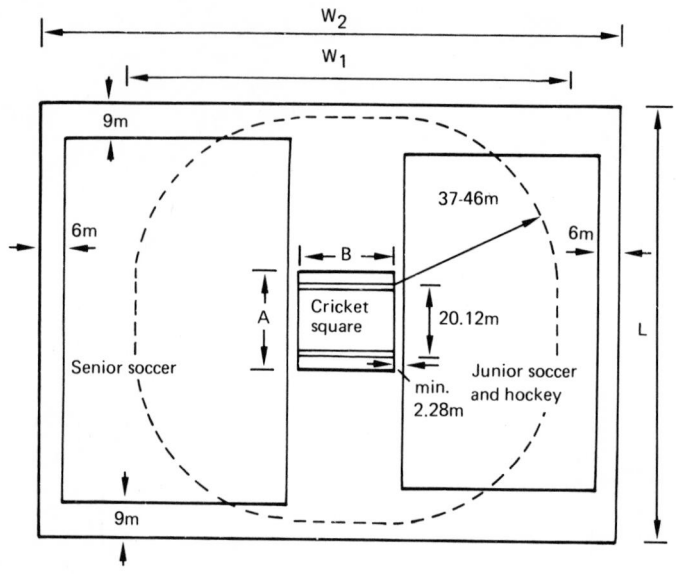

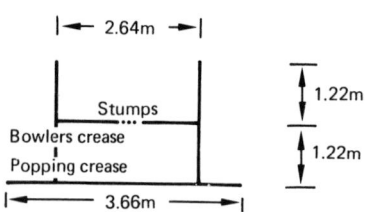

Cricket and winter games with details of ACC wicket (Law 26).

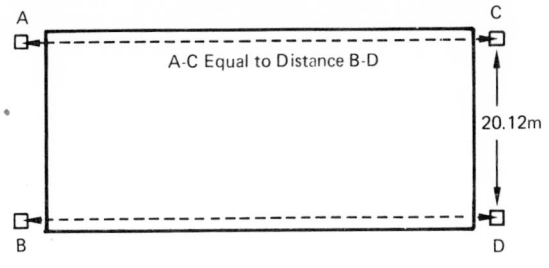

A-C Equal to Distance B-D

20.12m

☐ Corner pegs to keep wickets square

Squaring the square

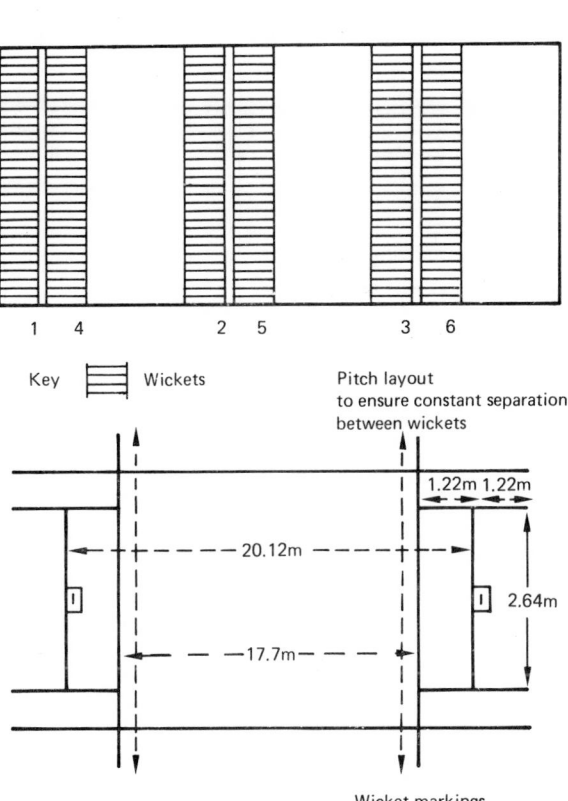

| 1 | 4 | | 2 | 5 | | 3 | 6 |

Key ▤ Wickets

Pitch layout
to ensure constant separation
between wickets

1.22m 1.22m

20.12m

2.64m

17.7m

Wicket markings

Cricket wicket.

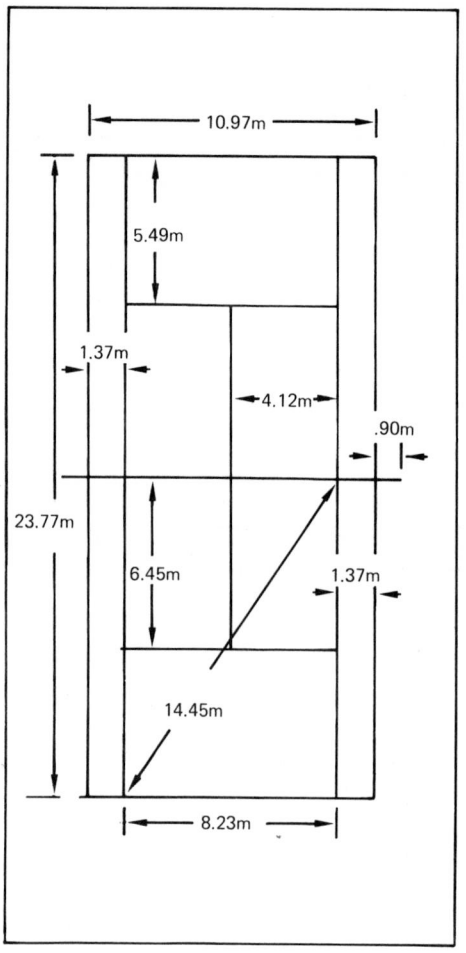

Tennis.

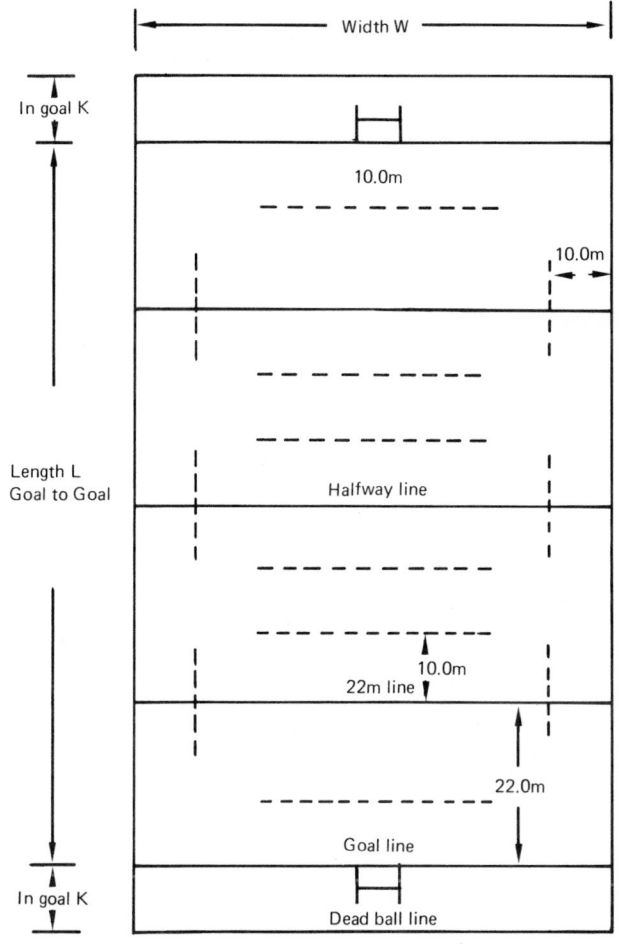

Width W

In goal K

10.0m

10.0m

Length L
Goal to Goal

Halfway line

10.0m
22m line

22.0m

Goal line

In goal K

Dead ball line

10m dotted lines to be minimum of 13.72m
in length

Rugby League football for seniors, the length L = 96–100m, W = 64–68m, the marginal clearances = 6m and 'ingoal' distance K = 5.5–11m.

265

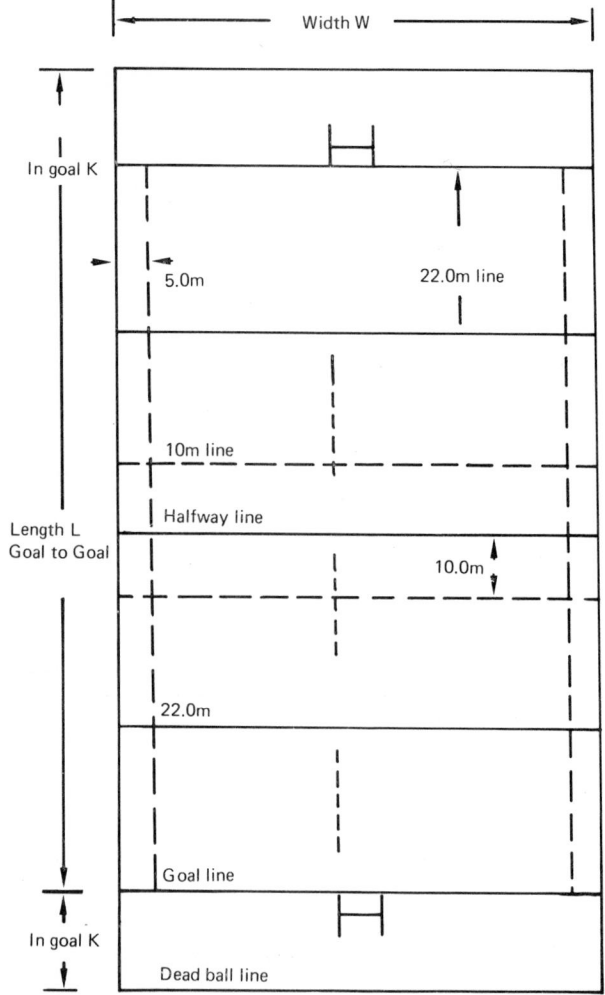

Rugby Union football. For seniors, the length L = 100m, W = 69m, marginal clearances at sides and ends = 6m and the 'ingoal' distance K = 22m.

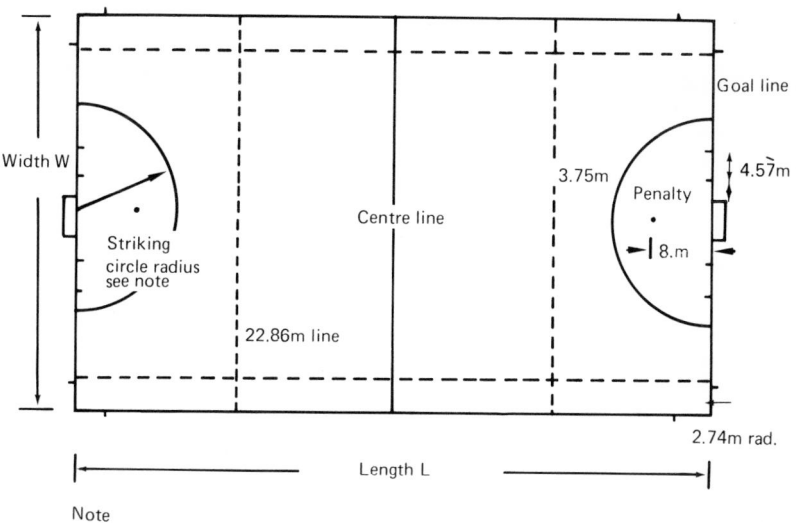

Hockey pitch. For mens' hockey, the dotted lines are known as 6.40m lines.
Being this distance from side lines striking circle radius for men is 14.63m.
L = 90m, W = 50–55m and marginal clearances and ends = 3–4.5m. For
women's hockey, the dotted lines are known as 4.57m lines. Being this distance
from side lines striking circle radius for women is 13.70m. L = 90m, W = 55m
and clearances, etc. as for men's hockey.

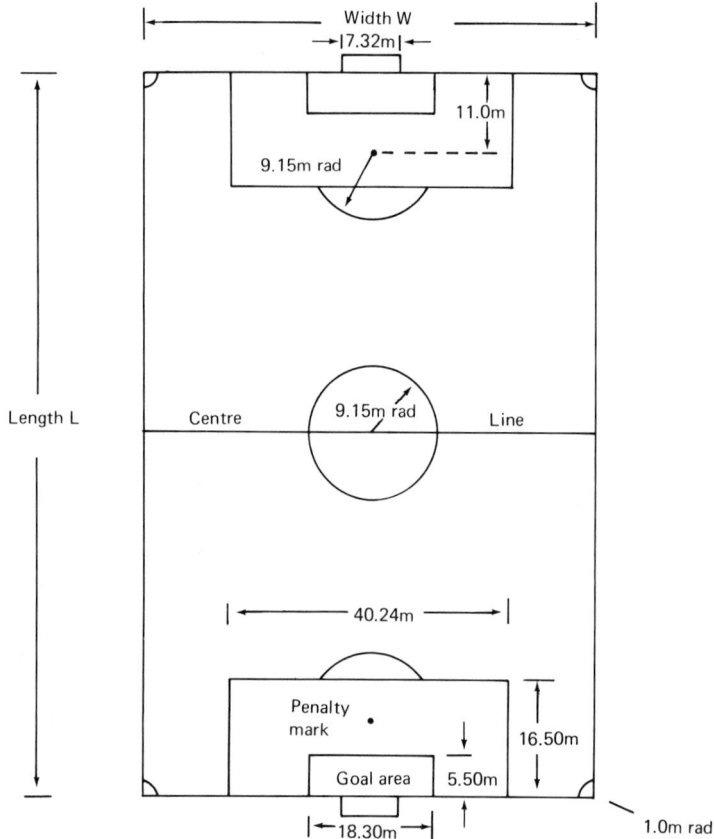

Soccer pitch. For seniors, L = 96–100m, W = 60-64m, marginal sides = 6m and end clearances = 9m. For juniors, L = 90m, W = 46-55m and marginal sides and end clearances are as for seniors. (The F.A. International Board decision on Law 1 says that L may vary from 90–120m and W can be 45–90m.)

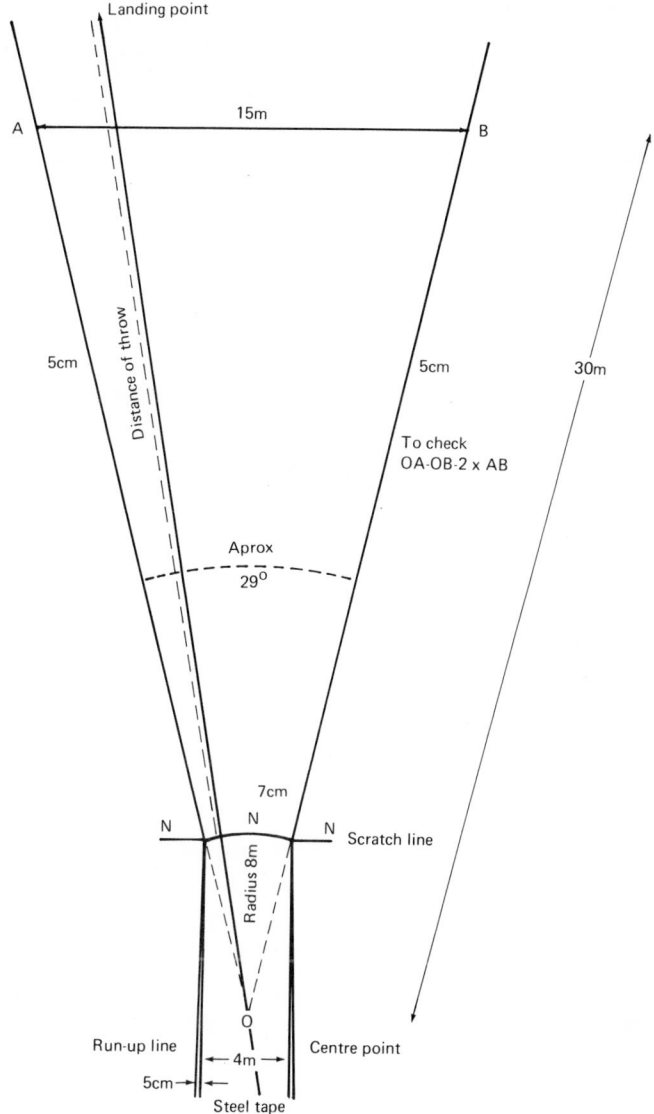

Landing point

15m

A ———————————————— B

5cm

5cm

Distance of throw

30m

To check
OA-OB-2 x AB

Aprox
29°

7cm

N   N   N   Scratch line

Radius 8m

Run-up line   Centre point

O

5cm

4m

Steel tape

Javelin.

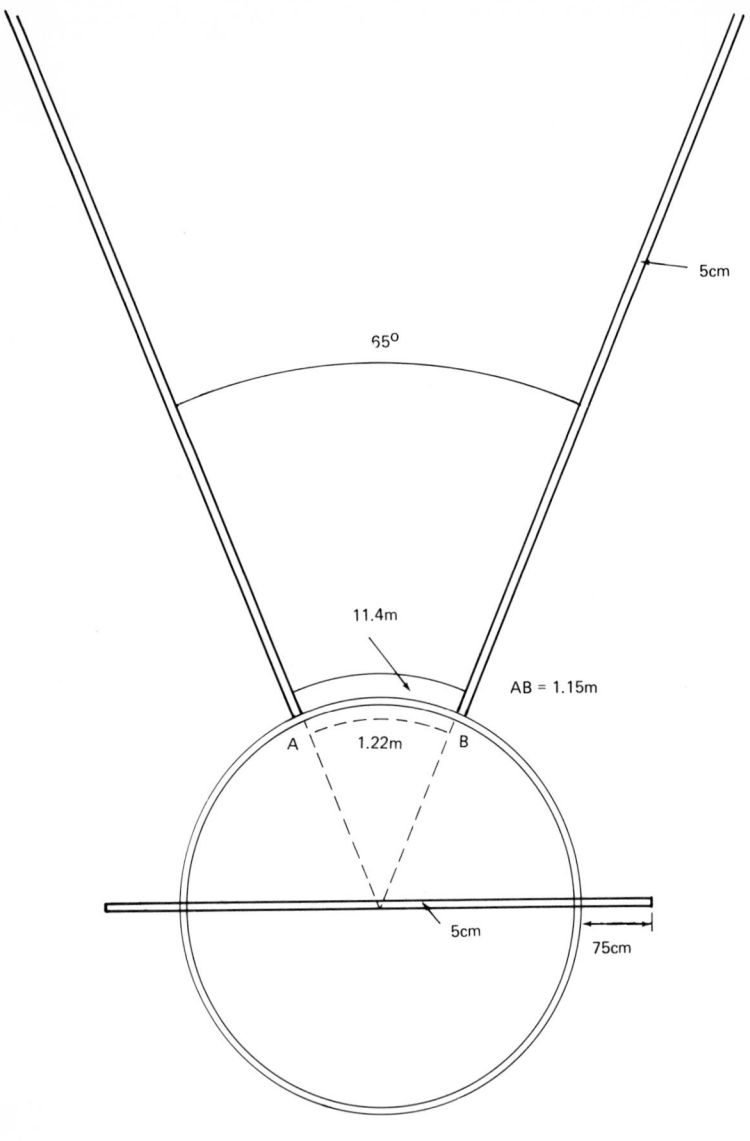

5cm

65°

11.4m

AB = 1.15m

A   1.22m   B

5cm

75cm

Shot-putt.

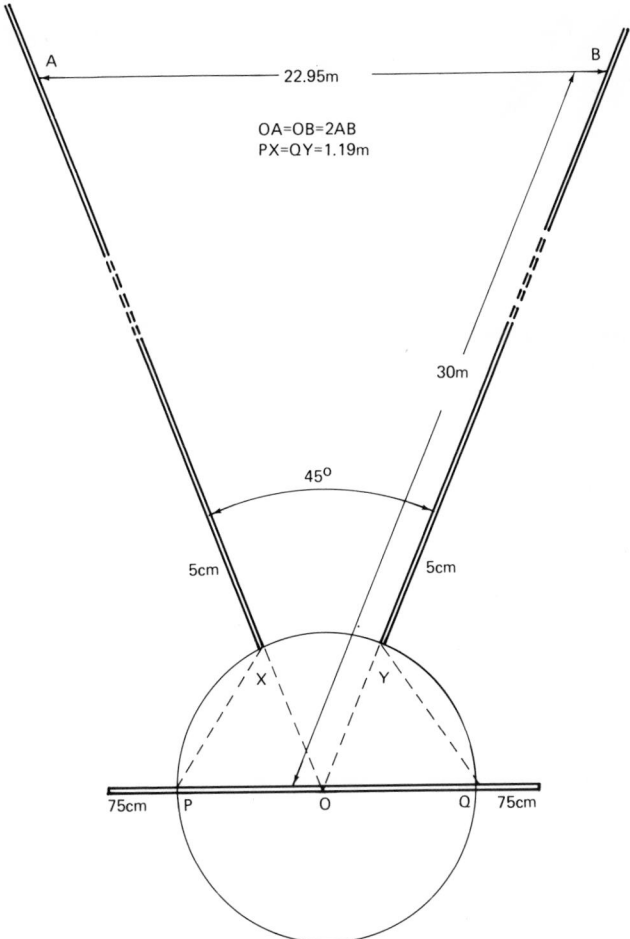

A   22.95m   B

OA=OB=2AB
PX=QY=1.19m

30m

45°

5cm   5cm

X   Y

75cm P   O   Q 75cm

Hammer throwing.

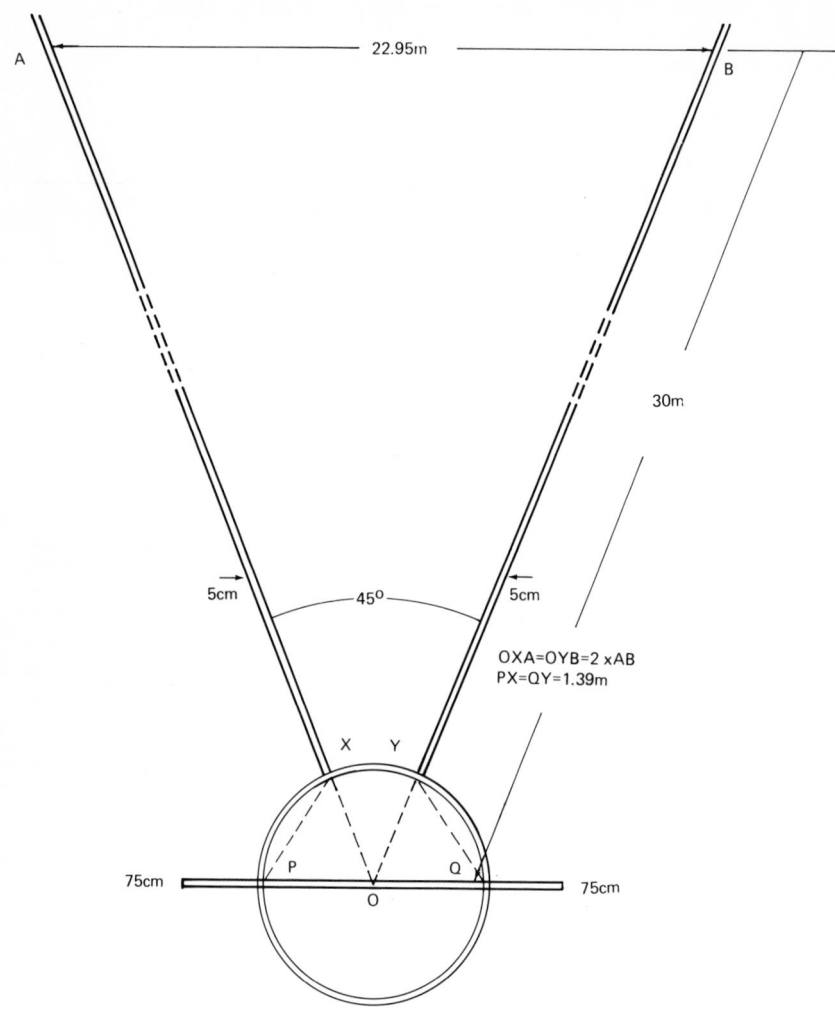

Discus.

1ft = 0.3048m

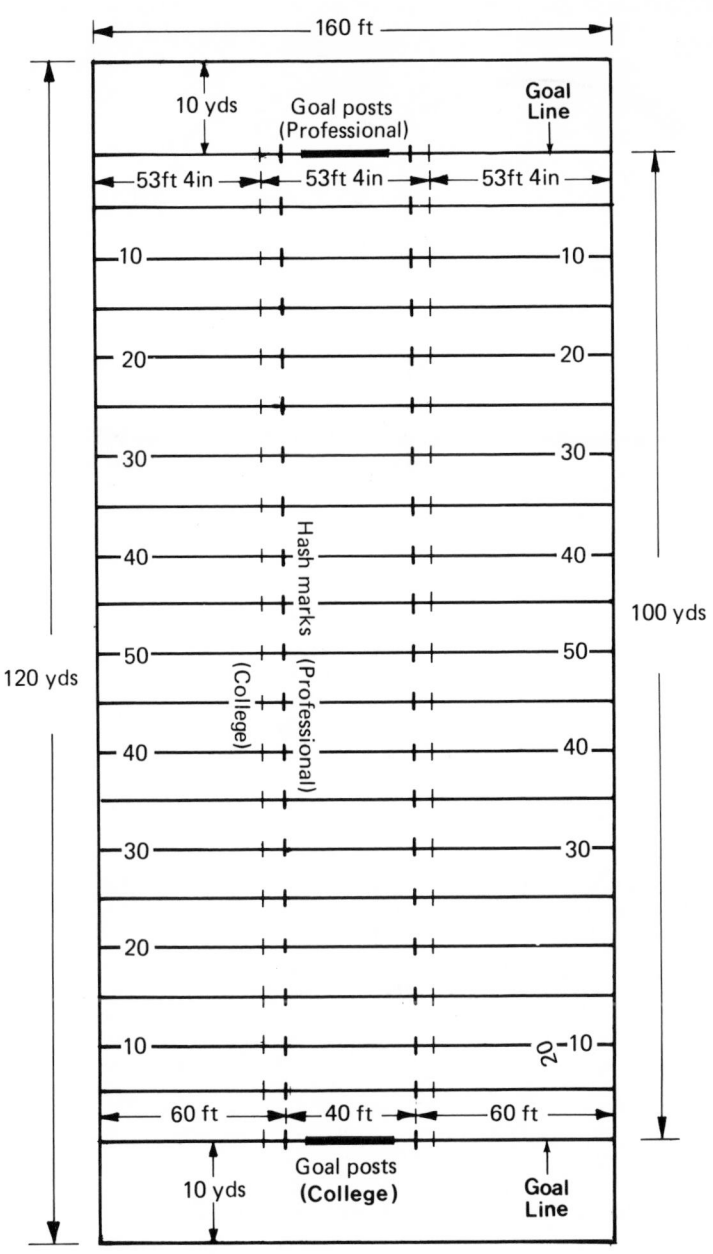

Football, U.S.A.

273

1ft = 0.3048m

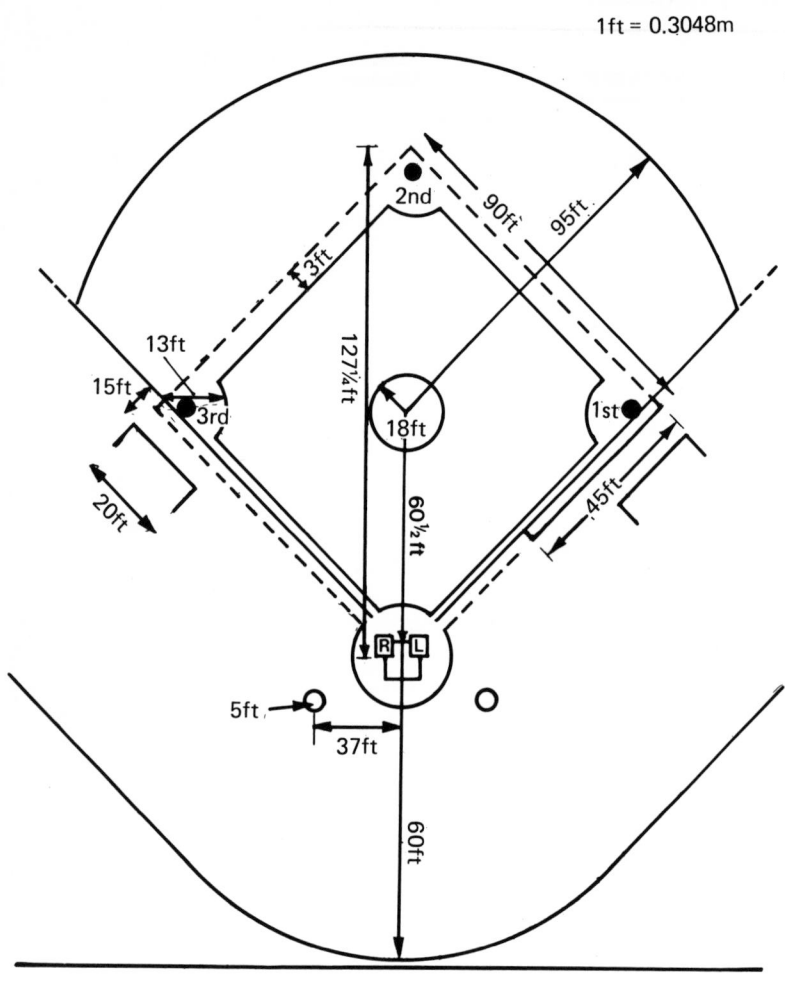

Baseball.

Appendix 3

Ornamental Plants for Various Situations

Plants for Damp Sites

Alnus glutinosa
Alnus incana
Betula pendula
Poplar species
Salix species

Cornus alba
Hippophae rhamnoides
Sambucus nigra
Metasequoia glyptostroboides
Taxodium distichum

Plants for Seaside Areas

Crataegus monogyna
Griselinia littoralis
Laurus nobilis
Quercus ilex
Sorbus aria

Choisya ternata
Elaeagnus pungens
Garrya elliptica
Hebe armstrongii
Phormium tenax

Ground Cover Plants

Ajuga reptans
Cotoneaster horizontalis
Dryas octopetala
Hypericum calycinum
Pachysandra terminalis

Santolina virens
Symphoricarpos x *chenaultii*
Vinca major
Juniperus sabina tamariscifolia
Podocarpus alpinus

Plants with Ornamental Bark

Acer griseum
Arbutus x *andrachnoides*
Parrotia persica
Prunus serrula
Salix daphnoides

Euonymus alatus
Leycesteria formosa
Salix irrorata
Cryptomeria japonica
Pinus bungeana

Plants with Ornamental Foliage

Ailanthus altissima
Magnolia macrophylla
Populus lasiocarpa
Sorbus mitchellii
Trachycarpus fortunei

Eriobotrya japonica
Hydrangea quercifolia
Mahonia lomariifolia
Osmanthus yunnanensis
Viburnum rhytidophyllum

Plants with Ornamental Fruits

Arbutus unedo
Cercis siliquastrum
Malus Golden Hornet
Robinia fertilis
Sorbus Joseph Rock

Clerodendrum trichotomum
Daphne mezereum
X Gaulnettya wisleyensis
Mespilus germanica
Ruscus aculeatus

Plants for Autumn Colour

Acer nikoense
Amelanchier laevis
Cercidiphyllum japonicum
Liquidambar styraciflua
Malus tschonoskii

Ceratostigma willmottianum
Eucryphia glutinosa
Fothergilla monticola
Rhus typhina
Viburnum opulus

Winter Flowering Plants

Acacia dealbata
Chimonanthus praecox
Hamamelis mollis
Lespedeza thunbergii
Mahonia x media

Prunus subhirtella Autumnalis
Rhododendron dauricum
Sorbus megalocarpa
Ulex europaeus
Viburnum x bodnantense

Aromatic Plants

Cinnamomum glanduliferum
Laurus nobilis
Salix pentandra
Sassafras albidum
Clerodendrum bungei

Hebe cupressoides
Lippia citriodora
Myrtus communis
Ribes sanguineum
Ruta graveolens

Climbing Plants

Actinidia kolomikta
Hedera canariensis
Jasminum officinale
Lonicera japonica
'Aureo-reticulata'
Meuhlenbeckia complexa

Polygonum baldschuanicum
Trachelospermum jasminoides Variegatum
Vitis riparia
Wattakaka sinensis
Wisteria sinensis

Conifers

X *Cupressocyparis leylandii*
Ginkgo biloba
Juniperus communis
Larix decidua
Picea smithiana

Pinus ayacahuite
Taxodium distichum
Taxus baccata
Thuja occidentalis
Tsuga canadensis

Bibliography

Beard, James B. *Turf grass: Science and Culture. 1973,* N. J. Prentice-Hall Inc., Englewood Cliffs.

Bleasdale, J. K. A. *Plant Physiology in Relation to Horticulture.* 1973. Macmillan, London.

Brade-Birks, B. and Graham, S. *Good Soil.* 1966. English Universities Press, London.

Clapham, Tutin and Warburg. *Flora of the British Isles.* 1962. Cambridge University Press, London.

Essex Institute of Agriculture *Lecture Notes.* 1974. Essex Institute of Agriculture, Writtle.

Fryer, J. and Makepeace R. *Weed Control Handbook.* 1972. Blackwell Scientific Publications, London.

Hawker, M. F. J. and Keenlyside, J. F. *Horticultural Machinery.* 1971. Macdonald, London.

H.M.S.O. *Approved Products for 1977 Farmers and Growers.* H.M.S.O. London.

Hubbard, C. E. *Grasses.* 1974. Penguin, London.

Ingold, C. T. *The Biology of Fungi.* 1969. Hutchinson Educational, London.

MacKean, D. G. *Introduction to Biology.* 1971. John Murray, London.

Martin Keble, W. *The Concise British Flora in Colour.* 1965. Ebury Press and Michael Joseph, London.

Parry, R. and Jenkins, W. R. *Land Surveying.* 1970. Estates Gazette, London.

Phillips, P. M. and Hardiman, W. *Glimpses of Groundsmanship.* National Association of Groundsmen, London.

Royal Horticultural Society *Dictionary of Gardening.* 1956. Oxford University Press, London.

Russel, Sir E. John *The World of the Soil.* 1961. Collins, London.

Russel, E. Walter *Soil Conditions and Plant Growth.* 1968. Longmans, London.

Skytte Christiansen, M. *Grasses in Colour.* 1978. Blandford Press, Poole.

Smith, J. Drew and Jackson, N. *Fungal Diseases of Turf Grasses.* 1965. The Sports Turf Research Institute, Bingley.

Townsend, W. N. *An Introduction to the Scientific Study of the Soil.* 1973. Edward Arnold, London.

Vose, James *Dumpy Level Work.* 1966. Macmillan, London.

Winter, E. J. *Water, Soil and the Plant.* 1974. Macmillan, London.

278

Index

2-(4-chloro-2-methylphenoxy) proprio-
acid, *see* Mecoprop
Chlorophyll, 15
Chlorotic tissue, 196
Cinquefoil, appearance and control
measures, 118-19
Cirsium acaule, appearance and control
measures, 114
Cirsium arvense, appearance and control
measures, 115
Cladochytrium spp., 157
Clay soils, 2-3
no rolling, 205
suitability for mole drainage, 39
Click Beetles, 146, 147
Climbing plants, 275
Clostridia, 7, 8
Clover, 110
Cockchafer, 147, 148
Collimation, line of, 21
Collimation method, 31
Collybia butyracea, 164
Common Storksbill, appearance and
control measures, 125
Common Tormentil, appearance and
control measures, 118
Communications, 247-50
clear wording, 249-50
written, preparation, 248
presentation, 249
stages, 247
Complete metamorphosis, 145
Compositae, appearance and control
measures, 113-15
Compost for top dressings, 104
Compound fertilisers, 99-100
Conidiophores, 159
Conifers, 277
Connecting rod, 167
Construction of sports areas, 250-1
Contact breaker points, 169
Contact herbicides, 71, 108, 110
Contravating, 200
Control function of management, 232,
237
Copper, 11, 13, 97
Copper sulphate, for earthworm con-
trol, 154

Coring, *see* Hollow-tining
Corticium fuciforme Berk., 160, 162
Couch grass, 69
discouraged by close mowing, 187
Cowley level, 25, 26
Crane Flies, 144
Crankcase induction, 170
Crankshaft, 167
Creeping Bent, 55, 64, 88
Creeping buttercup, appearance and
control measures, 117
Creeping Red Fescue, 56-8
Creeping soft grass, appearance and
control measures, 127
Creeping thistle, appearance and con-
trol measures, 115
Crested Dogstail, 63, 65, 74, 77, 80, 82
Ioxynil contra-indicated, 110
Cricket squares
dimensions with winter games areas,
262
seasonal maintenance, 217-19
Cricket wickets
dimensions, 263
preparation, 219-20
rolling, 205
Crowfoot, appearance and control
measures, 116
Cryslic acid, 146
Culms, 48
Cultural control of weeds, 111-12
Cumberland Marsh Fescue, 58, 75
Cut-and-fill technique of soil movement, 19, 20
Cutworms, 149-50
control measures, 150
damage, 149
life-cycle, 149-50
Cylinder mowers, 187, 188-9
correct adjustment, 188-9
for high quality turf, 187
Cylinders, 167
Cynodon dactylon, 88
Cynosurus cristatus, 63, 65, 74, 76, 77, 80,
82, 110

2, 4-D, 108, 109
D.D.T., 146, 149

281

Daisy, appearance and control measures, 113-14
Damage repair, *see* Repairs
'Damping off' diseases, 157
Dandelion, 106
  appearance and control measures, 115
Dart Moth, 149
Data collection, 237
Data handling, 233
Datum line, 19-20
Dazomet, 111
Decision making, 233-6
  process, 235-6
Decomposition, 6, 8
De-nitrification, 8
Derris dust, 152, 153
Deschampsia flexuosa, 66
Detergent oils, 176
Development function of management, 232
Dew, 204
Dicamba, 109, 110
3, 6-dichloro-2-methoxybenzoic acid, *see* Dicamba
2, 4-dichlorophenoxyacetic acid, *see* 2, 4-D
2-(2, 4-dichlorophenoxy) proprionic acid, *see* Dichlorprop
Dichlorprop, 109-10
Diesel engine faults, 183-4
1, 2-dihydropyridazine-3, 6-dione, *see* Maleic hydrazide
Dilophus febritis, 150
Dilution rates of chemicals, 132-3
Dimensions of sports areas, 260-74
Dimexan, 71, 108
Discus, dimensions of area, 272
Disease control, 112
  on cricket squares, 218, 220
  See also Fungal diseases; Pests
Divots, 222
Docks, 110
Dogstails, 63, 65
Dollar Spot, 162-3
  control measures, 162-3
  symptoms, 162
Dovesfoot Cranesbill, appearance and control measures, 125

Downland turf, 82
Drainage, 35-47
  backfilling, 43-4
  depth of drains, 43
  equipment, 41
  fall of drains, 43
  football pitches, 226
  good, advantages, 36
  poor, indications, 35
  related to Ophiobolus Patch disease, 164
  systems, 44-7
    fan, 46-7
    grid, 45-6
    herringbone, 44-5
  to control Dollar Spot, 163
  trenched method, 41
  trenchless method, 41
  types, 36-44
    mole, 39-41
    sand slitting, 37
    sub-surface, 38-44
    surface layer, 36-7
    tile, 41-4
  types of pipe, 41-2
Dressings, 101-5
  See also Base dressings; Topdressings
Dry sump lubrication system, 174
Dumpy level, 22-4
  setting up, 22
Dust form of chemicals, 132
  application equipment, 133

Earthworms, 151-4
  conditions governing worm activity, 152
  removal of worm casts, 112
  species creating problems, 151-2
  strychnine-covered, to destroy moles, 154
  worm casts, 204
  See also Worm control
Engines
  diagnosing faults, 179-83
    engine difficult to start, 179-80
    engine failing to start, 179
    engine overheating, 182
    excessive fuel consumption, 181

excessive oil consumption, 183
  irregular running, misfiring, 180-1
  loss of power, 183
  pre-ignition of fuel, 182
  lubrication, 172-6
  routine maintenance, 177-8
  See also Diesel engines
Epigynous flowers, 117
Equipment
  drainage, 41
  for application of chemicals, 133-4
  Ses also Machinery
Erodium circutarium agg., appearance
  and control measures, 125
Erodium moschatum, appearance and
  control measures, 125
Euxoa nigricans, 149
Exhaust valves, 167

Fairy rings, 164-6
  control measures, 165-6
  symptoms, 164-5
Fall of drains, 43
Fallowing the soil, 70-1, 111
Farm manure, 105
Fenoprop, 109, 110
Ferrous sulphate, 166
Fertilisers
  calculating amounts required, 99
  compound, 99-100
  containing calcium, 5
  inorganic, 91
  on bowling greens, 224, 225
  on cricket squares, 218, 219
  on football pitches, 226, 227
  on golf greens, 223
  on tees, 222
  on tennis courts, 228, 229
  organic, 90
  slow·release action, 91
  timing applications, 101
Fescues, 55-9, 64-5
  Fusarium Patch disease, 158
Festuca spp., 55, 64-5
  Fusarium Patch disease, 158
  susceptible to Red Thread, 160
Festuca ovina, 55, 58, 64, 65, 82

Festuca ovina tenuifolia Sibth., 59
Festuca rubra, 162
Festuca rubra var 'Fallax', *see Festuca
  rubra commutata* Goud.
Festuca rubra commutata Goud., 53,
  55-6, 64, 75-7
  effect of close mowing, 187
Festuca rubra genuina, 57
Festuca rubra genuina var. *glaucescens*, 58,
  75
Festuca rubra rubra, 56-8
Fever Fly, 150
Fever Fly larvae, 150-1
  control measures, 151
  damage, 150
  life-cycle, 150-1
Field capacity, 9
Field Woodrush, appearance and con-
  trol measures, 126
Filters in lubrication systems, 174-5
Fine-leaved Sheeps Fescue, 59
Flail mowers, 194-5
Floats, 84
Flywheel magneto ignition system, 169
Football pitches
  dimensions, 265, 266, 268, 273
  maintenance, 226-7
  selection of grass species, 226
Foresight, 21, 30
Formalin, 166
Four-stroke engines, 167-9
  cycle, 167-9
  for rotary mowers, 190
  ignition system, 169
Friction, 172
Fritted trace elements, 97
Full-force feed lubrication system, 174
  pressure gauges, 175
Fungal diseases, 155-66
  of established turf, 158-66
  of seedlings, 156-8
    control measures, 157-8
    symptoms of attack, 157
Fungi, 8-9
  creating bare patches in sward, 112
  reproductive methods, 155-6
  structure, 155-6
Fungi imperfecti, 156, 157, 159

283

289

2, 4, 5-T, 109
Talpa europea, 154
Tana-grass, 82-3
Taraxacum officinale, appearance and control measures, 115
Tees, maintenance, 221-2
Telephone communications, 247
Tennis courts
  dimensions, 264
  maintenance, 228-9
'Thatch', 112, 163, 196
  factors affecting production, 196
Thiophanate-methyl, 160, 162, 163
Thiram, 157, 158, 162, 163
Thistle, *see* Creeping Thistle; Stemless Thistle
Tile drainage systems, 40, 41-4
Timothy, 65, 66, 77
Tipula spp., 144
Tipula oleracea, 144
Tipula paludosa Meig., 144
Tipula vernalis Meig., 144
Topdressings
  application methods, 102-3
  autumn, to control Red Thread, 161
  benefits, 102
  bowling greens, 224
  bulky, 102-5, 205
  football pitches, 226
  for turves, 88
  materials, 103-5
  on cricket squares, 218
  on fairways, 221
  on golf greens, 223
  on tees, 222
  on tennis courts, 228
Tractor-mounted sprayers, calibration, 138-9
Translocated herbicides, 71, 108, 109
Transmission lubricants, 176
Transpiration, 208-9
Transpiration stream, 208
Trapping moles, 154
Trenched drainage method, 41
Trenchless drainage method, 41, 42
2-(2, 4, 5-trichlorophenoxy)proprionic acid, *see* Fenoprop

2, 4, 5-trichlorophenoxyacetic acid, *see* 2, 4, 5-T
Tricholoma gambosum, 164
Trifolium spp., 110
Trifolium dubium Sibth., appearance and control measures, 123-4
Trifolium repens, appearance and control measures, 124
Trolley sprayers, calibration, 138
Turf
  application of chemicals, 132-3
  boxing, 85
  laying, 86-8
  lifting, 84-6
  sizes and thicknesses, 85
  sources, downland, 82
    lagoon turf (Tana-grass), 82-3
    meadow, 82
    parkland, 81
    sea-washed, 82
  storage, 85-6
Turfing, 80-8
  selection of turves, 81
  sward degeneration, 81
Turfing irons, 84
Turgidity, 9
Turnip Moth, 149
Two-stroke engines, 169-72
  cycle, 170-2
  for rotary mowers, 190
  in reciprocating blade mowers, 191

Underdrainage, *see* Sub-surface drainage
Underground water, 210
Urea, 98

Vegetable matter, 1
Velvet Bent, 54-5, 64, 88
  susceptible to Ophiobolus Patch disease, 163
Veronica spp., 106, 110
Veronica chamaedrys, appearance and control measures, 123
Veronica filiformis Sm., appearance and control measures, 122-3

292

Viscosity, 172
Vitamins, 15

Water, 9-10, 14
  See also Irrigation
Water-potential gradient, 208
Water table, 10
  effect of laying drains, 43
  high, 35
Watering cans, calibration, 135-6
Water-displacing compounds for rust
    prevention, 177
Waterproof greases, 176
Wavy Hair Grass, 66
Weathering agents, 1-2
Weed control
  chemical, 71, 107-11
    See also Chemical control of weeds
  cultural, 69-70, 111-12
  during lawn preparation, 69-71
  fallowing the soil, 70-1
  in turf, 107-12
  on bowling greens, 225
  on fairways, 221
  on football pitches, 226
  on newly-seeded lawns, 80
  on tees, 222
  on tennis courts, 228
  soil sterilisation, 71
Weeds, 106-27
  features rendering them successful,
    106-7
  species and control measures, 112-27
  types varying with soil, 111

Welsh Chafer, 147, 149
Wettable powders, 132
  application equipment, 133
White Clover, appearance and control
    measures, 124
Wilting, permanent wilting point, 9-10
Winter flowering plants, 274
Wireworms, 146-7
  control measures, 147
  damage, 146
  life-cycle, 147
Wood Meadow Grass, 61, 65
Woodrush, appearance and control
    measures, 113
Worm casts, 204
Worm control
  by copper sulphate, 154
  chemical methods, 152-4
  cultural methods, 152
  on bowling greens, 224, 226
  on tennis courts, 228

Yarrow, 126
  appearance and control measures,
    113
Yorkshire Fog, 111
  appearance and control measures,
    126-7
  discouraged by close mowing, 187
  discouraged by scarification, 197
  Fusarium Patch disease, 158

Zinc, 11, 13, 97
Zygomorphic flowers, 122

293